D1058619

WIDOW CLICQUOT

ALSO BY TILAR J. MAZZEO

Mary Shelley's Literary Lives and Other Writings

Plagiarism and Literary Property in the Romantic Period

Romantic Travel Writing and the Middle East

WIDOW CLICQUOT

The Story of a Champagne Empire
and the Woman Who Ruled It

TILAR J. MAZZEO

COLLINS
An Imprint of HarperCollinsPublishers

HarperCollins books may be purchased for educational, business, or sales promotional use. For information please write: Special Markets Department, Harper-Collins Publishers, 10 East 53rd Street, New York, NY 10022.

Image on page x by Drian.

FIRST EDITION

Designed by Renato Stanisic

Library of Congress Cataloging-in-Publication Data

Mazzeo, Tilar J.
The widow Clicquot: the story of a champagne empire and the woman who ruled it / by Tilar Mazzeo.
p. cm.
Includes bibliographical references and index.
ISBN 978-0-06-128856-2
1. Clicquot-Ponsardin, Barbe-Nicole, 1777–1866. 2. Vintners—France—Champagne—Biography. 3. Champagne (Wine)—History. I. Title.

TP547.C55M39 2008
641.2'224092—dc22
[B]

2008005086

08 09 10 11 12   OV/RRD   10 9 8 7 6 5 4 3 2 1

FOR NOELLE AND ROBERTA, MORE THAN EVER

Contents

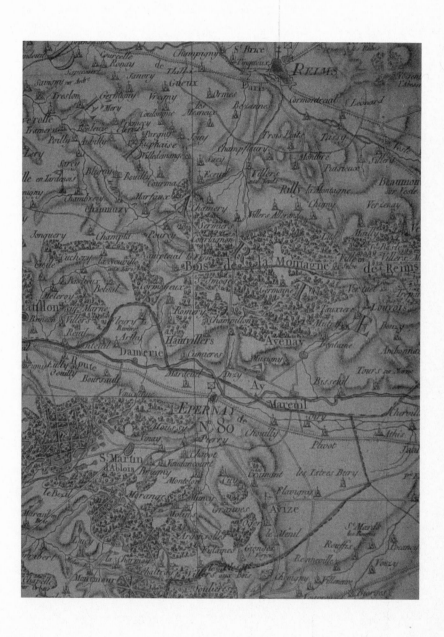

Prologue

This is the story of French champagne, but it didn't start amid the splendor of a countryside château. Its origins were a more modest little luxury: the aisles of a well-stocked wine shop. It was a remarkably simple way to have begun an obsession with the history of one of the world's great wines—and one of the world's great women. As much as we associate champagne with celebration and the good life, I should also tell you that, for me, it was a passion that began without fanfare in a small town in the American Midwest, where I was trying to weather what turned out to be the last months of a less than glamorous job.

It was in the midst of this daily living—and those occasional splurges that any sensible woman uses to temper it—that I discovered the Widow Clicquot. Although the writer in me wishes to tell you that my love affair with the Widow began in the spring, with the loosening of the earth and the promise of new life, that is not true. Winter had the Midwestern plains firmly in its Anglo-Saxon grasp, and I found myself gazing wistfully at a row of bubbly, dreaming of distant appellations and the sun-soaked vineyards of France.

I already knew the champagne. I don't mean that. My girlfriends and I drank it with a degree of enthusiastic regularity that might not be wise to detail. It was the story of Barbe-Nicole Clicquot Ponsardin that I discovered that afternoon, printed on a small card tucked into the box of the 1996 vintage Grande Dame that I had decided I certainly deserved.

The elegant little biography was less than thirty-five words, but it was a story that even in its outlines captured my attention that winter. It was the story of a woman raised to be a wife and mother, left widowed before thirty with a small child, with no training and little experience of the world, who grasped firmly at the reins of her own destiny and, through sheer determination and talent, transformed a fledgling family wine trade into one of the great champagne houses of the world. Here, I thought, is a woman who refuses to compromise.

In the years that followed, her story stayed with me, even after we had left the Midwest and settled in my then husband's home state of California in the hills of Sonoma County, where the winters are green-misted and indescribably soft. Something about this woman who took such immense risks to pursue her passion still resonated deeply, and I began odd little researches, hunting down nineteenth-century references to the Widow Clicquot in the local wine library in Healdsburg, practicing my rusty French reading old travel narratives written at the height of the Napoleonic empire. And, of course, never one to stint on rigorous research, I made sure that we tasted all the sparkling wine we could find, locally at first, and later in France, where I spent a windy January in a sprawling old farmhouse surrounded by nothing but muddy vineyards.

The trouble always was how to find the woman herself, this young widow with the unwieldy name of Barbe-Nicole Clicquot Ponsardin, the Veuve— or Widow—Clicquot. At the beginning of the nineteenth century, when Barbe-Nicole was settling into her adulthood and all the compromises that come with it, the lives of entrepreneurs and commercial innovators rarely made the history books. This was especially true if that entrepreneur or innovator happened to be a woman. The archives are filled with the letters and diaries of statesmen and princes, but few librarians thought to collect the personal records of businesspeople, even businesspeople who did exceptional things. It is still true today. Most of us will never see our love letters preserved in the world's great libraries. For a young woman in the nineteenth century it was particularly true, unless she was a queen or a duchess or the sister, wife, or mother of some great man.

Barbe-Nicole was none of those things. She was simply a formidable and independent woman, making her own name in the humdrum, dog-eat-dog world of business. When I finally made my way in the early months of 2007 to the Veuve Clicquot Ponsardin company archives in Reims, confident of discovering her private secrets, I found that the walls were lined with shelf after shelf of careful account books, all evidence of Barbe-Nicole's singular resolve. But there were few clues as to the woman behind the trademark yellow label.

So, instead, I dragged willing friends around the countryside of the Champagne that winter, looking for some trace of the life Barbe-Nicole must have known. Something that would explain not just *how* a young, sheltered woman broke free from the life other people had charted for her, but *why*. We bumped down rutted dirt roads in the rain, looking for the Widow's vineyards in the fields above the village of Bouzy. In a fit of collective charm one afternoon, we persuaded the reluctant winemaker at Château de Boursault, once her favorite country home, to give us just ten minutes in the private grounds she had loved. I sat for hours in the cool silence of the cathedral of Notre-Dame de Reims, thinking that Barbe-Nicole knew these same walls well. Throughout it all, I found myself staring at buildings and street corners, stealing glimpses through windows like some thief, looking in vain for a woman and the finely woven texture of her life.

Sometimes I wondered if finding her private life—rescuing her from the silence that engulfed her story—would be possible. Before my quest was over, I would meet with women winemakers and company presidents in sunlit Napa offices, searching for the modern incarnation of the Widow Clicquot, hoping to find in their experiences of a woman's life in wine some way to untangle the past. Later, there was France. In small towns throughout the Champagne, La Veuve—and in France there is only one—lives in the shadowy half-life of oral folk legend. Frustrated with the dusty books and the archives, some days I simply asked the locals in bars and bistros to remember, knowing that remembering and inventing are close cousins, especially at the distance of two hundred years. We passed the wine from table to table in open bottles, and the chef came out from the kitchen to relax with a cigarette and to listen. In those moments, her presence was with us.

I like to think that the life of the Widow Clicquot has been slowly ripening in quiet darkness like some rare and wonderful vintage. Some of that darkness has been my life and my imagination. Some of it has been the darkness of history and the role of entrepreneurial men and, especially, women in it. But now—at last—is the time to enjoy it. As we all know, over time, wine becomes something different and more precious. The hard tannins mellow into smoothness; the flavors mature and ripen. In the nineteenth century, much of the Widow's story wasn't worth saving. Today, its mere outlines are breathtaking. It is a tale that will change the way we think about the history of champagne and the role of one woman in it.

We all know the wine that Barbe-Nicole helped to make famous. No wine in the world brings to mind so many immediate associations as champagne. The pop of a cork and the bright sparkle of bubbles mean celebration and glamour and, more often than not, the distinct possibility of romance. It is the wine of weddings and New Year's kisses. It is beautiful and delicate, and above all, it is a wine associated with women.

It has ever been thus. The poet Lord Byron famously proclaimed that lobster salad and champagne were the only things a woman should ever be seen eating. Byron was an unrepentant chauvinist, but it is still a delicious idea. In the first decades of the eighteenth century, not long after champagne was discovered, the voluptuous and powerful Madame de Pompadour, mistress to the king of France, put it best: Champagne is the only wine that leaves a woman more beautiful after drinking it. According to legend, the shallow goblet-style champagne glasses known as *coupes* were modeled after this lady's much admired breasts. In the twentieth century, it was the perfect wine with little black dresses, and it still evokes Jazz Age flappers and the elegance of old Humphrey Bogart films.

But one look at the business of champagne tells a very different tale. In the boardrooms and wine cellars, champagne is a man's world. Today, there are only a handful of women in senior positions in the French wine industry, and only one of the elite and internationally renowned champagne houses known as the *grandes marques* is run by a woman—the house of Champagne Veuve Clicquot Ponsardin, headed since 2001 by Madame Cécile Bonnefond.

The familiar stories about the origins of champagne tell us that men have always controlled the business of wine. Indeed, champagne enthusiasts quickly learn that it was a man who discovered it. History credits a seventeenth-century blind monk with the now famous name of Dom Pierre Pérignon with having discovered the secret of champagne's bubbles in the cellars of his hillside abbey, perched at the edge of the village of Hautvillers. According to legend, he is the jolly mad scientist of champagne, relentlessly pursuing a way to transmute ordinary local wines into a sparkling liquid gold.

If Dom Pérignon discovered how to produce champagne, other talented and prosperous men learned how to market it to the world. Men such as Jean-Rémy Moët, who used his personal connections with Napoléon, fostered during wine country weekends at Moët's luxurious estates in Épernay, to build one of the first commercial champagne empires. Picture postcards of this celebrity friendship, with images of Moët and Napoléon touring the wine cellars in good spirits, were popular souvenirs as early as the nineteenth century. Even more famous was Charles-Henri Heidsieck, who rode two thousand miles on horseback to Russia as a marketing gimmick. His son Charles Camille was later immortalized in popular song as "Champagne Charlie," and before long, Champagne Charlie was slang for "any dissipated man or noted drinker of *fizz*."

With men like these in the business, no wonder champagne is one of the world's most familiar products. This one small region of northeastern France, with less than 85,000 acres of vines—the only place where true champagne is made—has been blessed with more than its fair share of entrepreneurial talent. The trouble is that the story of how these men slowly built a global champagne empire is only half-true. Dom Pérignon was certainly a talented winemaker and probably one of the great tasters of winemaking history, but he did not discover how to capture the bubbles in a bottle of champagne. In fact, when they occurred naturally, he tried to get rid of them. His goal was not developing a new product, but meeting the needs of the market he and his clerical brothers already controlled: a trade in good-quality still wines.

Even more shocking, champagne wasn't discovered by the French. It was the British who first learned the secret of making wine sparkle and first launched the commercial trade in champagne wine with bubbles.

The legend of Dom Pérignon was manufactured only in the late nineteenth century—and eventually registered by the estates of Moët and Chandon as a trademark. And while Champagne Charlie came onto the scene with genuine gusto, champagne was already big business by the time he was celebrated in cabaret tunes, and he was not quite the young upstart he pretended to be.

Champagne was not always big business, however. In the second part of the eighteenth century, champagne was in a slump, destined to become a regional curiosity. Local winemakers were struggling to drum up even modest sales, and champagne might have faded into obscurity, suffering the same fate as its unfortunate counterpart *sekt*—another sparkling wine now all but forgotten except among connoisseurs.

All that changed in the first decades of the nineteenth century, thanks to the determination and resourcefulness of less than a dozen important brokers and winemakers, who saw a bigger potential for the sparkling wines grown in the sloping vineyards running south from the cathedral city of Reims. Within the space of a single generation, champagne went from skidding toward the commercial sidelines to a powerful economic engine. From 1790 to 1830, sales increased almost 1,000 percent, from a few hundred thousand bottles a year to over five million. By the dawn of the twentieth century, even before the Jazz Age made champagne the symbol of an era, the world was already buying twenty million bottles of bubbly a year.

At the beginning of the nineteenth century, however, champagne was still a small-time enterprise, and these decades would prove to be a defining moment for the champagne industry. At the crossroads of its cultural history, one entrepreneur deserves much of the credit for establishing this sparkling wine as the most famous luxury product in the world market: the Widow Clicquot.

Widowed at the age of twenty-seven, with no formal business training and no firsthand experience, Barbe-Nicole transformed a well-funded but struggling and small-time family wine brokerage into arguably the most important champagne house of the nineteenth century in just over a decade. It is thanks to her technical innovations in the cellars that today we can find modestly priced bottles of champagne on store shelves around the world. Had she not discovered the process known as *remuage*, champagne would have remained the drink only of the very rich or the very lucky. I would not have been able to drown my sorrows that Wisconsin winter—and I would never have begun this quixotic search for the lost details of another woman's life.

By forty, Barbe-Nicole was one of the wealthiest and most celebrated entrepreneurs in all of Europe and one of the first businesswomen in history to lead an international commercial empire. Recognizing an industry in crisis, she was unafraid of entering into a new business and new markets when the entire social structure of old France—the ancien régime—was crumbling and Europe was in a collective panic. More experienced entrepreneurs resolved to wait out the crisis—or to find another line of business entirely. But the story of the Widow Clicquot has its roots in sheer audacity. Risking her financial independence for a future in champagne, she changed the history of French winemaking. In the process, she also helped to make the product she sold a byword for luxury, celebration, and the good life.

She opened these new horizons for women in business and forced those around her to reconsider the gender stereotypes of her day more or less despite herself. But the public figure of this enterprising widow, who resisted the limited domestic role society demanded of her, is in marked contrast with the private woman. Barbe-Nicole quietly defied the expectations her culture had about what women were and what they were capable of achieving. Meanwhile, at home and in her opinions, she was anything but a revolutionary.

In her personal beliefs, she was a deeply conservative and sometimes rigid woman. Her family remained staunch Catholics, even when the religion was outlawed and dangerous in republican France. She did not advocate for the rights of women, although she lived in the era when feminism was born. Instead, she surrounded herself with men, as employees, partners, and even friends. She was a devoted but frankly domineering mother, whose only child—a daughter—she undervalued intellectually and excluded from the family business, preferring instead to marry her off to an idle and flamboyant aristocratic playboy—one to whose charms

Barbe-Nicole herself was dangerously susceptible. And, in the end, she gave away a large part of the family business and most of her vineyards to her male business partners.

She was a mass of contradictions, but her genius as a businesswoman was in refusing to see her options as black and white. Her success was not in bucking the system, but neither did she slavishly follow convention. As the daughter of a local politician with a cunning instinct for survival even in the midst of an ugly revolution, she had a talent for seeing the opportunities that existed in moments of cultural and economic instability, in the space between where the old structures and old ways of doing business (and those who stubbornly stuck to them) disappeared and innovative new approaches took hold. Hers is the portrait of a woman with the courage to step into the breach, emotionally, physically, and financially.

Because of her willingness to take risks without fanfare, the Widow Clicquot became one of the most famous women of her era. Like the other great widow of her day, Great Britain's queen Victoria, she helped to define a century. For decade after decade, her name was heard on the lips of soldiers, princes, and poets as far away as Russia. Before long, tourists came looking for a glimpse of the woman whom the writer Prosper Mérimée once called the uncrowned queen of Reims. In the Champagne, she was known simply as *la grande dame*—the great lady. Rare Veuve Clicquot vintages are still called "La Grande Dame" in tribute to her fame. She remained a contradiction to the end: a generous philanthropist and a hardheaded business owner; a small, gruff, and decidedly plain woman with a sharp tongue who sold the world an exquisitely beautiful wine and an ethereal fantasy. Then she disappeared, becoming little more than the name on a bottle of bubbly.

Before this complex and sometimes contradictory woman was reduced to a brand name—or in twentieth-century caricatures to nothing more than a dancing bottle with legs—the Widow Clicquot defined the industry to which she was dedicated. At a time of increasing cultural rigidity, she opened the way for a second generation of enterprising women in the champagne business, women who had wit and talent as sharp as her own. Following in her footsteps, the young widow Louise Pommery went on to build one of the world's great champagne houses, which reached dizzying heights of wealth and promise just as Barbe-Nicole's own story was coming to an end. In doing so, the Widow Pommery invented the dry brut champagne that wine drinkers still adore today. It was a path Barbe-Nicole had opened for her. Sadly, there would not be a third generation of women with such scope in the champagne business. There would not be other women who transformed small family businesses into astonishing commercial empires. Those who came after—women like Lily Bollinger and Mathilde-Emile Laurent-Perrier—were above all stewards of enterprises first raised to public prominence by an earlier generation. By the first decades of the twentieth century, the wine industry in the region had become a large-scale commercial affair, controlled almost exclusively by men who could already be counted among the rich and the powerful, with few opportunities for untrained and untested fledgling entrepreneurs.

But for nearly a century—the first century of its global transformation into the iconic symbol of luxury and celebration—the champagne business was a woman's world. At the most critical juncture in the history of this celebrated wine, Barbe-Nicole dominated the industry. The result was a different future for women in the commercial arena. Today, the champagne house she founded gives a prestigious award in her name that celebrates the accomplishments of talented international businesswomen. And because of the Widow Clicquot, historians still claim that "no business in the world [has] been as much influenced by the female sex as that of champagne."

Chapter 1

Child of the Revolution, Child of the Champagne

What people in the Champagne remembered later about the summer of 1789 were the cobbled streets of Reims resounding with the chanting, angry mobs calling for liberty and equality. The French Revolution had begun, although no one would use those words yet to describe one of the most monumental events in the history of modern civilization. Democracy had taken root in the colonies of America only a decade before, and a new nation had emerged, aided in its war for independence from Great Britain by the military and financial might of France, one of the world's most powerful and ancient kingdoms. Now, democracy had also come to France. It was a bloody and brutal beginning.

The young girls in the royal convent of Saint-Pierre-les-Dames, just beyond the old city center of Reims—a bustling commercial town of perhaps thirty thousand inhabitants, at the heart of the French textile industry and only ninety miles to the east of Paris—had little to do with this larger world of war and politics. Two centuries before, Mary, Queen of Scots had been a student in the abbey from the tender age of five, under the care of her aunt, the noble abbess Renée de Lorraine. The other girls at this Catholic convent school often came, like Mary Stuart and her noble aunt, from the ranks of the aristocracy, and they spent their days learning the graceful arts expected of the wealthy daughters of the social elite: embroidery, music, dance steps, and their prayers. The cloistered courtyard echoed with the light steps and rustling habits of nuns moving silently in the shadows, and the garden was shady and welcoming even in the summer heat.

Their parents had sent them to Saint-Pierre-les-Dames to be educated in safety and privilege. But in July 1789, a royal abbey was just possibly the most dangerous place of all for these girls. The nobility and the church had crushed the peasantry with crippling taxes for centuries, and suddenly that summer, long-simmering resentments finally broke out into an open class war that changed the history of France. Old scores were being settled in horrifying ways. It was only a matter of time before the nuns and these young girls—the daughters of the city's social elite— became the targets of public abuse. Already, there were stories from Paris of nuns being raped and the rich being murdered in the streets. Now, wine flowed from the public fountains, and the laughs and cheers of the crowd in Reims had become more and more feverish.

Behind the shuttered windows, cloistered within the royal walls of Saint-Pierre-les-Dames, one of those girls may not have known that the world and her future were being transformed until the mob was nearly at their doorstep. Barbe-Nicole Ponsardin was eleven years old when the Revolution began. She was a small and serious girl, with golden blond hair and large gray eyes, the eldest daughter of one of the city's wealthiest and most important businessmen—an affluent and cultured man who dreamed of moving his family into the aristocracy and had sent his child, accordingly, to this prestigious royal convent to be educated with the daughters of feudal lords and princes.

Now, the streets of Reims were alive with angry crowds, and it seemed that Barbe-Nicole would share the fate of her aristocratic classmates. The shops everywhere were closed, and the fields were empty. In the center of the city, in the grand family mansion on rue Cérès, just beyond the shadow of the great cathedral, her parents—Ponce Jean Nicolas Philippe and Marie Jeanne Josèphe Clémentine Ponsardin, or more simply Nico-las and Jeanne-Clémentine—were frantic. Even if there were a way to send a carriage through the streets of Reims to fetch Barbe-Nicole, such a display of wealth and fear would only advertise her privilege and increase her danger on the streets.

Their last hope rested with the family dressmaker, a modest woman but with remarkable bravery. Arriving quietly at the convent door with a small bundle of garments, anxious not to be observed, she knew the only way to spirit a wealthy daughter through the streets of revolutionary France: in disguise. After she dressed the child in the clothes of the working poor, they hurried. The shapeless tunic must have itched, and Barbe-Nicole's first steps in the coarse wooden shoes—so different from her own soft leather slippers—were surely unsteady.

In another moment they had slipped out into the frenzied streets of Reims, praying to pass unnoticed. No one would bother a dressmaker or a peasant girl, but the convent-educated daughter of a bourgeois civic leader—a man who had personally helped to crown the king only a decade before—would make a compelling target for abuse. Much worse would happen to some of those whom Nicolas and Jeanne-Clémentine had entertained on those long summer evenings in the splendid halls of their family estate before the Revolution.

The roads beyond the convent were a brilliant red tide of men in Phrygian caps, classical symbols of liberty once worn by freed slaves in ancient democracies, singing familiar military marches with new words. In the distance was the sound of beating drums, and heels striking the cobble pavement echoed off the stone facades of the grandest buildings in Reims, as the men organized themselves into makeshift militias. There were fears throughout France of an imminent invasion, as the other great monarchs of Europe roused themselves to send troops to crush the popular uprising that had electrified the masses across the continent.

Hurrying through those chaotic streets must have been terrifying for a small girl. All around her was uproar as the mob gathered. They moved quickly past. Then, perhaps in the crowds of angry men, one or two looked at Barbe-Nicole with the perplexed stare of dim recognition. Perhaps she witnessed some of the many small atrocities of the Revolution—the vandalism, the beatings. The day was something no one who experienced it would ever forget.

. . . .

We can only speculate about what small horrors made up Barbe-Nicole's memory of that day, and we will never know precisely what happened next. Only the broadest outlines of this dramatic story have survived as family legend. We have one other fact: After their escape, during the first days of the Revolution, the dressmaker hid the girl in the small apartment above her shop, not far from a small, dingy square on the southern out-skirts of Reims, where there are still a few eighteenth-century buildings. Not much in Reims survived the bombings of World War I, but looking at these tilting structures, I find myself wondering if one of those apart-ments, with the faded linen curtains, was where Barbe-Nicole looked out on a changing world. The square is still known today as Place des Droits de l'Homme—Plaza of the Rights of Man.

After more than two hundred years of retelling, some people now even question whether it was Barbe-Nicole or her little sister who made this dramatic escape through the streets of a city in the grip of a revolu-tion. But in the few early documents that record the details of her private life—a nineteenth-century biography of her family by a local historian and a breezy mid-twentieth-century sketch by the aristocratic wife of the company president—this has been the central legend of Barbe-Nicole's childhood.

In fact, this one family anecdote is the only story about that childhood to survive. Apart from the barest outlines of birth and parentage, nothing of Barbe-Nicole's girlhood remains. This silence might be the most im-portant part of her story. Like other girls from privileged genteel families of the time, she was meant to be invisible. She should have lived a quiet and unexceptional life in a small city in provincial France. There would have been days filled with the duties of a wife and needs of children and aging parents. There would have been hours spent planning pretty dresses and dinner parties. There would have been the triumphs and tragedies of daily living. Had everything gone according to plan, Barbe-Nicole would have lived and died in relative anonymity.

We know, of course, that she did not. The Revolution, which ultimately transformed the entire social and economic fabric of France, is part of the reason her life story took such an unexpected direction. All politics are local, even in the midst of great world events. As so often is the case in the small rural region of northeast France known as the Champagne, the vineyards played a role in the turmoil that summer.

In 1789 the world changed, but the Revolution had been a long time coming. These men and women were in the streets of Reims for a reason. For more than a decade, the agricultural economy had stagnated. The laboring classes, whose subsistence was always held in balance by the slenderest of margins, had lost ground. Entire villages were on the brink of starvation, their crops blasted by a long drought and erratic temperatures that in the Champagne had turned the chalky fields as hard as stone. The land was so dry that even when the rain came, it brought only suffering: The parched soil was unable to absorb the water, and spring flooding throughout the Marne River valley brought more misery to the working-men and -women of the region.

By summer, those who tended the vines and grew the grapes that made champagne—the vignerons—were frustrated and resentful. That year had brought some of the coldest and most miserable weather in a century, and the crops had failed throughout France. The peasantry faced the real possibility of mass starvation, the wine growers among them. Even when there were crops to harvest, the taxes imposed on the working people of France were crippling. A typical vigneron—even one who owned his own land—might easily pay more than 40 percent in taxes to the local noblemen and clergy just for the right to be permitted to harvest and crush his grapes. In rural France, the vestiges of an ancient feudalism remained, and the law gave the local lord the exclusive right to control the village mill or its winepress. So the vigneron paid monopoly prices at harvest-time. And that was before he even tried to sell his wares. Among the most miserable of them all were the growers who lived outside the walls of the Benedictine abbey at Hautvillers, where a century earlier the craft of winemaking had been transformed into an art by the talented monk Dom Pérignon.

But Barbe-Nicole did not come from a family of peasants, and her father had no ties to the winemaking business. It was quite the opposite.

Born December 16, 1777, she was the eldest child of Nicolas Ponsardin and his nineteen-year-old bride, Jeanne-Clémentine Huart–Le Tertre. The economy of the Champagne region at the time depended for survival not on its now famous sparkling wine, but on the manufacture of cloth—especially soft, sturdy woolen goods. A family business in the textile trade, founded by Barbe-Nicole's grandfather, had made her father a rich and increasingly important man. According to one historian, Nicolas was "the town's largest employer of textile workers." On the eve of the Revolution, he employed nearly a thousand people in his factories and could boast annual sales of around 40,000 livres—the equivalent of perhaps $800,000 a year.

A socially ambitious man, Nicolas had also been laying the groundwork for a political career for more than a decade. Only recently, he had achieved an important position on the city council of Reims, but his star had been on the rise since at least as early as 1775, when, at only twenty-eight years of age, he had been chosen to serve on the local committee responsible for hosting the coronation of King Louis XVI and his now infamous queen, Marie Antoinette. He was even part of the retinue of town worthies who welcomed the royals at the door of their carriage. The king and queen came to be crowned at Reims because the church still housed a treasure known as the Sainte Ampoule, a mystical vial of sacramental oil used to transform men into kings, delivered, it was said, by an angel in the form of a dove some eleven centuries before and guarded throughout the millennium.

His role in planning the king's coronation ceremony marked Nicolas as a devoted subject and a man with a brilliant future in the city of Reims. It was also probably an excellent business opportunity. For the royal occasion, yards upon yards of the finest crimson cloth, embroidered with gold, were ordered from local textile merchants—Nicolas no doubt among them—to drape the nave of the great cathedral of Notre-Dame de Reims.

Nicolas had been deeply impressed by this passing contact with the royal family. In tribute to the king, he had spent vast sums of money building a sprawling mansion in the center of Reims, known simply as the Hôtel Ponsardin, constructed in the formal and extravagant style forever associated with Louis XVI. Today, the imposing structure houses—appropriately enough—the local Chamber of Commerce and seems to echo with the footsteps of the family that once inhabited these walls. The house faces rue Cérès, one of the city's main boulevards, with a symmetrical facade of endless airy windows. Barbe-Nicole was born here, on a street named after the Roman goddess of bountiful harvests. The gardens are in the classical eighteenth-century French style, with low hedges snaking down the lawns in intricate designs, and the courtyards must still be intoxicatingly fragrant in the early summers. It was here, surrounded by luxury in the heart of an important commercial center, that Barbe-Nicole spent her childhood, along with her younger brother, Jean-Baptiste Gérard, born in 1779, and her little sister, Clémentine, born in 1783.

While the outside of the Hôtel Ponsardin is forbidding in its cool grandeur, the inside remains luminous. The woodwork is fanciful and intricate, and the glowing parquet floors that Barbe-Nicole raced across as a girl still greet visitors. The ground level boasted elegant salons and ballrooms, where Nicolas entertained distinguished guests. The construction was vastly expensive. At times, Nicolas shuddered to think of the sums of money it was costing him to build and furnish such a magnificent home. Even with his very deep pockets, he could never afford to finish it.

Nicolas dreamed of the day when the Ponsardin family name would also be noble. This must have been part of the reason for sending his daughters to the royal convent school at Saint-Pierre-les-Dames, where they would rub shoulders with the children of the higher classes. Surely he dreamed of nothing less than a grand match for his first child. Of all his children, she was the one who had inherited his features and his air, and it was his eldest daughter who captured a special place in his heart. But if Nicolas had been dreaming of grand aristocratic matches for his daughters, those dreams ended in the summer of 1789. No man with even a modicum of foresight would give his daughter to a nobleman in the months and years that followed, and Nicolas was no fool.

Political events in France had unfolded quickly that summer. A bread riot in Paris that June grew into a grassroots political movement, and within weeks, the people of France had had enough. In a direct challenge to the king and the nobility, they demanded a role in the collection of taxes. By July, Louis XVI, tone-deaf as usual, had managed only to antagonize and infuriate the revolutionaries, and there were tens of thousands of citizens in the streets of Paris, calling for change. Then, on July 14, the notorious Parisian prison, the Bastille, was stormed by a bloody, murderous mob, and the king and his queen, the despised Marie Antoinette, became prisoners in their palace at Versailles.

Reims is only a short distance east of Paris, and word of events in the capital spread quickly. The result was instantaneous. Suddenly, all of Reims was in the streets. The Revolution was at its heart a class war, and aristocrats and clerics were abused and stripped of their estates. The fabled vineyards at Hautvillers were among those confiscated and returned to the people. In the days that followed, public squares throughout the Champagne were given over to protest marches, jubilant celebrations, and the mobs. When the first news of the unrest reached Reims, Nicolas Ponsardin joined the Revolution.

Being known as a friend of the aristocracy was a dangerous situation at the dawn of the Revolution. Men were killed for less in these turbulent and lawless times. Suddenly, the very fact of being wealthy and socially prominent—the fact of having participated in the feudal systems that had governed life in rural France for centuries—placed one's family in jeopardy, and Nicolas was among the first to grasp the implications for life in Reims.

Nicolas was no martyr and did not intend that his family should become martyrs, either. Astonishingly, he not only weathered the complete about-face in the political climate, but also prospered under it, rising to even greater local prominence and power in the years of Barbe-Nicole's early adolescence. The Revolution, it transpired, would be a boon for anyone in the wealthy industrial classes able to keep his wits about him. Nicolas did a quick political calculation and decided without hesitation that the best chances for him and his family—his gracious and demure wife, Jeanne-Clémentine, and his three young children—was to support the Revolution with open enthusiasm. Assessing his options, he probably decided that he did not have much of a choice.

Nicolas not only joined the protesters, but he joined the most radical fringe, the Jacobins, whose members called for a permanent end to the monarchy in France. He became a representative of his city in the new National Assembly, joining thousands of other prominent local citizens from around France in the exercise of democratic politics. In those first heady days of the Revolution, he surely took to the streets. The broad avenues of Reims were the hotbed of political activity, much of it bitterly retributive. The citizens were celebrating, but there was a nervous tension in the air. The wisest of the nobles made plans for a hasty flight into exile.

The cathedral of Reims, with its ancient royal treasures, was the target of public fury from the mobs that now filled the streets. The National Assembly and the new revolutionary government—with Nicolas as a member—outlawed all the churches of France and renamed them "temples of reason." Perhaps he stood watching as the vial of sacramental oil used to anoint the kings of France, guarded for centuries, was carried by an ecstatic crowd through the cool air to the central square of the city—once called the Place Royale but now renamed the more patriotic Place Nationale. It was only a few minutes' walk from the quiet splendor of the Hôtel Ponsardin. There, under the vacant stare of a statue of Louis XV, the sacred glass vial was publicly smashed.

Carried along with the crowds, Nicolas must have also watched as the ancient church and the nearby royal Palace of Tau, home to the kings of France during their coronation, were looted and vandalized. The cathedral was stripped of its heraldic decorations, and the portraits of the kings of France were burned and trampled underfoot. Today, the cold stone walls of the cathedral still bear the evidence of this distant turmoil, although it pales in comparison with what all of the city and its Gothic masterpiece suffered in the first decades of the twentieth century. Only the delicate carved floral decorations remained unscathed. They were said to depict every plant that grew in the fields of the Champagne and on the mountain and vine-laced hills that rose over the city to the south. The people of Reims never forgot their ties to the land or their respect for it.

In the open spaces where the city's broad boulevards meet, men like Nicolas soon erected festive altars to the goddess of a new secular religion. There, old married couples renewed their vows on the streets as a symbol of faithfulness in a new order, and in the central square children decorated liberty trees with ribbons and flowers. Nicolas is said to have planted one of these trees himself. In Paris, the women marched bare-breasted through the streets, and even in Reims young women were lifted indelicately aloft by the crowds and paraded along the avenues, scantily draped in loose-fitting togas and wearing crowns with a simple word on their foreheads: LIBERTY. The image of these young women is still a familiar symbol of freedom and democracy: Look no further than America's Statue of Liberty, a gift from the people of France.

Although other parents decked their daughters in white gowns and flowers to parade through the streets, Nicolas was not about to put his children on public display. In fact, despite his political prominence in the new revolutionary movement, he would do everything in his power to calm local politics and keep his family from drawing any unnecessary attention. Perhaps it is another reason we know so little about the childhood of Barbe-Nicole.

Nicolas had the best motives for wanting to keep his family out of the public eye, for shrouding life at the Hôtel Ponsardin in silence. Anything else was simply too dangerous. Behind the precarious facade of republicanism, the Ponsardin family guarded an explosive secret for the next decade. Despite her father's public role as a Jacobin patriot and willing convert to the cult of secular reason, there was a very different reality. Barbe-Nicole was less a child of the Revolution than a child of the Champagne—a place rich in the legend and mysteries of kings, where, even from the distant rolling vineyards, the eye could find on the horizon the spire of the great cathedral of Reims.

Chapter 2

Wedding Vows and Family Secrets

B arbe-Nicole was the member of a uniquely important generation, perhaps one of the most important in Western history. Scholars tell us that modern society—with its emphasis on commerce and the freedom of the individual—was invented in the wake of the French Revolution. For a thousand years, the social fabric of France had remained essentially the same. People thought of themselves as part of an extensive network of relationships that stretched back over generations. They were defined by the social roles they had inherited, roles they accepted as absolute.

For this new postrevolutionary generation, which grew to adulthood after 1789, that network unraveled. What the Revolution taught them was that the world could change in the most radical ways. Peasants could become politicians. Kings—once esteemed as gods—could face the executioner. The young Italian soldier Napoléon Bonaparte, who would soon rule one of the world's great empires but had spent much of his childhood at an impoverished boarding school in the Champagne, became one of his generation's best representatives.

The structure of society in this new modern era was based on commercial relations and on the display of commodities. In many ways, it was not very different from the world in which we now live. Because people started to see their dreams reflected in the goods they purchased, there was a second economic revolution. Before long, champagne would become one of those defining products that told people who they were. The explosion of the fashion industry hit closer to home for Barbe-Nicole and her family. Their luxurious lifestyle, after all, depended on the textile trade.

In the 1780s and 1790s, the world went crazy for fashion in a way it never had before. A generation earlier, clothes were a sign of whatever good fortune you had inherited. The aristocracy had always spent recklessly and famously on fashion, of course. Marie Antoinette couldn't get enough diamond shoe buckles or silk petticoats. They were symbols of power and privilege that she manipulated shrewdly. Now, middle-class citizens embraced fashion, which also became democratic. For the first time, the dresses of working people imitated the styles of the rich. And in revolutionary France, the upper classes, if they had any sense, pretty quickly started imitating the style of the peasants.

Fashion was at the heart of the Revolution. Another word for a member of the radical Jacobin Club was a *sans culottes*—someone who didn't wear a rich man's pants. During the months when people were haphazardly guillotined in the streets of France as public entertainment, ladies mimicked the look, cutting their hair in dramatic bobs and wearing blood-red ribbons around their necks. In Paris, the wives of republican politicians made a competition out of such fantastic costumes. In Great Britain, there was a special word for the men who imitated the revolutionary fashions of France and the United States: dandies. The word lives on in the old tune "Yankee Doodle Dandy."

As a young woman, Barbe-Nicole was not immune to fashion or to the social statements that it could make. Her sister, Clémentine, a local beauty, was notorious in Reims for her love of the latest styles. When she learned that everyone in London was wearing their hair stacked to towering heights and decorated with ribbons and trinkets, Clémentine had her portrait done, her granddaughter later remembered, "wearing a cloudy coiffure of white tulle and celestial blue ribbons."

No one has identified a picture of Barbe-Nicole as a young woman, although there must once have been one. Small miniatures painted on ivory were common—the snapshots of the era. Even without a portrait, it is easy enough to imagine Barbe-Nicole at sixteen. Unlike her willowy sister, she was not conventionally pretty. She was plain and tended to be chubby. Her citizen identification card describes her at that age as very petite, a mere four and a half feet tall, but with gray eyes and hair that even the stern bureaucrat conceded was a poetic "ardent" blond. The word in French evokes the color of live coals or a glass of tawny spirits.

Like so many other daughters of revolutionary France, she wore the simple white muslin gowns that were patriotic symbols of a rustic and more egalitarian future. These white dresses were more than just a popular—and populist—fashion. Almost immediately, the more dogmatic leaders of the new republican government began calling for a required national dress code. By the end of the 1790s, it was foolhardy to wear anything else. Men wore their trousers tucked into working boots. Women's simple gowns often had just one ornament: the national cockade. In her missing portrait, Barbe-Nicole surely has one pinned at her breast, in imitation of the great hostesses of Paris—a tricolor festoon of ribbons in the revolutionary colors of red, white, and blue.

If Barbe-Nicole appeared as the daughter of a French revolutionary and committed radical, appearances were deceiving. The Ponsardin family was living an elaborate lie—or at least a carefully constructed public deception. Her father had not only saved the family fortune; he had prospered during a peasant revolt. Embracing the revolutionary cause of the common man, he had risen to even greater political prominence while continuing to live a private life of upper-middle-class affluence and privilege that was essentially unchanged from the days of the ancien régime. This was all because Nicolas and his family understood the importance of keeping their secrets.

Barbe-Nicole's marriage was part of that collective silence. In 1798, the new century was swiftly approaching, and so was a new chapter in Barbe-Nicole's life. Although the most terrible excesses of the Revolution had waned, France remained politically and socially unsettled in this new era of republicanism. In this climate, the twenty-year-old Barbe-Nicole was about to be married. Her intended was a catch—the dashing François Clicquot, handsome son of another wealthy and prosperous textile merchant, a man who also dabbled increasingly in the local wine trade.

Barbe-Nicole must have dreamed of a church wedding, with candles and a choir and the strong scent of incense in the air. Perhaps she and the family's loyal dressmaker, the woman who had saved her from a revolutionary mob, now pored secretly over fashion plates from Paris, astonished at the fanciful dresses worn by the vibrant Madame Tallien and the other women who helped create the patriotic costumes of the new French Directory government. She knew, of course, that her father would never approve of such provocative attire for his daughter. It would only attract attention.

Besides, her dreams of a church wedding were illegal and dangerous. The practice of religion had been ended officially in France in 1794, and the Catholic rites were criminal. Her father had been part of the National Assembly that outlawed them. But the Ponsardin family was still Catholic. In fact, despite Nicolas's public embrace of radical party politics and a new secular society dedicated to reason, he remained not only a Catholic but a staunch royalist. Nicolas, after all, had helped to crown a king, and he still dreamed of the day when he could boast a noble coat of arms. Privately and with great secrecy, Catholic families throughout France began to arrange dangerous, furtive religious ceremonies, while conforming outwardly to the new civic rituals of the republic.

So, in the early hours of a June morning, Barbe-Nicole, dressed simply but not unfashionably in the plain white muslin gown of a young revolutionary, married François, the only son of Philippe and Catherine-Françoise Clicquot, in a damp cellar before a small and anxious group of their families. Perhaps it was even in the cellars beneath her family's grand estate: Since one of the passageways led underground to the new home where she and François would begin their lives together on rue de l'Hôpital, it would have been an obvious and convenient place for a secret gathering of the two families.

Interconnected cellars like this ran for three hundred miles underneath the city of Reims. According to legend, when the Romans built the ancient city of Reims (pronounced unaccountably to the Anglo-Saxon ear as "Rans"), then known as Durocortorum, they set thousands of enslaved men to digging out great blocks of limestone from quarries. These stones formed the foundation for the lively city of Barbe-Nicole's girlhood, with its cool white-and-gray palette and soaring Gothic cathedral.

The vast empty spaces these Roman quarry workers left behind—dark and silent underground cathedrals of a different kind—became the town's cellars and caverns. Businessmen such as her father employed them as storage depots, and for generations the monks, priests, and Knights Templars, whose presence in Reims dated back centuries, had used them as passageways beneath the cathedral and its nearby palace. The Hôtel Ponsardin stood in one of the most ancient and holy parts of the city, in what once was the heart of medieval Christendom. In modern times, wine merchants had already discovered that these passageways could serve as the climate-controlled wine cellars absolutely necessary to the production of the local sparkling wine that we enjoy as champagne.

Barbe-Nicole surely carried that day the traditional French bridal bouquet of roses and orange blossoms, and the soft breezes, which began somewhere in the distant tunnels that ran for miles underneath Reims, would have infused their summer scent into the empty coolness that surrounded this small party. The priest spoke quietly, conscious of the resounding echoes. The nerves of the assembled party were alert to every noise from outside. Discovery meant certain arrest and imprisonment. Later, the families completed the required secular contract, which confirms that Citizen Clicquot married Citizen Ponsardin on June 10, 1798—on 22 Pairial, in the sixth year of the new French republic.

Although this secret wedding may have seemed an inauspicious beginning, no place could have been more fitting than a cellar to celebrate a marriage that would change the history of wine. It would be in cellars such as this that Barbe-Nicole would craft her first vintage. Until the moment she married François, she had no personal connections to the sparkling wine with which the name Clicquot would one day be synonymous. She was simply the daughter of a wealthy and well-connected textile merchant, living a quiet life in a small city in the northeastern corner of France, and her marriage into a family with a wine brokerage was all more or less a matter of chance.

But Barbe-Nicole had been named after her maternal grandmother, a woman who would have been very pleased with all that this marriage would bring. Because Marie-Barbe-Nicole Huart–Le Tertre had been born a Ruinart—the daughter of Nicolas Ruinart, already a famous man in Reims. Although, like so many in the extended Ponsardin and Le Tertre families, he, too, had started life as a woolen dealer, this Nicolas was famous for champagne. He was the nephew of the monk Dom Thierry Ruinart, the friend and sometime collaborator of that legendary figure Dom Pierre Pérignon. As the story goes, before his death, Dom Pérignon imparted his winemaking secrets to Thierry, who passed them on to his nephew Nicolas, who founded in 1729 the world's first champagne house. Barbe-Nicole's great-grandfather had invented the industry that she would someday revolutionize.

The couple's respective families had negotiated this marriage. If Nicolas no longer entertained ideas of an aristocratic marriage after the Revolution, he certainly intended to arrange an advantageous one. François's family had also made their fortune in the local textile trade, although his father's wine brokerage, established some time in the 1770s, was becoming an increasingly important sideline, advertised in national news circulars. By 1777, the year of Barbe-Nicole's birth, the Clicquot wine brokerage was already selling a modest ten thousand bottles of wine a year, and a significant part of it was the local sparkling wine.

The Ponsardin family surely purchased wines from Philippe Clicquot during this period—perhaps even some of the champagne that their daughter would one day make famous. When Nicolas and Jeanne-Clémentine enjoyed a bottle of bubbly to celebrate the birth of their first child in 1777, perhaps it was a Clicquot family wine. The two families, after all, were near neighbors. The impressive Clicquot home, built along the gray cobblestone street known as rue de la Vache, was only a stone's throw from the Hôtel Ponsardin. More important, the two fathers worked in the same business. Despite the wine sideline, Philippe Clicquot was first and foremost a textile merchant, and in Reims this was a tight business community. Nicolas and Philippe were local industry leaders, with their commercial offices next door to each other. Competitors and neighbors, the families undoubtedly lived in each other's pockets.

By the time of their marriage, Barbe-Nicole and François had known each other for years, and it would be pleasant to imagine a childhood romance. The reality, however, was probably less sentimental. Marriage was an economic decision and not a romantic one, and it involved the future of an entire extended family. Children were not typically forced into marriages that they despised, but the first duty of a young girl especially was obedience and submission to her father: Love was something that blossomed within marriage and not a prelude to it. At its heart, this was a match arranged by their respective fathers, calculated to extend the complex web of social and entrepreneurial ties that connected the prominent merchant families of Reims.

Studying her new husband in the first days of their marriage, however, Barbe-Nicole had reason to be optimistic. François was an energetic young man, and he played the violin beautifully. He had been given a liberal and expensive education, and he could boast many accomplishments. Not only did he know the sums and figures of a businessman's son, he could also quote from the great works of French literature and had read the famous philosophers of the Enlightenment, men like Diderot, Voltaire, and Rousseau. Barbe-Nicole's private passion was reading, and it was common ground. François's spelling, however, was dismal, and his command of the foreign languages necessary to the family business was not quite what his father wished. Still, he had big ideas and great enthusiasm, and unlike many husbands, he was willing to share both with her.

Compared with Barbe-Nicole, however, it seems François was sensitive and moody, and she must also have noticed immediately the way in which his mother and father coddled him. She soon understood why. He could be cheerful and energized one moment and apparently turn melancholy and despairing the next. This was a side of her husband she would not have expected. Despite the close connections between their families, she had not seen much of him for several years. François had finished his education abroad, working as a business apprentice in the firm of a banker and merchant in Switzerland who was one of his father's friends. This sort of hands-on business training was the norm for the sons of successful entrepreneurs, and he had returned to Reims only the year before their wedding.

She heard, of course, the stories of his time in Switzerland. His parents had been anxious to help him avoid the military when the Revolution spiraled into war. The whole point of sending François to complete his education in Switzerland in 1792, just as conscriptions into the army were becoming inevitable, was to dodge the draft. Young men in France were being forcibly rounded up to serve in the military, and Philippe was anxious to get François out of the country. Like Barbe-Nicole's father, Philippe put on a show of being a radical patriot. His revolutionary politics, however, did not go so far as having his son on the front lines. Having lived a double life as a Catholic and royalist during a decade of republican purges, Barbe-Nicole had learned to expect a different reality behind any public facade. It made her something of a cynic.

She could also understand that with François as their only son, his parents had staked their financial future on the day when he could take over the family business. They would face an uncertain old age if he died in the muddy fields of Austria, and it was clearly in their best interests to keep him safe. What she could not have known and would have found less reassuring were the other reasons Philippe and Catherine-Françoise must have had for wanting to keep François out of the army.

François's letters home from 1792 to 1794 are filled with patriotic zeal. He had a romantic view of war and was naturally an idealist. He was also apparently prone to illness and—more worryingly—to depression. Philippe wrote urgent letters to his son in Switzerland, reminding François of his "weak temperament" and history of hernias. In other letters, he begged his son to fight melancholy and eat well. There was a darker side to François's ebullient personality that his parents knew only too well.

The result of it all was that the idea of their son facing the rigors of war sent them into a panic. Philippe was desperate to find a way out of the military for François, and his son's enthusiasm for the service only worried him more. Soon they were caught up in the power struggle that seems to have defined their relationship. His father was a coolly rational man who, with the best of intentions, must have undermined his son's confidence by questioning François's characteristic zeal for every new plan. Doubting himself and seeking approval, François would always back down.

So when a mandatory draft was announced, Philippe started pulling strings wherever he could find them, and François went along with it. When a medical waiver proved impossible, Philippe set about buying his son a noncombat commission. The young man had learned something about botany. Perhaps he could serve in the army's pharmacy. Philippe wrote anxious letters urging his son to consider it, while he struggled to arrange an appointment to the medical corps. Later, he would consider any branch, as long as it did not mean sending his son into the battlefield.

In the end, Philippe did manage to keep his son out of harm's way. Whatever bribes he paid were effective. In the spring of 1794, François began his military service on French soil, working in commercial import and export administration offices. There was no great glory in any of it, and it was hard for François to feel that he had not missed out, although in the years to come, this experience in the export business would lay the groundwork for the new directions in the family business.

When François was discharged in the final months of 1796—in the euphemistic words of one early biographer, "retired from active service"— he returned to Reims, and whatever courtship the young couple enjoyed took place in those eighteen months between François's return and a June morning in 1798, when they were wedded in a secret ceremony in the dank cellars that wound for miles underneath the ancient city of Reims.

Now a married woman with her own home and a lively young husband, whose company and conversation she enjoyed, Barbe-Nicole looked forward to the future with happiness. But even if she did not realize it yet, she and François were essentially mismatched in at least one fundamental way. She had inherited all her father's—and Philippe's—ruthless pragmatism and keen business instincts. Barbe-Nicole, however, had married a dreamer. And he had his heart set on the wine business.

In the first year of their marriage, François was determined to reinvent the family business. He was immediately brought into his father's company as a partner, and before long he was preoccupied with developing the small wine trade that his father had started more than twenty years before. It was a commitment that Barbe-Nicole would come to share.

The company had what should have been the most important asset for a wine trade: vineyards. The Clicquot family owned a good deal of property, including several excellent parcels of land in the countryside southeast of Reims, perfect for growing grapes. There were family vineyards in Villers-Allerand and Sermiers, on the northern slopes of the mountain that divides Reims from the nearby village of Épernay, in Bouzy to the east, and farther south along the river, in the *grand cru* village of Tours-sur-Marne.

The French system of the *échelle des crus*—the ranking of vineyard growths—is a time-honored tradition still used today to indicate the quality of the grapes used by the winemakers. The title of *grand cru* ("grand growth") is reserved for the highly select localities (currently only seventeen in the Champagne region) where the very finest grapes are grown, those rating a perfect 100 on a percentage scale. The second category, *premier cru* ("first growth"), refers to the next forty-three best wine-growing regions in an area and is given only to those rating from 90 to 99 percent excellent.

It is an admittedly arcane system, and the laws governing it are occasionally comic to the uninitiated. In his authoritative work *French Wine, Revised and Updated*, for example, Robert Joseph explains that, today, "unless a wine is from a *premier cru* vineyard . . . the vineyard name must be printed in characters no more than half the height of the ones used for the village name." Details like this make for superb satire, and I defy anyone to find them useful when confronted with the acreage of local wines found on the shelves of any sizable French grocery store. But the distinctions they represent are important.

The soil and microclimate in which grapes are grown, after all, are almost as important to the final wine as the skill of the winemaker, and it was already well-known by the eighteenth century that these environmental conditions—known in French as the *terroir*—shape the character of the wine as distinctively as any house style. Perhaps François and Barbe-Nicole owned a copy of the philosopher Diderot's famous encyclopedia, published in the 1760s and still popular during the 1790s. There, under the entry for "wine," they could read: "The climate, sun, and other causes contribute to the goodness of wine . . . [and] the nature of the *terroir* contributes greatly." It is the potential of this *terroir* that the *cru* system is intended to rank and describe.

The young couple personally owned a surprising amount of real estate when one considers that they were just beginning in life. Upon his daughter's marriage, Nicolas gave the newlyweds a large farm and two windmills, along with a large dowry of cash. As a wedding gift, her father-in-law, Philippe, gave them more land and more capital—a small forest in Quatre-Champs and extensive fields in Tours-sur-Marne and in the nearby river town of Bisseuil, excellent properties in the heart of the French wine country. They had the resources to dream, and it was a dream of wine from the beginning.

There were long afternoons when they could explore these small villages and study their prospects. Traveling in an open carriage along the dusty side roads, they soon became a familiar sight. In those first days of taking stock, of their future and each other, they doubtless stopped in the hillside village of Chigny-la-Montagne, where the family owned property. The village clings today to its steep incline and affords breathtaking views of the vast fertile expanses of valley below, although its name was changed at the end of the nineteenth century to Chigny-les-Roses, in tribute to Louise Pommery—later known as one of the great women of champagne but remembered by the locals for her love of roses. Everywhere in the Champagne the roses come tumbling out of the sides of the vineyards still. Unfortunately, it's hard to make romance out of the reason for this glorious summer profusion. None of the celebrated French lover's passion here, it seems. These roses are nothing more than the winemaker's canary in the mine shaft, an early signal of impending disease and blight in a vineyard. They are planted because roses get sick with everything and usually before anything else in the garden.

Here in Chigny-la-Montagne, Barbe-Nicole and François would have sought out the famous walled vineyards of the late Monsieur Allart de Maisonneuve, a former officer for Louis XV and one of the first men to produce champagne on the mountain of Reims. The grapes grown in this enclosed field, or *clos*, spread out beneath a small stone mill, were already among the most famous in the region. It has always been known as fabulous *terroir*, and

Allart had developed it with talent. Wine connoisseurs would write about this special vineyard well into the nineteenth century, and no one with a passion for the wine business would have missed the opportunity to see the Allart vineyards—and to wonder what they could learn.

Barbe-Nicole and François likely knew and sought out some of the local winemaking families as well, families such as the Cattiers. The wine business depended on a network of personal connections, especially between distributors like themselves and the local growers. When Barbe-Nicole and François first visited these hillside wine-growing regions in the early years of their marriage, the Cattiers were well established and respected vignerons in these small mountain villages and had owned vineyards in Chigny-la-Montagne at least as early as 1763. The young couple would have been eager to meet successful and reliable growers, already looking forward to new sources of wine when they had larger orders. Ironically, the Cattier family—still producers of a world-class champagne with a celebrity following—now owns the legendary Allart vineyards, known as the *clos du moulin*, after the mills (*moulins*) that have stood in these walled fields since before the French Revolution.

Despite their enthusiastic beginnings in the wine trade, Barbe-Nicole and François did not yet have a personal role in making any of the wines they sold, although the family owned excellent vineyards. The textile trade was still the primary focus of his father's company, and they were a long way yet from the day when François could focus all his attention on wine. The Clicquots were simply small-time wine brokers—people who made their money distributing the wines made by local growers like the Cattiers. Sometimes the wines were purchased directly from the vignerons, and sometimes they used a wine expert known as a *courtier* to make their selections for them. Even when the grapes were grown in the family vineyards, they relied on someone else to craft the vintage.

Despite his vast reserve of energy and enthusiasm, moreover, François was proposing only a modest revision to his father's business strategy in the beginning. The family company—now officially Clicquot-Muiron and Son (the Muiron a customary gesture to his mother's family)—had a small secondary focus on wine distribution. For decades, Philippe had been supplementing his textile shipments in France with wine sales, charging a small commission of around 10 percent on each bottle. François wanted to increase those sales so they were more than a sideline, and he wanted to find those new clients internationally, in capital cities as far away as Germany and Russia.

His father must have had his doubts. Sensibly enough, Philippe saw that most of Europe had been at war for nearly a decade. There were better moments for trying to reenter the international market. Even in the best circumstances, shipping overseas a fragile product like wine—so easily destroyed by changes in temperature or rough handling—was a risky business. Philippe had been in the trade long enough to know. But this time, François was determined not to let anyone spoil his enthusiasm, and, remarkably, the new partners came to an agreement. As soon as there was peace, François would have his way. If it was going to succeed, the young man had a lot to learn. He would have to develop an expertise in finding the best local wines. Above all, he would have to find a new way of marketing wine to the fashionable trendsetters of his generation.

Chapter 3

Champagne Dreams

W hen François first set out to learn about the local wine industry, he hoped to find a wine that he could sell to the international luxury market. His father had once sold wines around
the world. But after the Revolution, Philippe was reluctant to take on
the headache of shipping across war zones, refocusing his small sideline
in the wine business instead on selling wines at home. The war was still
dragging on in 1799. In fact, it would be an on-again, off-again affair for
the next fifteen years. François, however, had the idea that his military
service in the national export office—ungallant though it had been—had
taught him something about the ways around closed ports.

Considering his goals, it was inevitable that the local sparkling wine
caught François's attention. Clicquot-Muiron was in a good position to
expand its sales in champagne. Most of the wines sold in this northeastern
corner of France left the region in wooden casks, destined for a midrange
market. It was quality table wine, which a family or an innkeeper would
plan to consume within the year. Bottled wines were still rare. With all
the additional costs—labor, glassware, storage, breakage—bottling made
sense only if the wines could be sold at a premium.

Selling premium wines had been Philippe's business model from the
beginning. He was one of the earliest distributors in the Champagne to
see the advantage of specializing in fine bottled wines, especially. Since

the local growers who supplied his business did all the actual winemaking, he could cleverly avoid many of the obvious technical risks of the craft. By the 1790s, the offices of Clicquot-Muiron were shipping about 15,000 bottles of wine a year—and, of course, some of it was the local bubbly.

We know this wine as champagne. François and Barbe-Nicole would have called it just *vin mousseux*—sparkling wine. It wasn't regularly called *champagne* even in France until the 1860s, when it had all become big business. What is most surprising is how different champagne looked and tasted at the end of the eighteenth century. It would have been virtually unrecognizable to most of us.

We have to imagine that François conducted some of his market research at home. Any sensible businessman would have wanted to know his product. Marital harmony would have been the obvious casualty of greedily conducting this research alone. So François and Barbe-Nicole surely taste-tested some of the local wines. What filled their glasses was nothing like the crisp champagnes that we enjoy today. In fact, dry—or what the specialists call *brut*—champagne, like the word *champagne* itself, did not become popular for another sixty years. It certainly wasn't served as a predinner aperitif. Instead, people drank champagne as a dessert wine, sometimes so cold that it was almost frozen slush. And it was shockingly sweet.

Today, champagne is ranked from driest to sweetest in categories that progress from *brut nature* (naturally strong), *extra brut* (extra strong), and *brut* (strong) on the dry end and then—despite the hopelessly misleading names—on into the categories of *sec* (dry), *extra sec* (extra dry), *demi sec* (half dry), and *doux* (gentle) on the sweeter end. Essentially, *brut* is dry and *sec* is sweet. Our *demi sec*—one of the sweeter champagnes on the market—has up to twenty grams of sugar per bottle.

François and Barbe-Nicole sampled wines that were at least ten times sweeter than today's *demi sec* champagne. Champagne sold in France during their lifetime often had two hundred grams of residual sugar. The Russians liked it sweeter still. François hoped that Russia would become an important market for the future of Clicquot-Muiron wines; there, three hundred grams of sugar was common. To get an idea of what this must have tasted like, consider that even our most sugary dessert wines are positively tart in comparison. An ice wine or a sauternes only rarely has two hundred grams of sugar. The 2001 vintage sauternes made at the legendary Château d'Yquem in France, one of the most concentrated harvests in years, has only 150 grams of residual sugar. One of the sweetest wines around—the late-harvest dessert wine made in California's Napa Valley by Grgich Hills known as Violetta—has just 250 grams in an average year. Imagine it with bubbles, and that's more or less what a glass of champagne in the eighteenth century tasted like.

The champagne that François and Barbe-Nicole tasted wouldn't have been a pretty light blond color, either. We would probably describe it as rosé. But it was an earthy sort of rosé. The finest wines from the region were a brownish pink. In fact, one of the earliest uses of the word *champagne* as a color described it not as the pale golden straw hues of the twentieth century, but as "a faint redish colour like Champane wine." The locals had a better term for it. As one eighteenth-century wine lover put it, the color of the "natural Wine of *Champaign* . . . they call Oiel du Pedrix.[*sic*]" This translates as "eye of the partridge," and it was a kind of tawny pink, with rich honey highlights.

The colors came from the winemaking process. To give customers the jarringly sweet champagne they wanted, winemakers added generous dollops of sugar syrup and brandy to the bottle before the final corking, and the brandy often tinted the wine a light golden brown. The pink color came when the skins of the grapes stained the clear juice inside. It was a sign that the red grapes had not been crushed quickly enough at harvest or early enough in the morning to produce a perfectly clear white liquid, known as the *must*. A bit of staining was so common that even when the technology improved, some winemakers began deliberately coloring their champagnes a brighter red, using elderberry syrup. People had come to expect color in their bubbly.

Sometimes people also described their champagne as gray, which doesn't sound like the most appetizing color for a glass of sparkling wine. Eighteenth-century wine manuals talk about the *gris de perle*, or pearl gray tints. Pearl gray at least begins to sound almost glamorous. Fortunately, champagne never actually looked like dirty dishwater. The word here is deceiving. These authors are describing not the color of the wine but, rather, the grapes that went into its production. As one wine tourist in the 1760s tried to explain: "In the Champagne gray wine refers to those wines which in other places are called white Champagne. Gray wine is made with black grapes." The logic was simple: Black and white makes gray. So gray wine was a white wine crafted with some black—or what people today often call red—grapes. Under current French law, champagne is still made in this same way. Strict regulations assure that real champagne can use only three grape varietals—the black *pinot meunier* and *pinot noir* grapes and the white *chardonnay* grape.

The blend of these grapes creates the style of the wine, and today, there are two styles of champagne. *Blanc de noirs* is a white wine made with at least one of the black grapes in the mix, while *blanc de blancs* is a white wine made only from white grapes. Since chardonnay is the only white grape used in champagne, blanc de blanc champagne is essentially a sparkling chardonnay. Since pinot meunier doesn't hold up particularly well in aging, a lot of vintage blanc de noirs are actually just sparkling pinot noir wines. In our modern era, the style is designated on the label, along with information about whether it is vintage (using grapes from a single harvest) or nonvintage (using grapes from a blend of harvests). At the end of the eighteenth century, when Barbe-Nicole and François were first imagining a future in the wine business, nobody put labels on their bottles. And champagne was made only as a blanc de noirs—the style then known as *gris de perle*.

At least the champagne that François and Barbe-Nicole tasted would have bubbled like ours. Or if not exactly like ours—poor glassmaking in the eighteenth century meant that bottles started bursting at about half the pressure champagne makers use today—it did bubble. This would not have been the case had they lived only a century before. Even today, the history of how champagne got its sparkle is an astonishing tale, filled with deception and controversy.

The story of champagne begins sometime in the seventeenth century, although people had been making wine in this region for at least a thousand years. According to legend, the Romans first cultivated vineyards in the chalky fields of the Champagne. Others date the appearance of vines in the area around Reims to the fourth century AD. By the seventeenth century, the Champagne was already famous for its wines.

The best wine-growing areas in the region were either in the little villages that grew up along the banks of the river Marne or along the sunny slopes of the mountain to the southeast of Reims. Today, these two areas are in the heart of the Champagne wine country, and wines made in this microregion—crafted mostly from pinot noir grapes—are labeled simply with the appellation "Montagne de Reims."

It was here that many of the Clicquot family properties were located, and the names of most of the best winemaking villages are still famous. Modern guidebooks direct tourists and hopeful wine tasters to villages such as Aÿ, Dizy, Cumières, Ambonnay, Verzenay, Chigny-les-Roses, Bouzy, Sermiers, Épernay, and, of course, Hautvillers. Long before consumers could turn to the familiar rankings we now find in *Wine Spectator* or pasted to grocery-store shelves, customers had to depend on the reputation of the region—or even the particular village—where the wine was grown. In the seventeenth century, wines made in the heart of the Champagne were known for their excellence, said to rival even those grown farther to the south in the verdant Saône valley of Burgundy.

This was a business in still wines, many of which were hearty reds. Winemakers in the region did not look on the development of bubbles with any happiness. Wine that sparkled was wine that had gone wrong. By the seventeenth century, it seemed to be happening more and more often. So in the 1660s, Dom Pierre Pérignon, the legendary father of champagne and cellar master of the abbey at Hautvillers, was given the task of finding a way to get rid of the bubbles ruining the local wines. Had he been successful, champagne in France might have ended before it ever got started.

This curious sparkle that appeared in the wines of the Champagne region first began to plague the local vintners during the Middle Ages, and it was apparently the result of unexpectedly cold weather. By the end of the late fourteenth century, Europe was experiencing what has been called "the little ice age." This shift in climatic patterns, which lasted well into the nineteenth century, transformed winemaking in France as dramatically as scientists now predict global warming will.

The trouble with this extended cold spell was that the Champagne had always been a cool climate. Today, hovering along the forty-ninth parallel latitude, it is still one of the most northerly wine-growing regions to produce excellent fruit. (Although perhaps not for long. Scientists think it might take only another few degrees before this northerly range extends across the English Channel to Great Britain.) With this further drop in temperatures during the little ice age, at its worst from about 1560 to 1730—in other words, during the long seventeenth century—winemakers found that the natural process of fermentation needed to transform grape must into wine often stalled over the winter.

Normally, the process of winemaking is simple. The ripe grapes, with their rich fruit sugars, are harvested and crushed. The must from the earliest pressings is used to make a good-quality still wine. The later pressings are used to make local farm wines of descending quality. In the eighteenth century, the peasants even drank a wine known as *piquette*, a watery pomace wine made from the pulp that remained after all the richness and flavor had been pressed out of the grapes at harvest.

Next, the must is placed in unsealed wooden casks. Here, within the right temperature range, the yeasts naturally lurking on the grape skins begin to consume the fruit sugars. There are two important by-products of this "hot" organic reaction: carbon dioxide, which escapes into the air; and alcohol, which thankfully stays put. When the fermentation runs its course—when the yeast has consumed all the sugar—the wine is then racked and clarified to remove the residue, including the yeast cells, which begin to die and decompose. At this point, we could drink the wine, although it would taste quite sharp. So instead, eighteenth-century wines were usually put into sealed wooden casks sometime during the winter and stored until the next autumn, letting them mellow. During the freezing cold winters of the seventeenth century, winemakers in the Champagne discovered that they had live yeast showing up again in the spring, pumping out more carbon dioxide and more alcohol after the wines had been placed in those sealed casks. Since now the carbon dioxide had nowhere to go, the result was fizzy wine.

What had happened was that the temperatures went too low in the winter for the yeast to finish consuming all the sugar. It had just gone dormant. Without the technology to test the amount of sugar remaining in a barrel of wine, the winemakers were at the mercy of the seasons and their intuition. When the warmer temperatures returned in the spring, the process of yeast fermentation just picked back up again. Winemakers today refer to this as a "secondary fermentation." Winemakers in the seventeenth century had a less charitable phrase for it. They called a bubbly vintage the devil's wine.

This process of a second fermentation where the bubbles get trapped is still the basis for the production of sparkling wine in the *méthode champenoise*, or champagne method. Today, owing to legal restrictions on use of the word *champagne*, which allow only wines made in the Champagne region of France to be identified in this way, it is often also known as the *méthode traditionnelle*, or traditional method. At its most basic level, champagne is a still wine that has been coaxed into undergoing a secondary fermentation process in a bottle. This time, the carbon dioxide is concentrated in the wine, giving it the celebrated sparkle.

For winemakers in the rural Champagne during the little ice age, this second fermentation was occurring by accident. In time, winemakers and wine lovers would discover that it was possible to make wine sparkle on purpose by adding dissolved sugar, brandy, and yeast before bottling. New sugar and yeast would kick-start the fermentation process again. This mixture is known in champagne production as the *liqueur de tirage*, and it is essential to producing those nose-tickling bubbles that we enjoy in fine champagne.

In the seventeenth century, however, winemakers were anything but delighted by the voluntary sparkle that developed in their casks come spring. When Dom Pérignon was cellar master of the ancient hillside abbey in the village of Hautvillers in the 1660s, no one in France wanted fizzy wines, and the bubbles were ruining the abbey's lucrative wine trade. The monks were not crazy. In truth, the bubbles could turn a bad wine into something undrinkable. Sealed in casks rather than bottles, these wines fizzed only lightly: They did not have the exuberant sparkle that we associate with commercially produced champagne.

Perhaps more important, only rare wines are improved by the addition of bubbles. Making wine sparkle takes some knowledge; making champagne requires the art of a master blender. The base wine used to make champagne is often a blend or, in French, *assemblage* of over forty different growths, and a master blender is like an alchemist of the senses, capable of transmuting the lowly grape into a silky liquid gold. Dom Pérignon was justly famous for his superb skills as a blender—but his legendary wines did not have bubbles.

This is one of the great ironies—we might even say great deceptions—of wine history, for conventional wisdom tells us that Dom Pérignon was the delighted inventor of champagne. He is supposed to have quipped to one of his sandal-shod brothers, "Come quickly! I am drinking the stars!" Yet it only made sense that Dom Pérignon wanted to rid champagne of its bubbles. There was no market for sparkling wines yet. In France, nobody wanted them. So, over the course of the next decade, Dom Pérignon dedicated himself to experimenting with ways to stop the development of bubbles.

In fact, the idea that Dom Pérignon invented champagne was always just imaginative marketing. It was a brilliant but misleading sales pitch. The popular legend has its origins in a late-nineteenth-century advertising campaign, started at a time when sparkling wine was already big business. In her book *When Champagne Became French*, scholar Kolleen Guy shows how it wasn't until the 1889 World Exhibition in Paris that the region's champagne producers saw the marketing potential and started printing brochures about Dom Pérignon. From that point on, the role of the celebrated monk became a truism.

The truth is that no one in the seventeenth or even the eighteenth century associated Dom Pérignon with the discovery of sparkling wine. His friend Dom François, writing the biography of the famous monk, never mentions bubbles, and even the abbey's lawyers in the nineteenth century—looking for things to claim rights to—didn't think they could convince anyone that Dom Pérignon had anything to do with making wine sparkle. As the lawyers knew, the monks at Hautvillers didn't even start bottling their wines until the 1750s.

For those who enjoy the romance of the Dom Pérignon legend, there is even worse news. Wine historians now claim that champagne did not even originate in France. Champagne was first "invented" in Great Britain, where there was already a small commercial market for sparkling champagne by the 1660s. British enthusiasts were investigating ways to control the production of its so-called *mousse*—the fizz—several decades before the wine was sold at all in France. It seems that wealthy British consumers, anxious to prevent their imported barrels of wine from turning to expensive vinegar, first bottled wines from the Champagne region and, in doing so, discovered sparkling wine.

What would happen is this: Seventeenth-century British connoisseurs would order their fine table wines from vintners in the Champagne region, and, as required under French law in those days, it would be sold in wooden barrels. The wines arrived without a hint of bubbles. Winemakers in the Champagne, in fact, were not legally allowed to sell their wines in glass bottles until the passage of a special royal decree given to the city of Reims in the 1720s. Unfortunately, without a sealed bottle, there is no sparkling champagne. It just takes leaving a bottle open in the fridge overnight to learn how fast bubbly goes flat. Likewise, it did not take these British consumers long to discover that once a sealed cask of wine was tapped, it went off quickly, a result of the same oxidization process that spoils opened bottles of wine after a day or two in our own kitchens.

So these wily merchants and consumers began considering ways to preserve their wines. It was no mystery that brandy could act as a preservative. They also began bottling. Great Britain was producing far stronger and less expensive glass than could be found on the other side of the English Channel, giving British wine lovers the advantage. After bottling their imported wines and maybe dosing them with brandy, people inevitably found that some of this wine—wine where a bit of yeast happened to be present—started to fizz. In their efforts to preserve imported still wines from the Champagne, they had haphazardly started the process of secondary fermentation required to make sparkling champagne.

This, we now believe, was how champagne was discovered. This oenological curiosity soon developed a cult following, and one of history's great gourmets, a Frenchman by the name of Charles de Saint-Évremond, helped to create its new celebrity. He had made an enemy of the king and was forced to flee for his life into exile in Great Britain. The consummate

Frenchman, he brought with him a love of fine wines and good food. So when a small group of people learned about this new sparkling wine, he started spreading the news with an infectious enthusiasm. Soon sparkling wine became the status symbol of in-the-know London high society. While Dom Pérignon was laboring in the cellars of his chilly abbey at Hautvillers to get rid of the bubbles in his wines, British scientists were working hard to understand how to produce them.

As a result, the process of making sparkling wine didn't remain haphazard for long. When people want evidence that the British were making champagne first, they usually turn to the lecture presented in 1662 to the Royal Society of London by a scientist named Christopher Merrett. In his treatise, he explained how adding sugar to wines would help produce the desired fizz. But Merrett's lecture on winemaking, *Observations Concerning the Ordering of Wines* (1662), which borrowed some of its ideas from the ancient English tradition of cider making, was just one of several sources from which hobbyists and gentlemen could learn the essentials of making champagne. Many of the same principles for making sparkling liqueurs in the bottle are described, for example, in contemporary texts such as John Evelyn's *Pomona; or, An Appendix Concerning Fruit-Trees in Relation to Cider*, published by order of the Royal Society in 1664. Most wine experts now believe that the British were converting their barrels of imported wine from the region around Reims—wine with a natural tendency to fizz easily—into sparkling champagne by the 1670s, a full decade before the wine was first produced in France.

In France today, the idea that the British discovered champagne is naturally controversial. Among those who support the French claims, there are some who contend that whatever the British role in developing a gourmet and commercial market for sparkling champagne, the monastic tradition of winemaking in France was already centuries old by the late seventeenth century. Obviously, monks like Dom Pérignon knew that the local wines could sometimes sparkle, even if they considered it a nuisance. And scientific and historical records show that the climatic changes of the little ice age—those decades of unusually cold weather that stalled the fermentation process in the winter and allowed for the natural and unwelcome springtime emergence of bubbles—had been disrupting agriculture in Europe since the end of the sixteenth century. Surely French winemakers had not managed to escape the cold-weather effects on their wines for over a century.

Even if Dom Pérignon and his predecessors did not discover champagne, by the end of the seventeenth century the royal court at the Palace of Versailles certainly had. King Louis XIV of France now wanted nothing more than bubbles in his wine. Suddenly winemakers on both sides of the English Channel were scrambling to find ways to make champagne sparkle, and in order to support his taste for bubbly, the king gave the city of Reims an exclusive license to sell their wines in bottles. It was the beginning of a regional monopoly that would survive, in one form or another, for centuries. In the 1720s, Barbe-Nicole's Ruinart ancestors founded the first champagne house, but soon there were a dozen more, and dealers selling "foamy" wines from the Champagne enjoyed a period of rocketing sales until as late as the 1740s. After all, if Louis XIV began the fashion for sparkling wine, his successor Louis XV turned it into a royal frenzy. He would do anything to please his mistress, the powerful Madame de Pompadour—a woman whose family conveniently owned lucrative property in the Champagne. For more than thirty years, local winemakers could command astonishing prices by supplying the king of France and his friends with bubbly.

Although these were heady times, in reality the royal court was still a tiny and very elite market. The entire Champagne region sold fewer than twenty thousand bottles of sparkling wine a year in the 1730s, and often more than 50 percent of it was sold directly to the palace at Versailles. The customer base was limited to the trendsetters among Europe's nobility, who were enjoying a passing fad. From the beginning, champagne was always the drink of celebration for the lucky few. But even at the height of its first popularity, during those twenty years of royal fame, it never became a broader cultural phenomenon. The average person on the street never dreamed of tasting it. Only the richest of the rich knew its sensuous appeal.

Champagne's iconic status would only emerge much later, because the boom times ended as suddenly as they had begun: By the 1740s, fashion suddenly changed. The growers and distributors, counting on regular extravagances in Paris and looking to make easy money, had planted too many vines, many of them cheap, and the wine market in the Champagne crashed. As bad wines flooded the market, the reputation of the entire region suffered. By the middle of the eighteenth century, the local sparkling wine that François had dreams of once again selling to the world was little more than an extravagant curiosity, known only at the royal courts of Europe. It might well have stayed that way. Had the local wine industry not been reinvented by a handful of talented entrepreneurs—and had champagne not been transformed into the world's most powerful symbol of celebration and the good life—this sparkling wine would have soon faded into the background of world history. And Barbe-Nicole's amazing story would have disappeared with it.

Chapter 4

Anonymity in Their Blood

Despite the grim state of the wine industry in the Champagne during the last decades of the eighteenth century, François and Barbe-Nicole were looking forward to the future with optimism. Not many people in France shared that optimism.

The country had been at war since the early days of the Revolution—for nearly a decade when Barbe-Nicole and François were married. Now, in the first year of Barbe-Nicole and François's life together, the Austrians drove the French across the Rhine at Stockach in a bloody battle that left less fortunate men than François maimed, and the British forced a French retreat in Holland. British admiral Horatio Nelson destroyed almost the entire French navy in the Battle of the Nile, leaving nearly forty thousand young soldiers not very different from François stranded in a war zone with no way of getting home.

Despite the unrest that spread across the European continent, in this small corner of northeastern France the future seemed bright. Barbe-Nicole and François were young and wealthy, and passion for expanding the family's wine business quickly united them. Dreaming of a life in the wine trade and watching the harvest that first year, caught up in the spirit of gaiety that it always occasions for those whose lives are spent watching the slow and uncertain progress of a vintage, they had every reason to be thankful.

To another young man with his roots in the fields of the Champagne, the future also seemed bright in the last year of the century. In early November 1799, when the peasants were at work clearing the debris from the vineyards, word came of monumental changes in Paris. The young general Napoléon Bonaparte—so crushingly defeated in the Battle of the Nile that summer—had overthrown the government in a stunning coup, declaring himself the first consul of France. These were the first heady and frightening days of what would soon become the Napoleonic empire.

Under the new consulate, the dazzling lifestyle that Barbe-Nicole had known as a girl became fashionable again. For an affluent young woman from one of the most ambitious families in Reims, now the mistress of her own home, it should have been an exciting time. But despite her enviable good fortune—and despite even François's obvious pleasure in sharing his passion for the wine business with her—Barbe-Nicole's world in 1799 was quickly closing in. As the wife of an important business owner and the daughter of a man with great political ambitions, the future imagined for her was a luxurious but narrow one. She was on her way to achieving the respectable anonymity for which women of her class were praised. It was a future spent largely in nurseries and drawing rooms.

Already that spring, she had given birth to a baby girl, born at the family home on March 20, 1799, and named, like her mother and her sister, Clémentine. This should have been the beginning of a relentless reproductive life, like the one that left many women at the end of the eighteenth century maimed or dead, either from complications of childbirth or from the barbaric medical interventions meant to save them. A woman had a one-in-twenty chance of dying as a result of the delivery, perhaps a victim of septic infection or puerperal fever, both agonizing deaths. If things took their natural course, Barbe-Nicole could expect in the years to come as many as half a dozen pregnancies, making those death rates a sobering statistic. Her baby had even slimmer chances of survival. French doctors estimated that nearly a third of the children born would die before the end of their second year of life.

Perhaps it was because of this frightening outlook that some young women made a point of dancing at balls until dawn. Even as a new mother and wife, there were undoubtedly plenty of parties. That year,

Barbe-Nicole's brother, Jean-Baptiste, married a twenty-four-year-old widow named Thérèse and moved into a sprawling new home on rue de Vesle, not far from the Hôtel Ponsardin, which he was destined to inherit. Within months, there was word that her sister, Clémentine, now seventeen, would marry the young widower Jean-Nicolas Barrachin in a secret and still dangerous Catholic ceremony at dawn, in the cool splendor of the nearby cathedral.

Clémentine and Thérèse quickly established themselves as elegant hostesses and social trendsetters. While Barbe-Nicole was plain and petite, Clémentine was lovely and statuesque, with a passion for the splendid silk dresses that had made French fashion famous. At extravagant parties and soirées, the young people rubbed elbows with the social elite of industrial Reims and with important and exciting visitors from farther abroad. Increasingly, those visitors spoke of Napoléon, the man destined, it seemed, to rule France and perhaps finally to bring peace.

It was a privileged life, but it was still life in a gilded cage. And think how astonishing it is that we know anything about the lives of these young women at all. Barbe-Nicole and her sister had learned from the time the were small girls studying catechism in their convent school that the only women with public reputations were prostitutes or queens. Even the two most famous women of Barbe-Nicole's day—Marie Antoinette and Joséphine Bonaparte—were famous only because of their choice of husbands. It is probably not a coincidence that the public still thought of them both as whores.

Musing on the invisibility of women like Barbe-Nicole and her sister, Clémentine, the novelist Virginia Woolf wrote simply, "Anonymity runs in their blood." Even one of Barbe-Nicole's contemporaries, Lady Bessborough—born into one of Great Britain's most important and most progressive political families—herself believed that "no woman should meddle with . . . any serious business, farther than giving her opinion (if she is ask'd)." Barbe-Nicole undoubtedly took a similar line with her husband. No man wanted to hear his wife rattling on about how he should run his business, especially when she didn't have any training and knew nothing about it.

. . . .

Exactly how Barbe-Nicole, a woman destined for a sheltered life of domesticity, became educated in the gritty essentials of the wine trade has always been viewed as a great mystery. In fact, she lived at an especially unlucky moment. A century before, it was not impossible for middle-class women to participate in running the family enterprise. Most businesses then were still family affairs, run by an extended network of close relations. No longer. In nineteenth-century Europe, the combined forces of a postrevolutionary commodity culture, the rise of international manufacturing, and a new system of modern laws—the Napoleonic Code—meant a far narrower world for women. As the historian Bonnie G. Smith put it: "A prejudice against women acting in the marketplace appeared in the Napoleonic Code [which] pointed women toward an exclusively reproductive life."

But the Napoleonic Code was the invention of the first years of the new century, and Barbe-Nicole was beginning life as the wife of a wealthy industrialist at what we might think of as just the last possible moment. Industrialism already meant that most families were confining wives and daughters to the drawing rooms. Her fashionable sister, Clémentine, soon preoccupied with four small children—her infant son, Balsamie, and three stepchildren—would embody this new domestic pattern. Barbe-Nicole would follow in the footsteps of a fading commercial tradition, embracing the entrepreneurial family model that both she and François had learned as the children of old-fashioned businessmen. The different lives of these two sisters show how quickly the world was changing. If Barbe-Nicole had been more fashion-conscious or had she been beautiful, it might have seemed too great a sacrifice. Her decision must have marked her, even in those first years of the cult of domesticity, as a social eccentric. I will also hazard a guess that if François had had brothers—if there had been more than one son to carry on the family enterprise and if her interest had not actually been of some use—Barbe-Nicole would never have been allowed the haphazard commercial education that she found.

. . . .

In the beginning, I expect she was his sounding board. François himself knew next to nothing about the wine business when he first threw himself into developing the family sideline, and this was surely a critical factor. His period of self-education happily coincided with the early years of their marriage, when they were first getting to know each other. Like any two people thrown together, they were looking for things to talk about, and nothing could have been more natural than to talk about wine and his plans for the business.

So it would not have come to Barbe-Nicole as any surprise when, as soon as the news came in 1801 that France had signed a peace treaty at Lunéville, François decided that he would have to take to the road as a traveling salesman. Selling wines internationally still meant sending someone to get the orders, and in the beginning this would have to be François himself. The peace, they hoped, would change everything. The country had been at war with the so-called Second Coalition—Great Britain, Austria, Russia, the Ottoman empire, several of the Italian states—since the year she and François were first married. Now, with the peace at Lunéville, only Great Britain remained as the declared enemy of France, and that spring it looked for a moment as though life might soon return to normal. After years of waiting, it seemed as if the closed markets to the east and to the south would begin to open again. François intended to capitalize on the new opportunities.

Today, wine tasting is a multimillion-dollar tourist industry, but it was these traveling distributors, especially at the end of the eighteenth century—men like François and his competitors—who popularized wine tasting as a commercial strategy. At the time, caves and warehouses were not open for cellar visits, barrel tasting, and winemaker's suppers, and the branding of wines was only in its infancy. It would be another twenty years before consumers would even expect to find their wines labeled and identified. Customers had to rely on the judgment and integrity of agents for their wine purchases.

These agents, increasingly, brought the experience of wine tasting to their clients, discovering that it was, then as now, an effective way of selling wine. If on the road François would suffer rough conditions, broken carriages, miserable inns, and bad food, he would have little to complain about on his arrival. The goal of a wine sales agent was to discover the most alluring and fashionable hostesses of the city, charm them with his wit and grace, and persuade them to serve his company's wine. As often as not, this also involved some judicious sampling of the luxury wares—a *dégustation*, or wine tasting.

As a young mother and never a renowned beauty, Barbe-Nicole undoubtedly preferred not to dwell too long on this part of her husband's business. When François took to the road for an extended sales tour that summer, he was gone for months, traveling in Germany and Switzerland. In the days before the harvest, Barbe-Nicole kept an eye on the fields and the crops. She undoubtedly meant to keep an eye on the business as well, if her father-in-law would share news of it with her, because she had inherited her father's entrepreneurial instincts, even if no one else realized it yet.

She soon must have learned that there were other women in the wine business—the wives and daughters of those same old-fashioned family businessmen. Vineyards had always been a family undertaking, and even if spinning and weaving had been increasingly taken out of the rural cottages and moved into big factories like the ones her father owned, there was nothing industrialized about winemaking yet. In fact, women had played an essential role in the industry—and in the sales of sparkling champagne especially—since at least the middle of the eighteenth century, when sales had slumped so dramatically.

Ironically, the fact that champagne didn't look like a good way to make big money was part of the reason these small-time businesswomen had such an important role in the marketplace. Contracting businesses have always created opportunities for women and other newcomers ready to seize the initiative. In her book *Women of Wine: The Rise of Women in the Global Wine Industry,* author Ann B. Matasar points out that these periodic collapses in wine sales have created rare "opportunities for women to participate in rebuilding the industry." At a time when big money was to be made in businesses that could be industrialized and in commodities that could be mass-produced, wine—especially a finicky handcrafted product like champagne—had dim prospects.

Perhaps it was when François was on the road as a salesman that Barbe-Nicole first heard of working women such as Dame Geoffrey, a widow from the graceful bourgeois town of Épernay, just south of the river Marne, in the heart of some of the best vineyards in all of France. It is still known today as the capital of champagne. Certainly Barbe-Nicole already knew the estates of the Moët family, whose name had Dutch origins and was often spelled in the late eighteenth century just as it is pronounced: Moette. Everyone knew that their sparkling vintages had made them famous at the pleasure-loving court of Louis XV. Like François and his father, the men of the Moët family were distributors, not winemakers, and they bought their wines ready-made from small local craftsmen—or craftswomen. For, many of these vignerons, Barbe-Nicole must have discovered, were women. In fact, throughout the eighteenth century, the Moët family purchased nearly 50 percent of their fine wines from women. Dame Geoffrey, the widow of a local tax collector who managed extensive vineyards and crafted her own wines, was one of their largest suppliers.

Barbe-Nicole probably also learned before too long the story of the Widow Germon, an important wine broker who sold tens of thousands of bottles of champagne each year throughout the 1770s and 1780s. When Philippe Clicquot was just starting his small wine trade, the Widow Germon was already doing a brisk business and was even bottling her own sparkling wines. And, of course, Barbe-Nicole knew the Widow Robert and the Widow Blanc. The Widow Robert ran an important wine depository in Paris, where distributors could warehouse their wines for easy delivery to new customers in the nation's capital. The Moët family had used the services of the Widow Robert for more than twenty years, and François had recently considered the possibility of placing some wines in Paris. And because François and his father did not make their own wines, they had to purchase them from somewhere. The Widow Blanc, a local vigneron, was one of their regular suppliers.

If not these women, then Barbe-Nicole certainly learned of others like them. There were dozens more. Dame Geoffrey was only one of nearly twenty small-time women winemakers from Épernay whose names appeared in the Moët family account books during the eighteenth century but whose lives, like those of so many women from this period, are lost to history. No one has written their biographies, in part because at the time no one thought the ephemera of their personal lives worth saving for the archives. But their stories would not have been lost to Barbe-Nicole. In fact, increasingly, they would have been the cause of raised eyebrows in a small city like Reims. Businesswomen—once part of a bourgeois family economy—were quickly becoming something daring and faintly disreputable.

A generation older than Barbe-Nicole, women like the Widow Blanc and the Widow Robert were typical of the earlier tradition of family entrepreneurs, and the tradition was fading fast. Already in 1801, Barbe-Nicole's presence on the fringes of the Clicquot commercial concerns was an exception, especially for a woman of her class. Even a decade or two later, I think it would have been impossible for Barbe-Nicole to exercise an active interest in her husband's business and to have access to the essentials of the wine trade. It was in part because these other women came from the working and lower middle classes that they were able to run these small businesses in the new postrevolutionary climate. Barbe-Nicole came from the other end of the social hierarchy. Historian Béatrice Craig, who has studied the lives of women in Barbe-Nicole's day, found that "the wives of manufacturers were less likely to have an occupation than wives of craftsmen." The burden of supporting families trumped the demands of feminine delicacy, and for these independent women, working was a matter of financial survival.

Above all, Barbe-Nicole surely did not miss the other thing these women had in common: They were all widows, the only women granted the social freedom to run their own affairs. Having lost their husbands, they could make their own decisions—but it was hard to wish for opportunity at that price.

Perhaps part of the reason François was so willing to talk with his wife about his business ambitions was that he struggled with his father. All the evidence suggests that they were very different men. Philippe was a cautious and conservative businessman who couldn't muster much excitement for his son's plan to travel halfway across the continent, trying to sell luxury wines to people crippled by years of economic crisis. Even if François landed the sales, there was still the problem of how to ship the orders. François, however, had it in his head that this would be a great opportunity, and off he went. He even managed to drum up enough sales that his father couldn't point to the trip as an obvious failure, and while on the road, he did make—albeit by pure chance—the single most important discovery for the future of his family's wine business.

This discovery was named Louis Bohne. Louis was a short and portly traveling salesman from Mannheim, Germany, with red hair and a rare talent for closing a deal. François met him in the port town of Basel, where the Rhine runs out to the sea and at the crossroads where modern-day France, Switzerland, and Germany converge. Louis spoke half a dozen languages, had a head for numbers, and—most important—was immediately as enthusiastic about the Clicquot family wine business as François himself.

When François returned to Reims, he had to admit that Germany and Switzerland had been disappointing markets, but new prospects and a glittering future seemed just on the horizon. By the spring of 1802, especially, there was reason to be hopeful. In March, with the Treaty of Amiens, economic relations with even Great Britain were restored, and for the first time in nearly a generation, France was at peace. Now François and Louis came up with a grand plan for selling wines in Great Britain. They were certain there was an untapped market just waiting for French product. On the face of it, they weren't wrong. With the end of the war, after years in which luxuries like French wine and silk had been contraband, the British people were starved for these pleasures, and François and Louis were determined to capture their share of the sales. So in the first flush of collective enthusiasm, Louis set out for London to sell the high-end company wines, while François came home to run the business.

Although the British were hankering for French wines, champagne was a harder sell. London had been the commercial birthplace of champagne at the end of the seventeenth century, and there had even been a brief fashion for this special sparkling wine again during the 1770s, when François's father was first beginning his small trade as a wine broker; but the British passion for sparkling wine had cooled since the days of the

Revolution. Current demand was only for the most mildly effervescent champagne known as *crémant* or for the finest still wines of the region. There was even a brief resurgence of interest in the delicate red wines grown on the southernmost slopes of the mountain of Reims.

François's grandmother owned large vineyards and a farm in the most famous of those villages, Bouzy. A light red wine was often made from the grapes grown on the property, and some of it probably made its way to London in the years to come. Curious wine lovers can try something very like it today, because Bouzy red is still crafted in the Champagne. It is something of a rarity, and in my experience the quality of the wine varies dramatically from one producer to another. But no matter who makes it—and no matter how well or how poorly—Bouzy red commands the same steep prices as a bottle of sparkling champagne. The laws governing winemaking strictly limit the total weight of the grapes that can be harvested in the Champagne. Every grape in a bottle of this still red wine counts against the total harvest for the entire region. Bouzy red is as expensive as champagne because it is made from grapes that would otherwise have found their way into one of the region's famous sparkling wines.

We can still savor a Bouzy red. An authentic champagne *crémant*, on the other hand, is now forbidden. The rigid rules for controlling how wines are labeled in France, a system known as the AOC, or *appellation d'origine contrôlée*, today ensures that prestigious winemaking areas like the Champagne have a geographic monopoly on certain words. The word *crémant* now belongs to someone else, making the commercial production of champagne *crémant* impossible despite the local origins of this remarkable sparkling wine with froth like rich cream.

In spite of their hopes and the opening markets abroad during the peace, Louis's trip to Great Britain was a sales disaster. Plenty of people were buying French wines, but breaking into the market as a newcomer turned out to be impossible. Sales depended on access to aristocratic circles, where people had the money to buy extravagantly expensive wines. An average bottle of champagne was expensive indeed, easily costing 3 to 4 francs—more than half the weekly salary of many of the people who labored to produce it. In today's figures, this would be as much as $80 a bottle. It would take years to cultivate this clientele, and their competitors had the market locked up until then. Dukes and duchesses did not readily open their doors to traveling salesmen, even those peddling fine wines.

One of the competitors who dominated the champagne sales in Great Britain was the Moët family, headed at the time by Jean-Rémy Moët. If his portraits are any indication, Jean-Rémy was a trim and handsome man in his youth. The Moët family had been distributing the local sparkling wine since the heyday of the 1730s, but like everyone in the industry, they were struggling. In fact, newcomers like François, whose companies had not had to ride out a forty-year slump in the wine market, often had more financial resources than their established rivals.

It may be because of the Moët family contacts in the British market and the fashion for champagne *crémant* that François and his father ended up selling some of their 1800 vintage stocks to Jean-Rémy not long after Louis had returned with sorry sales figures. French scholar Michel Etienne, who has made an exhaustive study of the Veuve Clicquot company business records, has discovered on the books a deal for the sale of two or three thousand bottles of nearly flat champagne, made from the high-quality grapes of Aÿ, sold to the Moët wine company. Perhaps, recognizing that such wine was marketable only in England, where they had failed to secure orders themselves, François decided to move the product.

All things considered, François must have been discouraged with the results of his first few years in the wine business. Sales were only modest where he had hoped for stunning ones, and there was no way to put a good spin on the trip to London for his watchful father. But with the new peace, things could only get better, and although Philippe must have been reluctant to cede control of the business, it was time for him to step aside. François had his own energy and vision, and he had not actually done badly. Besides, at sixty-two, Philippe was tired. In the summer of 1802, his father retired from the business, leaving François for the first time completely in charge of shaping the direction of the company.

As luck would have it, François's first year solo at the helm was a disaster. This time the problem was not the lack of sales orders. After the disappointment in London, Louis had returned to central Europe, a territory that he knew far better, and that summer he returned from the extended trip abroad with solid orders for the wines they would harvest that fall.

The problem was now it didn't look as though they would be able to fill them. The weather conspired against the vintners in the Champagne that year. The final months of the growing season in 1802 were so hot that the vines shriveled in the fields. It was the beginning of a three-year period of exceptionally hot, dry summers that meant disastrous harvests throughout Europe. That summer, the English poet William Wordsworth and his sister Dorothy were in France, and Dorothy's journals make note of the sweltering weather. The heat in August was oppressive, even in a seaside town like Calais: "The day very hot," she writes, "the sea was gloomy . . . overspread with lightning . . . [and] calm hot nights."

By the end of August, François knew what the heat wave portended for his business. "In the memory of man," he wrote to a friend, "no one [can] remember a year this unfortunate." In nearly three-quarters of the Champagne there was no harvest at all that year. The Clicquot family found themselves, like all the other distributors in the area, hard-pressed to buy enough wine to fill the orders for which they had struggled and sacrificed. That year, all the profit went to the intermediaries and brokers with the foresight to store significant reserves.

In these early days of the wine industry in the Champagne, only a handful of dealers kept reserves of this sort. Most of the people who traded in wines purchased them—like François—ready-made from local vintners. François usually bought his wines by the bottle, although some enterprising businessmen had started purchasing cask wines to bottle themselves, taking on some extra risk in hopes of making a better return. Nobody wanted to store wines for extended periods unless they had to. Many of the wines from the region, especially those grown along the banks of the river Marne, didn't have a reputation for aging well. Even today, it is not wise to keep your champagne for too long.

Winemakers had recognized the fleeting qualities of the local wines as early as the seventeenth century. The local pinot meunier grape, grown in the river towns along the Marne, was particularly short-lived, although it made a satisfying, mellow wine. Ironically, the better-quality wines were often the most delicate. Wines that were fine and rich, with the subtlest flavors and made from the very first pressing of the grapes—the *cuvée*—were delicious but fragile. They rarely lasted in casks more than a year or two in the cellars.

In most cases, it was a much better idea to sell the wines quickly and be done with it. The risk of spoilage and the storage costs didn't make stockpiling wines an attractive idea to many businessmen. Wines only started to be bottled in the Champagne during the eighteenth century because brokers in the industry slump could extend the life of their product by a few years if the wines were stored in glass. Philippe had built the family business by selling the finest of these stocks.

More daring winemakers sometimes turned those bottled wines into sparkling champagne, hoping to add greater value to the product. The risks were huge, especially in warm weather. During the hot summer of 1747, Allart de Maisonneuve woke up to find that over 80 percent of his bottles—wines worth perhaps as much as $200,000—had simply exploded. During the heat wave that gripped the Champagne in 1802, things weren't much better.

In the midst of a ruinous summer, when most vignerons had nothing to show for an entire year's labor, Barbe-Nicole discovered that her husband was now seized with a new idea. Barbe-Nicole would always have a dangerous weakness for men who were gamblers, perhaps because she had married one. His intensity was exhilarating. When the chips were down, François wanted nothing more than to roll the dice—and reinvent the family business. One company insider later described how François "visited the neighboring vineyards, went down into all the cellars, compared, weighed, mediated, and then finally laid the foundation of an entirely different commercial system." No longer content with the modest commissions of a distributor, he wanted to play for bigger stakes. Despite the risks—and despite what he knew the town's more experienced businessmen must be thinking—François was determined to start bottling his own wines. As always, his timing would prove disastrous.

Chapter 5

Crafting the Cuvée

The nineteenth-century copy of Jean-Antoine Chaptal's treatise *The Art of Making, Controlling, and Perfecting Wines* in the wine collections of the Sonoma County Public Library is a thin and tightly gathered collection of gently yellowed paper, with the cramped and blurry type common of inexpensive books from the beginning of the nineteenth century. It was a book much like this one, however, that inspired François's decision to stake the family fortunes on a new bottling operation in 1802. *The Art of Making, Controlling, and Perfecting Wines* has been described as "a decisive turning point in the history of wine technology." It had been published the year before, and there was no way François and Barbe-Nicole could have missed owning a copy. Just as François was beginning his first experiments with blending and bottling wines in the family cellars, Napoléon ordered departmental prefects throughout France to distribute a copy of the treatise to everyone in the wine business.

Chaptal changed the future of winemaking with his slender scientific treatise. As both François and Barbe-Nicole knew, the greatest obstacle to the commercial integration of the winemaking cycle was the separation between the growers and the distributors. The problem for François's grand new plan was that the growers had all the skills: They made the wines, and they usually bottled them as well. Since bottling wines added significant value—sometimes making the same wine worth three times what it sold for by the barrel—François was eager to try his hand at it. He and Barbe-Nicole desperately needed the knowledge that came with generations of experience in the vineyards.

There was a rich lore and tradition that governed the production of wine in France, and nowhere was this folk wisdom more revered than in the making of that finicky and mysterious sparkling wine still known locally as *vin mousseux*. Winemakers watched the stars for portents of a good harvest, and traditionally vintners waited for the first full moon in March to begin bottling champagne. According to popular legend, the springtime moon had the power to raise a tide of bubbles in the bottles. Others put their faith in a higher source. Today, visitors to Reims in January can still witness the solemn and ancient festival of St. Vincent, the patron of winemakers. On a windy afternoon that winter in France, I stumbled upon the celebration unexpectedly and stood shivering on a street corner to watch as a thousand vintners made their silent pilgrimage from the Hôtel de Ville to the Basilica of Saint Rémi in scarlet cloaks and white bonnets, bearing before them the small icon of a harvest saint. It was a moving reminder of the reverence those who live in the Champagne have always felt for the mysteries of winemaking.

The finer details of this lore were not part of the personal experience that François brought to his new enterprise, however, and the secret traditions of generations of winemakers weren't likely to help him launch his new business plan anyhow. Although he had learned a good deal about the making and selling of wine during his years of business training with his father, trade was not the same thing as craft. What François needed was reliable technical information about the production of wine that would make them less reliant on the experience and knowledge of the rural craftsmen who turned grapes into fine wines.

This was exactly what Chaptal's treatise provided. *The Art of Making, Controlling, and Perfecting Wines* was an elegant synthesis of all the scientific and practical knowledge about winemaking available at the time, mass-distributed in a way that no other book on viniculture had been before. Among his most important discoveries, Chaptal is still famous for quantifying the chemical relationship between sugar, fermentation, and alcohol. Although winemakers since the seventeenth century had known that sugar was essential to champagne, the process of adding sugar to the must in order to make a better wine is known today as *chaptalization*. But Chaptal also advised his readers on everything from cleaning bottles to corking champagne. For anyone new to the business, his treatise was invaluable.

If it seems curious that Napoléon chose to distribute this pamphlet at just the moment when François and Barbe-Nicole were preparing to take new risks in the wine business, it really isn't. Napoléon had commissioned the book from Chaptal as part of a new government effort to expand the wine industry in France—and the champagne industry in particular. Everyone knew that Napoléon had a soft spot for sparkling wine and for the entrepreneurs who provided him with it. There were already stories about staggeringly expensive dinner parties in Paris where his guests consumed a thousand bottles in a night. Perhaps Napoléon remembered fondly those rolling hills and chalk fields of his own boyhood in the region. Perhaps his old friend Jean-Rémy Moët had his ear. Whatever the reason, champagne was one of Napoléon's passions, and with the same zeal for reform that led him to modernize the French legal system and improve the nation's highways, he set in motion a series of initiatives aimed at transforming the French wine industry into a national economic engine. Chaptal's book was part of that plan, and the right information—along with some attractive government incentives—undoubtedly played a role in François's thinking.

Despite François's eagerness and the recent return of peace in France, this new enterprise was a slow and tedious business. It would take more than a year to prepare their first "house" wines to bring to the market in 1803. Perhaps a bit rattled by his dawning understanding of the fabulous risks and steep learning curve that making their own champagne entailed, in the beginning François decided to limit their production to 25 percent of the annual stocks.

Some restraint was a good idea. As novices to the art of bottling wines, the Clicquots had a lot to learn. Perhaps, in addition to Chaptal's guide, François turned to books such as Jean Godinot's *Manner of Cultivating the Vine and Making Wine in the Champagne* or Nicolas Bidet's *Treatise on the*

Culture of Wines. In the cellars, they could turn for advice to the company cellar master, Monsieur Protest. All the hard labor of the bottling and blending would fall on his shoulders (and those of the other cellar workers) in the end. And, of course, they relied on Louis Bohne. He was the one who knew what the customers wanted.

Apart from the small batches of wine made from the grapes of the family estates, there was never any plan to start making wines from scratch that summer. François would buy his base wines by the cask from growers, as always. But some of that wine he now planned to blend and bottle, for resale either as luxury still wines or as sparkling champagne. Inevitably, crafting excellent wines in his cellars depended on finding the highest-quality casks possible.

And what Barbe-Nicole learned about winemaking in the first years of her marriage sparked a passion that would last a lifetime. Although she had to sit on the sidelines while François made the financial decisions, she was determined not to be excluded from the vineyards. In the early mornings of those hot, dry summers, family legend tells how Barbe-Nicole accompanied François as he drove through the fields of the Champagne, anxious about the fate of the harvest. They would stop to check the progress of the grapes or to talk with those who knew the land and the craft of winemaking best: the weathered vignerons and the peasantry. In the fall there was the harvest—the *vendange* in French. According to local custom, it lasted for twelve days, and the harvest began at dawn. The grapes were best when harvested on cool, foggy mornings, while the moisture of the dew left the fruit plump and full of juice. The early hours were critical for the production of champagne, because this *vin gris*—a white wine made with red grape varietals—depended on the immediate and gentle pressing of grapes unstained by the color of the skins.

Barbe-Nicole was there at sunrise. Her favorite haunt at harvest-time was in the village of Bouzy, where she could watch as the field-workers gathered in the grapes grown on the family vineyards. François's grandmother Muiron owned the vineyards, and the storeroom on the estate had a modern winepress, built in 1780 and now one of the oldest surviving presses in the Champagne. Here, Barbe-Nicole would sit for hours, watching as the grapes were slowly and gently crushed.

She was never happier than when studying wine. As the baskets were trundled in from the nearby fields, the grapes were spread carefully across the floor of the press, and, with the slow creak of heavy wood and the mixed scents of rope and warm fruit, she could anticipate the gentle aroma of the first pressing. The juice of this initial crush—the cuvée—was light, with little body but great delicacy, and it would make an excellent component of the final wine. Known as *vin de goût*, this was the wine made from the juice that flowed freely from the grapes when the heavy wood of the press was left to settle gently on the fruit, and it could not be exported alone. It made a delicious vintage, but without enough body to age or transport reliably unblended. It is in part because of the fragile nature of the finest must that it is said the French never export their best wines.

After the must from the cuvée was drained away into barrels, roughly filtered through plaited baskets, the *première taille*, or the first cutting, began. The man working the press would gently crank, adding enough pressure to break or "cut" the grapes, coaxing from them more of their ripe juices. Perhaps Barbe-Nicole tried her hand at the press, to the wry amusement of the farmworkers. The *première taille* gave what some considered to be the most valuable juice from the grapes—a fine and full-flavored must, rich with promise and strong enough to age deliciously.

With each successive cutting, the pressure exerted on the grapes would have to be increased, with consequences for the quality. The next pressing was the *deuxième taille*, or second cutting, and it gave full-bodied and clean juice, often with the tawny hue known as "partridge eye." For a superior wine, Barbe-Nicole knew that the winemakers would use only the juice from the first three pressings. By the time of the fourth and fifth cuttings, the must was ruddy and sharp. Most common cask wines were a blend of the third, fourth, and fifth cuttings, and they were sold inexpensively and as quickly as possible.

There were also family estates at Verzenay and Chigny-la-Montagne, where Barbe-Nicole could have learned the essentials of fermenting and clarifying cask wines as well. Although François would still depend on others to make the raw wines that he would blend and bottle, as wine merchant and speculator he had learned early in his career how to judge a well-made vintage. Perhaps as their carriage rolled along mile after mile through the fields of the Champagne, this was part of what François talked about during those summers.

After the harvest, fermentation began as a natural process. First, the must was racked and the bits of organic debris were allowed to settle. It was then moved to a new cask. Because making the best wines took considerable skill and some luck, winemakers had all sorts of tricks of the trade. One of those tricks can be a real headache even today. Winemakers would smoke their casks with "brimstone," gently lowering into the barrel a burning rag dipped in sulfur, in hopes of producing a bright, clear wine. Without knowing the reason, these early winemakers were on to something. Winemakers today still rely on sulfur's antiseptic qualities to prevent the natural bacteria at work in fermentation from taking over and ruining the wine, and sulfur is widely used as a preservative in many wines on the market. But some unlucky people find that it gives them a pounding headache, and for a small percentage of people it is even a life-threatening allergy.

Over the course of the next three months, the must would be allowed to ferment naturally in the barrels, slowly becoming a sharp young wine. With the dead yeast cells and other organic debris floating in it, however, this raw wine did not make for elegant drinking. Sometimes, clearing the wine was relatively simple. Racking was a straightforward business, relying on gravity. The wine was poured from one barrel to another, leaving the gunk behind. If the cellars were cool enough, all the sediment would fall to the bottom, leaving the wine clear and appetizing.

More often than not, however, the wines were still cloudy, and clarifying the wine from here was a hit-or-miss proposition, involving considerable ingenuity. When a wine wouldn't clear easily, winemakers had to turn to a *colle*—the French term for the secret concoction used to separate the particles from the wine. Usually in cloudy wines the problem was suspended tannins or yeast cells, and here the solution was a *colle* made of egg whites or bone-marrow gelatin. Sometimes winemakers used milk, cream, or blood. Or they could substitute a commercial mixture, probably quite unsavory in its origins, known as "powder number three" and thought to be particularly suited to the production of champagne.

Essentially, a *colle* acts as a positively charged chemical magnet, attracting the negative wayward particles and gathering them in a big mass that will settle to the bottom of the barrel when chilled. Anyone who has mastered the skill in French cooking of clarifying a consommé knows that a mixture of beef marrow and egg whites can be used to produce a perfectly clear broth with an exquisite flavor, because the coagulants trap the smallest impurities in an unappealing mass. The principle is exactly the same in winemaking.

Now that François was planning to bottle his own champagnes, getting the wines to stay crystal clear would be one of his biggest frustrations. There was no easy solution to the problem. A second fermentation in the bottle—when the sugar and yeast added in the *liqueur de tirage* are slowly transformed into alcohol and trapped carbon dioxide—is necessary to create the ebullient sparkle of champagne. But the process also created more dead yeast cells, which no one found any more attractive in the nineteenth century than we would now.

As with cask wines, the process of clearing champagne could range from the time-consuming to the downright tedious. After the bottles had rested on their sides for a year in the cellars, developing their sparkle, someone had to find a way to get rid of the debris trapped inside. The easiest way was to rely on gravity. The process was known as *transvasage*, but we can think of it as racking wines in the bottle. The cellar workers could just pour the wine from one bottle to another, leaving the debris behind. It worked in theory, but the sparkle of the wine wasn't exactly improved by all this pouring.

The other way to dispel the debris was called *dégorgement*. Nineteenth-century wine manuals make disgorging sound pretty arduous. The cellar worker had to invert the bottle and pop the cork off just long enough to let a bit of the wine and all of the debris come shooting out—but not a moment longer. The trick was in having a good eye to track the sediment and an excellent thumb, capable of stopping up the bottle fast, before all the wine poured onto the floor in an expensive puddle. Working bottle by bottle, disgorging champagne was a time-consuming and expensive process. Even with modern advances in winemaking, it is part of the reason champagne continues to command luxury prices.

Still, it would be foolhardy to wish for too easy a solution to this sediment—or to wish for too much cheap champagne. Ironically, experts today recognize that this irritating debris is actually crucial to the birth of great sparkling wine. During the year or more that the bottles are resting in the cellars, the fermentation is creating more than just alcohol and bubbles. The yeast cells also break down in the chemical process called "autolysis." Autolysis begins when wine is left in contact with the enzymes naturally produced during the decomposition process—in other words, when a wine is aged while containing the dead yeast cells. Winemakers elegantly call it "aging on the lees" or, in French, *sur lies*. The important thing to know is that the result is a happy one, giving fine champagne its characteristic rich, nutty flavors.

Now that the Clicquots were bottling their own wines, there was also the chance to experiment with blending the wines, creating a "marriage" of flavors. Making great wine—and making great champagne in particular—depended on skillful blending. Dom Pérignon may not have invented champagne, but he was a pioneer in the art of blending. World-class champagne today is often a carefully selected mixture of as many as forty different growths, or *crus*, with grapes from different varieties and grown in different parts of the region.

Barbe-Nicole already knew that blending depended on *terroir*. She had watched enough harvests and tasted enough of the juice to know that each grape was the product of the soil that had produced it. In winemaking, experts talk of the indefinable essence of *terroir*, the gift that the land gives to the grape and that creates the potential range of tastes and aromas it can express. Just as the minerals of the Dead Sea are thought to have inexplicable healing qualities for the sick and the infirm, so the soil of a great vineyard—from the composition of its clay and chalk to the wild plants that prosper in it—is spoken of reverently and in ways that can make it seem magical.

In the twenty-first century, scientists have undertaken chemical analysis of the vineyards of the Champagne and have confirmed their special properties. The chalky and acidic soil of the region develops the aroma of the fruit, and its northern location prevents the grapes from developing too many natural sugars. The moist springs and dry summers slowly deprive the grapes of water, allowing them to ripen gradually, without being overshadowed by foliage. The chalk in the soil lets the ground retain water in the winter and release it slowly in the dry summer periods.

Just as serving champagne at the right temperature—around 45°F or 7°C, best achieved by chilling the bottle in a mixture of ice and water for half an hour—will open up the flavors of the wine, so the right conditions in the vineyard will bring out the most striking qualities in the grape. It is because these conditions are so subtle and complex, depending on a combination of the right amount of rain and sun, at the right moments, in the right soil, that vintage years are rare. Vintage years are exceptional harvests, years when the winemaker does not need to rely on fine reserve wines, saved from a previous harvest, to round out the blending.

Perhaps above all, Barbe-Nicole and François soon learned that bottling wine—and especially the sparkling pink champagne that proved so popular—was a risky business. Breakage rates could be ruinous. In a hot summer, eighteenth-century vintners sometimes lost as much as 90 percent of their champagne stocks when the pressurized contents of the sparkling wine exploded. Unlucky vintners could awaken to discover their storerooms, filled with the wine on which they had staked their future, flooded with wine and broken glass.

Local growers like the Cattier family in Chigny-la-Montagne must have still remembered the legend of Allart de Maisonneuve's staggering losses in the sweltering summer of 1747, when his cellars were so toxic with the fumes of spilled wine that no one could enter them for months. Now, vintners again were faced with cellars throughout the Champagne awash in pools of ruined wine. The heat wave that began in 1802 would grip France for three consecutive summers. What could be saved from the wreckage was turned into *vin de casse*—breakage wine—but it had to be sold at rock-bottom prices and had little appeal.

They soon realized that the quality of the bottles was part of the problem. French glassmaking was often a shoddy business, and ordering bottles could be maddening. Staring down at misshapen and flawed glasswork, Barbe-Nicole and François must sometimes have despaired. If they put champagne in these bottles, there would be little left to sell come autumn. Yet glass bottles were absolutely essential to the manufacture of champagne.

The shapes of the bottles created more obstacles. It wouldn't be until 1811 that someone would invent a machine for molding commercial glassware. Until then, wine bottles were blown by hand. The result was bottles with inconsistent shapes and sizes. Customers might not have cared, but François had reason to worry when he saw them. In a cellar, bottles had to be stacked on top of one another, and uneven bottles did not stack steadily. Collapsed rows of ruined champagne were distressingly common, even when the cellar workers tried to stabilize the rows with wooden slats. When the bottles came with different-size openings, corking them became a tedious and time-consuming business as well. Sometimes, if the lip at the mouth of the bottle was wrong, it was impossible to tie the cork in place securely with string. Making a profit was difficult enough after a decade of war, but they were learning that winemaking had its own dangers.

These were simply the risks that came as a matter of course with the business of bottling wines. Barbe-Nicole and François still needed to learn whether he could blend wines good enough to justify the premium prices they would have to charge. Thanks to his father's first forays into the wine trade in the 1770s, François had been trained as a boy in tasting wines and evaluating their potential. But it would turn out that Barbe-Nicole was the one with the gift for blending wines.

Perhaps she was what wine experts today sometimes call a "supertaster"—someone gifted with a higher proportion of taste buds on her tongue than the rest of us. Women are more likely to be supertasters than men. Even more than this, however, it was her nose that mattered. While we can experience only five tastes—sweet, salty, sour, bitter, and the elusive "other" taste known as *umami*—we can recognize over a thousand smells.

All wine has a distinct bouquet, which chemists tell us is the result of a dizzying array of volatile compounds. These compounds are volatile because they react—with one another and with the air—and their aromas are largely responsible for the experience of taste we have when we drink a glass of wine. Lactones can be nutty, while phenols can be spicy. Sulfur gives a cool summer's glass of *sauvignon blanc* in the backyard its grassy notes. In his book *Molecular Gastronomy*, gourmet and scientist Hervé This explains in fascinating detail how this experience is intensified when white wines are aged "on the lees"—aged resting in the dead yeast cells, which have the highest sulfur concentrations. And as Eileen Crane, one of California's master winemakers and president of Napa's Domaine Carneros, explained to me one warm autumn afternoon, with champagne these aromas are doubly important. The popping bubbles in a glass of champagne are an unrivaled aroma delivery system, bringing a thousand scents and associations to our minds, all of them elegant and gleeful, before our first sip.

Barbe-Nicole probably knew none of this. Given the state of science in the beginning of the nineteenth century, she could have no conception of how sulfur molecules reacted with the enzymes in our saliva to create the experience of a great wine. But she did have the gift of blending great wines. While the science is amazing, there is nothing in winemaking that substitutes for the instincts of a connoisseur.

Perhaps the science of winemaking and the mysteries of craft were on Barbe-Nicole's mind the following year as she stood in the cavernous reception rooms of the Hôtel Ponsardin. She was proud, but she was also anxious. Already, row upon row of their sparkling wines were waiting in the cellars, slowly concentrating their small, delicate bubbles. But the tenuous peace, they now knew, had not lasted. The deal brokered with the British at Amiens was unraveling. It had been just the briefest reprieve—a mere fourteen months. She watched as her father worked the room, dreaming again his old aristocratic dreams. Clémentine and Thérèse swayed elegantly in their rustling dresses. At the center of the crowd stood a wiry man with sharp eyes. Napoléon had come to study the local wine industry—and he was staying for a few days as the guest of the Ponsardin family.

Perhaps on this visit, when he was feted at Reims with opulence and ceremony, Napoléon first tasted the Clicquot champagne, although it was not yet memorable. The young couple was working hard to make the winery a success, but theirs did not have the appeal of the more celebrated cellars at Moët. There would have been no reason yet for a great statesman to seek it out, but there would be. Before the decade was out, the Clicquot champagne and the soon-to-be-widowed young woman who was left to produce it would take Europe by storm.

Chapter 6

The Champagne Widow

By 1804, François had changed the direction of the family wine business emphatically. Sales in France were now a mere 7 percent of their sales, down from nearly 25 percent only a few years before. With the renewed hostilities with Great Britain, orders came largely from Prussia and Austria or not at all. And, at the beginning, things looked promising. At the end of 1803, when their first house wines were available to customers, total orders were up modestly, and Louis Bohne had managed to find buyers among the dukes and princes of these eastern empires.

Once again riding a wave of enthusiasm, François was planning to expand the market even farther to the east. Early that summer, the ruddy and good-natured Louis visited François and Barbe-Nicole in Reims, and all the talk was about Russia. Louis was going to open the market for them, and he was already preparing to set off on his third voyage for the company. The trip would last well over a year and would take him to the frontiers of the Russian Empire, in search of new clients for their wines.

Barbe-Nicole listened to it all from the sidelines, perhaps with their five-year-old daughter, Clémentine, growing drowsy at her knee on those summer evenings. She and François were learning the winemaking business together, and she wished for the success of these new prospects, which seemed just on the horizon, with a passion equal to his own. When at last Louis set off in July for Russia, he went with her good wishes and all her hopes as well. Within weeks, they would have his first letters and soon, they hoped, news of astonishing sales.

The news, when it arrived, was crushing. For François, it must have been a terrible disappointment and an embarrassment as well. He already had the bungled London adventure to live down. Now it was clear that Russia would be a disaster, too. Writing from Saint Petersburg in the first days of October, Louis discovered that they had misjudged the market: "The excess of luxury [here] means that the broker, after all the costs are deducted, gains nothing and in a bad year is lost." From Moscow, the news was worse. "The commerce in this place is excessively rotten and bad faith is the order of the day," Louis wrote, adding bitterly, "Foreign companies are seen as nanny goats ready for milking." Even if they got orders, he doubted they would ever get paid.

By the winter of 1805, François was undoubtedly depressed. The Russian numbers were miserable, accounting for just a small percentage of their sales. With Louis in Russia, moreover, they had lost ground in Germany. Then there was the war, which once again seemed endless and futile. The conflict with Great Britain, which had resumed in the summer of 1803, was pulling in more combatants, and some days it was difficult to know which foreign markets would stay open and which would close. The climate for international trade got worse with every passing week, with word of new battles and new blockades.

That winter was the sorry prelude to the period that historians talk about as the war of the Third Coalition—when Russia, Austria, and Sweden eventually joined Great Britain in a loose alliance against France. Napoléon wasn't doing anything to turn down the political heat. In December, he had crowned himself emperor—not in the cathedral of Reims, like the kings of France since time immemorial, but in Paris. Now he was amassing troops for a planned invasion of England, perhaps in the spring. At the moment, nothing was certain, but an intensification of the war already seemed inevitable in the coming months, and there was no reason to expect a sudden improvement in their affairs. Barbe-Nicole was powerless, left to spend quiet afternoons in her sitting room, bent over some piece of fine needlework or glancing distractedly at a new novel sent from Paris, worrying about the future and what it might bring.

When the spring orders arrived in Reims, they should have raised François's spirits. They were far better than expected. During those few months, they would ship over seventy-five thousand bottles of wine—more than their entire sales in 1804. Russia, not yet drawn into the simmering conflict, would account for an astonishing third of their sales. It had been a year of excruciating ups and downs, when they had begun to doubt in themselves and in the wisdom of François's dreams of an international marketplace for their wines. Now, they should have been celebrating this small victory. It was a sign that they were doing something right. But François remained discouraged and dejected.

When the summer arrived, it was wet. They had seen enough summers to know that it was already too late to hope for anything from the harvest. It would be another failure. François, thwarted at every turn, could only watch the vineyards with despair, calculating over and over what this would mean in losses for the company, in new obstacles that he must have doubted his own ability to overcome. He had tried to reinvent the company he had inherited from his father, and he had been given all the advantages—sufficient capital, excellent training, an enviable list of international clients, contacts ready to do business with him, even a brief but important period of peace in which to build the company.

What was the result of it all? He had disappointed. His father surely warned him against staking the future on the distant and unsettled Russian market. Already by now, Napoléon and the czar, Alexander I, were at loggerheads, and by September it was open hostility. The future of international commerce was dark. Perhaps giving up the textile business had been a mistake. Perhaps bottling wines had been too great a risk. For those looking at the wet, muddy fields and at the useless grapes rotting on the vines, the worries were everywhere.

Then, sometime in early October, when the low vineyards sloping away from the mountain of Reims were again silent in the early hours of dawn, in the gloomy aftermath of that harvest, François—if the family version of events is true—must have found himself exhausted and consumed by a kind of frantic anxiety. As he sank quickly and deeply into a darker depression, the family began to worry in earnest.

The public story was that François had contracted an infectious fever. Like so many in Europe, they had lived with fears of the epidemic since the beginning of Napoléon's wars, knowing that the disease was kept alive in the crowded and unhealthy conditions at the camps. In the nineteenth century, it was an easy death to imagine—far too easy and familiar. For two weeks, François suffered with what his doctors called simply putrid or malignant fever. Later generations would know the disease as typhoid. Only when the vomiting and chills began in the second week would Barbe-Nicole have understood the terrible truth about his illness. The resolute look of the doctor, when he came, must have told her what she already suspected. As François struggled to breathe, the ringing in his ears would have grown louder, and soon he was coughing blood, tormented by headaches. The telltale black spots soon covered his body, turning even his tongue to a black crust of infection, and everywhere, he ached. Barbe-Nicole could only watch his private agony.

For days, she suffered with him, surely sick with worry for the health of her little girl. She must have nursed the secret hope that he would be one of the lucky ones—one of the survivors. These hopes would soon be dashed. On October 23, after days of terrible torments, she could only feel relief to hear that François was dead. Three days later, numb with grief and horror, the Widow Clicquot buried her husband, after a funeral mass in the soaring Gothic cathedral of Notre-Dame de Reims. At twenty-seven, Barbe-Nicole would now need to begin imagining a future alone.

This, at least, is the usual story of François's death. If he was a victim of malignant fever, the doctor who treated him during his illness necessarily understood little about the actual nature of the infection. Typhoid remained a fearsome illness throughout much of the nineteenth century, and there was nothing reliable to be done for the patient unfortunate enough to contract it. If the doctor who tended to the Clicquot family during this sudden illness had been trained locally, at the medical university in Reims, he must have been struck by a cruel irony, however. The antiseptic properties of champagne were the subject of heated controversy among doctors and scientists in the region. Sparkling wine was thought to prevent—perhaps even to cure—the very illness that had struck down François Clicquot before the age of thirty.

In an eighteenth-century pamphlet entitled *Question Agitated in the School of the Faculty of Medicine at Reims . . . on the Use of Sparkling Champagne Against Putrid Fevers and Other Maladies of the Same Nature* (1778), Jean-Claude Navier cut to the heart of the controversy. Champagne was thought to possess particular curative powers. "It contains," Dr. Navier wrote, " . . . a particular principle, which the Chemists call Gas or air fixed, a principle that characterizes it essentially, a principle recognized today as the most powerful antiseptic that there is in nature."

Because Dr. Navier was a champagne insider, we might be forgiven for wondering if this was just another of the local marketing efforts, like the one that invented the legend of Dom Pérignon sixty years later. After all, Dr. Navier's brother-in-law was none other than Jean-Rémy Moët, a competitor in the wine business. But the unlikely assertions that champagne could cure fever were apparently widespread.

The idea was not even simply a passing medical fashion, not just one of those unaccountable and gruesome things doctors did at the dawn of the nineteenth century. For more than two hundred years, it had been conventional wisdom that the fermentation of wine was comparable to infections in the blood, leading to harebrained (but quite appealing) experiments with wine cures. Doctors still believed it as late as 1870, when Charles Tovey wrote, in a book called *Champagne: Its History, Properties, and Manufactures*: "Champagne, if pure, is one of the safest wines that can be drunk. In typhoid fevers, in weakness, in debility, when there is a deficiency of the vital powers, there is nothing which can take its place; it enables the system to resist the attacks of intermittent and malignant fever."

To think that a bottle of his own sparkling wine might have saved François! Or perhaps the doctor who attended him tried this champagne cure but found his illness too far progressed to be cured, even by bubbly of the best kind. Certainly, champagne would have been a more welcome treatment than the other nineteenth-century remedies for infectious fever—bloodletting and enemas—and one hopes that François's final moments were soothed with a healthy medicinal dose of the Clicquot sparkling rosé that he and Barbe-Nicole had found such pleasure in crafting.

Barbe-Nicole knew that Philippe was broken by the death of his son. The intensity of her own grief was nothing compared with the depression that gripped her father-in-law. He could speak of little besides his despair, even in the most routine business correspondence. "Nothing," he wrote in one of his letters, "can ever assuage the deep sorrow I feel. My loss is brought back to me every moment. Old age and increasing infirmity . . . have made me determined to retire and rest and have necessitated an interval between life and death." Past caring, Philippe settled down to wait and die.

Perhaps Barbe-Nicole considered doing the same when she heard the horrifying rumors circulating in Reims in the weeks after her husband's death. There is another story of how François died. People whispered that he had committed suicide. The scene is almost too terrible to imagine: François lying white and motionless in cool, bloody bathwater, perhaps, after the famous 1794 image of the slain revolutionary Jean-Paul Marat that hangs today in the Musée des Beaux-Arts in Reims. There is the scream of the servant finding François or perhaps just the dull shock of his father, Philippe, after seeing the knife that had dropped from his son's hand, the slow dawning of understanding, the terrible conviction of what it meant for his eternal soul—and, above all, the desperate hope of finding a doctor who would keep their secret, so François could be buried in sacred Catholic ground.

There is no direct evidence that the gossip was true. It may have been nothing more than vicious rumor or a confused sense of his other symptoms. The first sign of typhoid would have been a sense of hopelessness, after all. The very name *typhoid* comes from the Greek word for "smoke" and was chosen because mental confusion, irrational anxiety, and unspecified despair are the disease's earliest and most persistent signs. As eighteenth-century readers of William Buchan's *The Domestic Medicine* (1797) were told: "The malignant fever is generally preceded by a remarkable weakness. . . . This is sometimes so great that the patient can scarcely walk, or even sit upright, without being in danger of fainting away. His mind too is greatly dejected; he sighs, and is full of dreadful apprehensions."

But the story might equally have been true. There is no doubt that François was down that autumn. The business had been struggling. There had also been hints all along that François was prone to bouts of depression and mania that had less obvious causes. People described him sometimes as a man of irrepressible energies and enthusiasm. He loved big plans and big ideas, and he lived with an almost frantic exuberance. The other side of François seems to have been darker.

If Barbe-Nicole ever spoke of it, the letters have not survived. Some of Philippe's early correspondence with his son, however, hints that François's tendency toward "gloom" worried his father. In one letter, written on Christmas Day 1793, Philippe urged his son, "Do not abandon yourself to a sort of melancholy gloom that can harm you and retard the development of your faculties and prolong the weakness of your temperament. Your happiness, your existence is all that makes mine precious." We hear the resonance of a father worried about his son's mental health.

Whatever the truth—and one hopes it was fever that took François—Barbe-Nicole is sure to have resented the rumored cause of his suicide: business failure. Local reports circulated that in those first years of running the family business, François was busy driving the company into the ground. He had developed a new—and, it was said, fundamentally flawed—business strategy. He had committed himself to a risky commercial approach to selling wines and was failing. As one nineteenth-century historian tells the story, "While big with this magnificent project, death came and cut short the career of . . . [François] Clicquot, the former husband of the Widow Clicquot Ponsardin. Common rumor at Rheims tells a different story of the exit of this notable personage, saying that he cut his throat in despair of the success of the 'entirely different commercial system' with which his biographer credits him."

Barbe-Nicole herself surely despaired at moments that autumn. She could remember François as he had been—kind and generous to his family, alive with all the plans for the wine business that was his dream. Perhaps there were periods of serious depression, too. There certainly had been times of worry. Still, they had been, on the whole, happy, and now she saw that everything they had worked for in their seven years of marriage would be lost: all the risks in opening new markets abroad, the new adventures in making their own wines, the future of a business that, despite the more limited role she had been given to play, she cared about as deeply as François.

Her father-in-law, Philippe, could not bear to think of the future, and the entire company would be liquidated. It was said that he had also abandoned himself to the "profound depression" that perhaps was part of a family tendency. Maybe the very idea of a family business was just too painful a reminder of what he had lost. He did muster the energy to write Louis Bohne in Russia, telling him to return to Reims immediately. There was no point in Louis taking new orders when they would never fill them.

When Louis received the letter with news of François's death, he was stunned. He and François were more than just employee and employer. They were building a company together, and opening these new markets in Saint Petersburg had been a shared passion. It was a warm relationship, born of years of shared correspondence, which Louis posted from the road, with news of his travels and with perceptive, often witty accounts of their commercial prospects in each city. Only months before, they had spent long hours together debating the risks and the rewards of this excursion to Russia with his father, and Louis had fueled François's enthusiasm for this adventure.

They should have been still celebrating the success of the year's orders, even if the harvest had gone badly. A failed *vendange* would create real headaches a year or two down the road, when those wines would be coming to market, but it was not an immediate disaster. For now, sales were up, and they had stock to fill them. There was time. Then, suddenly, his instructions were to abandon everything. Looking out on a stark November day, conscious of the early signs of another northern winter, Louis wasted no time in obeying them. He would have set off for Reims instantly, even if Philippe had not asked it, for Louis hoped that there might be some way to prevent Clicquot-Muiron from closing its doors, if only he could return quickly enough.

Louis traveled hard, for he arrived back in the Champagne in less than a month. It was a journey of more than a thousand miles, accomplished alternatively by horseback, carriage, and barge. By the time he arrived in Reims in December, perhaps Barbe-Nicole was already beginning to formulate a daring plan of her own. She knew something about the family business, after all. She came from a family of entrepreneurs. Surely she remembered that there were other women in the wine trade—women like the Widow Robert, who ran the depository in Paris, or the Widow Blanc, who supplied some of their barrel wines at Clicquot-Muiron.

Barbe-Nicole also knew that her genteel-class background made striking out on her own complicated. These other women didn't come from proud and important bourgeois families, and increasingly, the daughters and wives of wealthy entrepreneurs were meant to decorate drawing rooms with their lovely looks and elegant manners, not to run businesses. If she needed a model, she had only to look to her sister, Clémentine, already a fashionable domestic lady of leisure. And she had her father's ambitions to consider. Nicolas was already on intimate terms with Napoléon, now emperor of France. Her father would certainly prefer to see his daughter married again safely—and perhaps, if she could manage it, splendidly.

Mulling over the possibilities, she recognized that the idea taking shape in her imagination was out of step with the tenor of her times. The moment when enterprising widows could respectably run a family trade was passing, in part because the very model of the family-run business was disappearing quickly as well. Nowhere was this truer than in textile centers like Reims, where the economic future was in the large, professionally managed factories that had created the Ponsardin and Clicquot fortunes. Everyone around her agreed that a genteel young woman and a mother had no place in the business world. Already, "the *bourgeoisie* of yesteryear who had tended the [company] books had . . . metamorphosed into the lady clad in silks and absorbed in social and religious life." The wiser course was to embrace a quiet and comfortable life of polite invisibility, dedicated to domestic motherhood and pious circumspection.

We have no way of knowing precisely when Barbe-Nicole first began to imagine a different future for herself—or when she began to believe that it might actually be possible. Perhaps it was only a vague plan that she thought about sometimes in those first weeks of mourning, when she grieved not only for François but also for the end of the enterprise to which he had been devoted so passionately. When Louis Bohne returned in December, recalled by that awful letter telling him of François's death, however, he found Barbe-Nicole very willing to hear what he had to say about the possibilities for the future of the company, and it appears that Barbe-Nicole was energized by his return. When it came to saving the business, Barbe-Nicole and Louis were soon of one mind. The problem would be convincing anyone else.

Chapter 7

Partner and Apprentice

Staring at the ceiling of her bedroom in the early morning hours of February 10, 1806, Barbe-Nicole was perhaps already feeling queasy. The church bells tolled six o'clock, and without turning to look, she knew the horizon was still only a dim wash of early gray.

It was her usual morning hour, yet this was anything but a usual day. Today—after months of hard thinking and secret anxieties, after weeks of persuasion and self-doubt—was the day she would sign over her assets to enter into an arranged partnership with a man she knew only in passing. It was the second time in her life she had done so. But this time, it was not a marriage. It was a business partnership. And if anything, the stakes were even greater. She was risking a family fortune on a commercial venture, and with it she was risking the independence that she had only recently realized was her right as a widow—especially as the widow of a wealthy industrialist.

As her gaze took in the room around her in the growing half-light of dawn—the high, decorative ceilings and airy windows, the luster of the polished furniture in the shadows—perhaps she thought for a moment about the life she could have chosen now that François was gone: summers at a country estate somewhere cool and delicious, winters here in Reims or perhaps even Paris, with her favorite cousins, members of the extended Le Tertre family to which her mother had been born. There would have been no worries about money or the future. No reasons to wake up with her stomach turning somersaults.

Swinging her feet to the floor, she also knew that what she was feeling was excitement. Rarely had she felt so alive or so determined. It had taken the same determination to persuade her father-in-law to let her take over the company. He had been the only obstacle she couldn't dismiss easily, and his doubts about a woman's ability to run a struggling commercial enterprise—about her complete lack of any business experience, above all—had sometimes seemed insurmountable. Still, in the end, she thought with a smile, he had agreed to let her try. She was glad that men of his generation could still imagine the possibility of a family businesswoman, even in this new industrialist era. She could never forget how kind he had been in the end; not only had he given her his blessing, but he had promised to be her first investor, to the tune of nearly half a million dollars. Afterward, they had both cried a bit, thinking of François.

Philippe had put his trust in her enthusiasm and persistence, with one condition, a condition that was non-negotiable. He would let her try to make a go of it, but she would need to serve her own kind of apprenticeship. For four years, she would have to work with a partner, someone Philippe would choose. After that, if she still wanted the hard life of a widow entrepreneur—and if she could persuade him that her instincts were sharp—then he wouldn't stand in her way.

So today, they would sign the financial agreements and legal contracts that would form her new business. Once again, she would enter into an arranged partnership with a man. His name was Alexandre Jérôme Fourneaux, and he was her father's age. In fact, both Philippe and her father knew him well. He was another of the wealthy textile merchants who made up their small circle in Reims.

But Alexandre was also a winemaker. Like Philippe, Alexandre had been dealing in local wines as a sideline for years. More important, he wasn't just a distributor. He knew the craft of winemaking. François had taken risks with the family business when he started bottling the company wines. Alexandre had been doing that and more. He had been growing his own grapes and making his own base wines as well, leading the way in the integration of the winemaking process and undoubtedly putting some of the small brokers out of business in the process. Barbe-Nicole had been eagerly learning all she could about winemaking, but she needed to master its secrets. She now had four years—and a hard-nosed teacher.

Her marriage had begun in a damp underground cellar. Today would also end in a cellar, she thought ruefully. But this partnership was a very different kind of marriage, and she would not be wearing the girlish white of a young patriot and bride. She was a widow, and that meant a future of blacks and browns and grays and perhaps someday the deepest purples. Looking at herself in the vanity mirror for the last time that morning, she decided that she didn't mind. She had never made much of a socialite. She would be perfectly happy to wear the somber widow's weeds forever. The public reminder of her mourning just might make people more willing to accept her exercising the new freedoms that came with it, as she fully intended to do.

As a widow, Barbe-Nicole was entitled to manage her own affairs. It was a unique situation in French culture at the beginning of the nineteenth century. Widows had all the social freedoms of married women—and most of the financial freedoms of a man. Under the laws of the Napoleonic Code, a married businesswoman had a shadowy legal existence. According to statute, a woman entrepreneur could not defend even a simple contract without her husband's permission. But as a widow—and especially as a recognized public trader—Barbe-Nicole could make her own decisions. Still, no one had really expected her to take control of the family fortune. Certainly, no one expected her to risk it on a business investment, much less on a company that she proposed to run herself.

While marriage was never an equal partnership in this era, this new business should have been. She and Alexandre had each invested 80,000 francs. This was a vast sum of money—eighty times the annual salary of an entry-level traveling salesman for the company. Exactly how much the investment was worth in modern terms is tricky to estimate. The standard of living was very different then, and the value of money fluctuated wildly during Napoléon's wars, but consider that thirty years later an unskilled laborer still earned less than 400 francs a year.

A one-to-twenty ratio of francs to modern dollars is probably a conservative calculation. That means an unlucky manual laborer earned something under $8,000 a year, and a young salesman earned closer to $20,000 annually, certainly little enough to persuade him of the value of his commissions. At an average of 3.5 francs at the beginning of the nineteenth century, a bottle of champagne went for something upward of $70. Using these figures, Barbe-Nicole invested over $1.5 million dollars in this new venture. Philippe brought to the table another 30,000 francs, almost $500,000, all in inventory and presumably in wine. It was a total of nearly $4 million in capital gambled on a company led—at least on the face of it—by a young woman with no business experience.

At this point in 1806, the Clicquot family officially went out of the textile business. Trading in bolts of wool like her father was not Barbe-Nicole's vision of her business future. The new partners were anxious not to lose all the old clients that Philippe and François had nurtured in the cloth trade, however. They were careful to keep their contacts and sent out an announcement to all their old customers. "Renouncing the commerce in textiles," the loose-leaf circular read, "we reserve only those of wines of our own vintage," both sparkling and still. While the new partners never made *all* their own wines, approximately 75 percent of the wines sold by this new company—Veuve Clicquot Fourneaux and Company—were crafted directly by the proprietors, far more than even François had ever been able to make.

Barbe-Nicole was starting this venture in a remarkably uncertain business climate: in the middle of a war that only seemed to get worse with each passing month. Success was not just uncertain, but unlikely. That first year, however, beginner's luck was with the partners at Veuve Clicquot Fourneaux. In the first flush of success, she and Alexandre negotiated the delivery of over fifty thousand bottles of champagne—an amazing $3 million worth of product—to be taken through the military blockades that constricted trade routes across Europe in 1806, a dazzling feat requiring sharp wits and strong heads.

In making these sales, they were defying Napoléon's newly established Continental System: a series of trade restrictions intended to create an economic stranglehold on his enemies in Great Britain, Prussia, Germany, and now, once again, Russia. The coalition retaliated by trying to thwart French traders in return, and running the blockades meant that a merchant risked losing everything. No insurers would cover a commodity as tempting as champagne in wartime. Their plan was to get the wines as far as Amsterdam, then a little used seaport on French commercial routes, avoiding the port closures at Dieppe and Brussels. From there, they would ship their wines on to Germany, Scandinavia, and even Russia, moving quietly through the small Prussian port of Memel in modern-day Lithuania. The partners must have chuckled to think of the surprise their competitors would feel. In a war that was ruining everyone's business, they had found a backdoor trade route.

At first, it looked as if they really had discovered a surefire itinerary. When Alexandre sent word late that spring that he had arrived safely in Amsterdam with the wine, Barbe-Nicole, managing the books back in Reims, was gleeful. The shipment had made it safely out of France and was far enough along the English Channel to avoid the worst wartime hazards.

Then came a crushing blow. As merchant traders stood on the docks, watching as the men loaded their cargo, the terrible news worked its way through the crowded seaport. Slowly, all the hustle and bustle of the docks faded to an uncomfortable and ominous silence. Amsterdam was blockaded. The port was being closed, and the ship that Alexandre and Barbe-Nicole had hired to take the wines the next stage would not be allowed to sail.

There had been only the narrowest of windows, and they had missed it. Determined to intensify the economic isolation of France and its allies, the British had closed dozens of ports, all the way to the North Sea. If their shipment had been only a few days—even a few hours—earlier, they might have avoided catastrophe. In despair, Alexandre sent the news back to Reims. "Sea commerce is totally ruined," he wrote, "and therefore all commerce on the Continent." Their only option was to store the wines in Amsterdam and pray that the ports would open soon.

By May, everyone knew it would be a long delay. The British were determined to close the ports indefinitely. But wine could not wait. The storage conditions in Amsterdam were poor, and wine is temperamental. Alexandre returned to France worried and resigned. Barbe-Nicole already knew the worst. It was a disaster.

There was nothing to be done but regroup and reconsider. Veuve Clicquot Fourneaux would have to move on. It was a crippling loss, but there were other sales to make, other orders to fill. There was always the new wine to worry about. Still, as the summer heat turned the fields of the Champagne a luminous gold that year and as the fruit in the vineyard grew dark and heavy on the vines, Barbe-Nicole, her heart still full with all the grief of the previous year, must sometimes have thought of all those other bottles of wine—nearly a third of their annual stock—sitting in sweaty storage in Amsterdam. Champagne exploding in the heat, and clear wine turning murky and muddy with sediment. It was awful.

Wine stored in poor conditions is easily destroyed. This is why serious collectors spend so much time worrying about the temperature and humidity in their cellars. Wine should ideally be stored in cool darkness at around 55°F or 13°C and at 70 percent humidity or higher. Still, even careful storage doesn't guarantee that a bottle of wine will taste its best when finally opened. The dirty little secret of the wine industry today is that 5 percent of the wine sold to customers is "corked"—ruined by the presence of a chemical known as TCA and its musty aromas. TCA stands for 2,4,6-trichloroanisole. The long scientific name suggests something far more complicated than the reality: TCA is the unfortunate result of fungus munching on corkwood. The cork will not smell, but a whiff of badly corked wine is unmistakable.

At the helm of a well-funded but still fledgling winemaking business in the early nineteenth century, Barbe-Nicole and Alexandre had bigger worries than TCA and cork taint. Changes in temperature could cause an entire shipment of her champagne to turn to a slimy mess that was impossible to sell. Customers wanted above all a wine that was clear and sparkling, and they would sacrifice taste in order to achieve it.

Sometimes it was obvious as soon as a bottle came out of the cellar that something had gone wrong. The wine was murky, with a glossy haze. Inside, greasy filaments floated like oily snakes, or there might be suspiciously colored deposits that would not settle and disgorge properly. Worst of all, the wine might be what Barbe-Nicole called "ropey," with the gelatinous consistency of loose egg whites.

Likely, the culprit was problems that had begun during the cask stage of production with the process of malolactic fermentation. Like the sugar and yeast fermentation that leads to autolysis, malolactic fermentation is an organic reaction that plays a role in creating the flavors of fine wine. Just as native yeasts are naturally present in grape must, so there are also native bacteria. These bacteria create a second kind of fermentation, in which the tart, fruity malic acid in the wine is slowly transformed into a smooth and buttery lactic acid—once again making more carbon dioxide and more delicious bubbles.

Malolactic fermentation was notoriously hard to get right in the nine-teenth century, especially with the less sugary grapes common in a north-ern climate region like the Champagne. The big problem was figuring out whether the malolactic reaction was complete before bottling. If not, the bacteria had a sneaky tendency to reappear in the finished wine, with far less desirable results. Smoking casks with sulfur, a natural antiseptic, helped some, but compulsive racking—letting the wine repeatedly and slowly settle over time in a cool cellar and then pouring it from container to container to leave behind the dregs—was the only real solution, and they couldn't be sure it had been done well enough until they saw the finished product.

If the champagne turned out cloudy, they knew they had failed. As long as the wines were still in the cellars, there were some options. One trick was to move the wines to a colder part of the cellar. Sometimes the suspended bacterial debris would settle out naturally. But if the wine turned muddy once it was already on the road, making its way to their clients, it was heartbreaking. A wine that came out of the cellars clear could instantly turn cloudy if the temperature shifted too dramatically. This was part of the problem in the Amsterdam disaster.

Even worse than knowing that so many bottles of fine wine were being ruined in Amsterdam was the bill. The storage costs and port fees were outrageous. Dozens of ships had been caught in the port closure, and warehouse and cellar owners could charge wartime prices. With every passing day, the financial losses were getting worse. Perhaps the wines were already a total loss, and now they were paying richly to store worth-less product. If the wine had already started to go off, it would be hard to sell, even if the ports did miraculously open. So in August, they finally had to send one of their salesmen to do something with the wines—even if it was just liquidate them.

When Charles Hartmann arrived in Holland, he confirmed their worst fears. The wine was in terrible shape. "I prayed to the Good Lord," he wrote to Barbe-Nicole and Alexandre, "to let me find our wines in such a way that I could send you good news, but my prayers were not at all answered. I opened the first case with trembling hands . . . I took out a bottle, trembling I removed the straw and tissue paper, but rather than the clear and brilliant wine that I had hoped for, I saw nothing but a deposit like a finger that I could not detach without shaking the bottle for a full minute."

It took him weeks to go through the stock, bottle by bottle, salvaging what he could. Cloudy bottles he gave a hearty shake, hoping that this might cause some of the suspended sediment to precipitate again, clearing the wine to an extent and making it possible to sell. Overall, the news was wrenching. It was not until the end of September that Charles was able to place the handful of wines that could be saved from the shipment. Once again, they would have to risk port closures to move the product. The wines were shipped to the open port of Copenhagen, to be sent from there, on nimble coastal cruisers, to the Prussian market. "I pray to the Good Lord day and night to send some corsair to take them," he wrote. At least then they would be done with this ill-fated shipment.

The total loss of Amsterdam was quickly followed by word that the entire market was on the verge of collapse. Louis Bohne had set off in April for Germany and Russia on another of his marathon sales tours. The German market, he now wrote, was hopeless: "This country has lacked even money for the worst vintage this past year and after fifteen years of war has given up on being able to procure our luxury drink. . . . The result is that it is necessary for all the world to head to the North. . . . All is war, war and war!" No one had the money—or the inclination—for champagne.

Finally, from Russia, a small bit of unexpected good news: Louis learned that Empress Elizabeth Alexeievna was pregnant. "What a blessing for us," he wrote to Barbe-Nicole and Alexandre, "if this is a Prince that she is brought to bed of . . . a tide of champagne will be drunk in this immense country. Do not mention it, all our competitors would come at once." In over a dozen years of marriage, the empress had given birth only once, to a daughter, and the baby had died as a very young child. The czar would celebrate the birth of a son and heir after all these years with lavish celebrations—celebrations that Louis hoped would include their stealthily exported champagne. By early autumn, he was heading for the Russian border, war or no war. It would turn out to be the most dangerous adventure of his career.

The life of the international salesman was treacherous even in the best of times. A commercial traveler took risks with his life on the road. Roads were generally in bad condition, deeply rutted and narrow. Carriages overturned frequently, in the modern equivalent of the deadly car crash. Ships were lost at sea. That year, another of Barbe-Nicole's employees had nearly been shipwrecked off the coast of Norway; his letter, describing the terror onboard a sinking ship, made for sober reading in Reims.

During wartime, all these dangers were intensified, and Louis knew that he was risking his life going to Russia. The risk was not simply being caught in the crossfire between opposing armies. The problem with a Frenchman arriving in enemy territory in the middle of a war that the Russians were on the verge of losing and setting out to ply the aristocracy with his sparkling wine and cultured charms was that it looked downright suspicious. Before crossing into Russian territory, Louis wrote to Barbe-Nicole and Alexandre, warning them to censor their letters. Avoid "talking politics," he pleaded, "this is dangerous in this country."

Despite all their precautions, Louis soon found that he was suspected of being a French spy. By the spring of 1807, having endured a bitter winter in Saint Petersburg, there was something like panic in his letters to Reims. He was afraid that he would be arrested at any moment, and he knew that his posted letters were being scrutinized. When the chance came, he seized the opportunity to send a hand-delivered note to his employers with a friend returning to France. "In the name of God, don't ever talk of politics," he urged them, "if you don't want to compromise my liberty or my life, deportation to the mines of Siberia is the chastisement for all indiscretions; all the letters are opened."

Perhaps a blistering winter in the capital had given him too clear an idea of what Siberia promised. Leaving precipitously, however, would certainly arouse almost as much suspicion as staying, so Louis was forced to remain at least through spring, when the roads were open for easy traveling. When warmer days returned, they found a relieved Louis promptly on the road, heading west out of Russia.

Despite it all, Russia turned out to be another colossal failure. The empress had given birth to a daughter in the autumn, and this child, like her first, died quickly. Besides, the child was rumored to be the daughter not of the czar, but of Elizabeth's handsome lover, and somehow the emperor wasn't in the mood to throw any fabulous champagne celebrations. Louis had taken some good orders, but the cost of doing business so far from home was turning out to be fabulously expensive, and it was still not clear how they would manage to get their wines into the country. If they couldn't deliver their wines, there would be no staying afloat.

Barbe-Nicole spent much of the next year trying to find some way to get their wines to customers overseas. By the time news came in the summer of 1807 that a Franco-Russian peace treaty was on the horizon, they were faced with a sickening dilemma. When the trade restrictions with Russia were lifted, there would be a mad rush for the border, and the wine merchants able to get product there first would take all the easy sales. They already had requests for champagne pouring in from Russia, Austria, and the Prussian Empire. But no one was going to wait for their wines if their competitor Jean-Rémy Moët got there first. The only option was, once again, to send a shipment of wine to Amsterdam, where it would be ready to sail for Russia as soon as trade opened—and where it would sit waiting in the meantime.

There would be a while to wait. By autumn, it was all depressingly familiar to Barbe-Nicole. No peace treaty still. Wines once again stuck in a warehouse in Holland. The account books were enough to leave her with a pounding headache, and there could be only so many disasters before Veuve Clicquot Fourneaux was out of business. Slowly, the company letters reveal Alexandre fading into the background. Perhaps he already suspected that his initial investment could not be saved. Or perhaps tensions between the two partners were mounting, because despite the setbacks, Barbe-Nicole stubbornly insisted that they needed to focus on international markets. She was so determined that she even considered breaking the law for the first time.

She started to toy with the idea of sending her wines as contraband. Up to now, they had simply been sending their wines in private ships around closed ports, hoping to avoid detection and confiscation at sea. Sending the wines as contraband was something far more serious. It meant cutting a deal with a foreign ship captain—usually someone on the other side of the war. In the final months of 1807, it began to look like the only remaining option, unless she wanted wines sitting in uncertain storage in Amsterdam for a second time.

For a heavy fee, it was possible to have foreign sea captains—and British and American sea captains especially—transport cargo into closed ports by disguising the French origins of the products. Barbe-Nicole was considering it. But she hesitated, probably because she realized some of the unique risks of contraband champagne: In the event these ships were stopped for inspection, it would be difficult to disguise the French origins of this sparkling wine.

Part of what had saved champagne dealers thus far was the exclusivity of the product. At the royal courts of Europe, a lucky few had enjoyed it for more than a century, and the war had perversely whetted their appetite for this luxury wine. It was an impulse pretty near to looting the wine cellars as the *Titanic* went down. Champagne has always had the advantage of coming from one place only—the French are insistent on this point. Real champagne is made only in the Champagne region of France. Today, the region is limited to 323 classified villages, and everything from the dates of the harvest to the pruning of the vines is strictly controlled.

This determination to protect the integrity of champagne, both as a product and as a marketing monopoly, was just getting its start in the early nineteenth century, much like the industry itself. It wasn't until 1844 that champagne makers—recognizing that a brand name was fast becoming a generic category—sued for the right to prevent other sparkling-wine makers from using the word. The legal battle is still not over. Hoping to avoid the branding destiny of products like Band-Aid and Q-tips, winemakers in the Champagne challenge all comers. Even the descriptive term *champenoise,* or "champagne style," used to describe sparkling wines crafted in the traditional style, is contested property.

In the first decade of the nineteenth century, the winemakers of the Champagne weren't yet worried about the misuse of their name. Champagne was not yet big business, and in the mind of the consumers—a select and mostly royal crowd—it naturally came only from this small part of the world. Even so, when it came to sending champagne through closed ports, the singularly French origins of the wine already meant that there could be no disguising its source. Barbe-Nicole would have hesitated to gamble on a ruse that had such an obvious and singular flaw.

The cruel irony was that by 1808, the wines of the Widow Clicquot were in great demand in Russia. It just goes to show that name recognition in the marketplace sometimes doesn't square with the actual sales figures. She owed much of this success to Louis Bohne. Political tensions had eased, and Louis was back in Russia again, hell-bent on capturing the market. In fact, for the next four years, France and Russia would maintain an uneasy and always fragile peace in the midst of the ongoing European conflict. Now, at the beginning of this peace, Louis knew that he had helped talk Barbe-Nicole into her international strategy, and his business judgment was on the line. Besides, Louis was working on commission. Although he wrote that "a large part of Europe [was] ruined by the famine, the exigencies of occupation," and that "the misery of the times is contrary to the effects of luxury," he had persevered doggedly.

Already, both the name of their company and the limited quantities of wine that they managed to get into the country had excellent reputations. Increasingly, it was Barbe-Nicole's name alone that the customers recognized. Ironically, the faceless Widow Clicquot was becoming a brand in Russia before she could even make her own decisions as an entrepreneur. Unlike the popularity of so many famous brands named after women in the years to come, this success owed nothing to conventional stereotypes of personal beauty or charm. The Russians can have had no idea that behind these wines was a hardheaded and diminutive woman of just thirty. As Louis told her, already in the most fashionable homes "there are rare advantages that give us a rising name brand among our competitors and which we need not wait for a general peace to realize. . . . [The] favorable reputation attached abroad to the name of Clicquot . . . is invariable and can be considered as the unique foundation of your establishment." "Your establishment." Already, it seemed, everyone understood who was at the heart of this commercial partnership.

In the autumn of 1808, for a marvelous few months, there was a reprieve. During those heady weeks, Barbe-Nicole could imagine what business might be like without all the obstacles. The blockades were lifted, and they scrambled to ship their wines. Fifty thousand bottles arrived safely in Saint Petersburg, and orders for more were pouring in. For a moment, it seemed the worst was over.

But by the spring of 1809, Barbe-Nicole knew that it was really just the beginning of another long haul. Suddenly, everything turned more ugly than anyone could have imagined, as economies across the continent unraveled. Trade came to a virtual standstill, and in letter after letter word came back from her travelers with the same report: "Everywhere . . . business is absolutely dead." In July, even Louis admitted defeat. There was no point in staying in Russia. Europe was on the verge of financial collapse, and the French were largely to blame. In the midst of it, Napoléon only turned the screws tighter. In Krakow, their sales agent was threatened with arrest and given "an order to leave the city and the states of Austria." Suddenly, no one was in the mood for luxuries like champagne. No one wanted anything to do with the French, either.

Barbe-Nicole now understood that the ports would stay closed for months, maybe even years. There would be no more sly exports. No amount of cunning or energy could get her wines safely to her international clients now—even if there had been clients waiting for them. And there were not. The business was in trouble. There was no question about it. In 1809, she managed to sell only forty thousand bottles of wine, many of them to markets no farther than France. She turned to the domestic market in hopes of staying in business, but few people at home had the money to indulge in champagne or expensive fine wines. Fewer still had cause to celebrate.

In the spring of 1810, the orders were once again a dismal trickle, and in July came the final blow. On the emperor's orders, all export trade would require expensive government licenses, and banks throughout Europe began to fail at an alarming rate. There had been no word at all from Louis for months, and Barbe-Nicole was beginning to worry that something terrible had happened. Finally, a letter arrived. We can only imagine what went through Barbe-Nicole's mind as she held the slender packet with its bright wax seal. Perhaps, she thought, Louis had once more saved them. Perhaps inside was news of stupendous orders or peace just on the horizon. Her hand hesitated a moment before she unfolded the sheets, and she read with devastating simplicity the only news he could send: "Business totally dead."

Looking at the letter for a long while, she must have dreaded writing her reply. There was no easy way to reassure Louis, nothing she could say to buoy his spirits that he would believe. And there was one other thing that she would need to tell him. On July 10, the four-year contract that had kept Veuve Clicquot Fourneaux in business expired. It would not be renewed. Alexandre couldn't see a future in this company, and he was taking the opportunity to walk away—with his half of the operating capital. The cycle of hope followed by crushing failure had taken its toll on all the partners at Veuve Clicquot Fourneaux. For the second time in her life, Barbe-Nicole found herself facing an uncertain future, and this time she really would be on her own.

Chapter 8

Alone at the Brink of Ruin

For Barbe-Nicole—indeed, for the entire Ponsardin family and the wine industry in general—1810 was a year of great transitions. Barbe-Nicole had known that the contract with Alexandre would expire that summer, and the decision not to renew the partnership was no mystery. The continuing war with Great Britain and Napoléon's Continental System were making export sales impossible, and profit margins were slender. She had known since spring that, soon, expensive licenses would be required for all shipments abroad.

Besides, Alexandre's son Jérôme had now completed his commercial education, and Alexandre was understandably eager to set up his son in the trade. There was no reason to commit Jérôme to a long-term partnership in a failing family business with a young widow several years his senior—especially one who clearly wanted to run the family business herself.

Barbe-Nicole, it seems, had no intention of marrying again, although if she had, Jérôme Fourneaux might have been a convenient choice. Perhaps some small spark of romance or admiration had been ignited, for although Jérôme and his father had turned their energies to expanding their own family wine business—founded in 1734 by Alexandre's grandfather under the name Forest-Fourneaux—the young man continued to help Barbe-Nicole with the finer points of winemaking in her first few years alone, despite the fact that she was now a competitor.

The family business to which Alexandre and Jérôme returned their attentions, now renamed simply Fourneaux and Son, never made either famous. If the direction of their company is any indication, they didn't have the same competitive ambition that always characterized Barbe-Nicole as an entrepreneur. Still, both were talented winemakers, and the tradition of delightful champagne wines that they initiated continues to this day. In 1931, the company they had nurtured was bought out by a family of winemakers who would turn it into one of the world's most prestigious estates. It is now known as Champagne Taittinger—thanks to Alexandre and Jérôme, the third oldest champagne house in existence.

That spring, when Barbe-Nicole's days were filled with preparations for the necessary liquidation and with plans for her own future as a sole proprietor, there were also monumental changes for the Ponsardin family. Their star was on the rise. Her father, Nicolas, always a charming and politically savvy man, had been currying favor with Napoléon since the early years of the century, when Napoléon and Joséphine had stayed as guests at the Hôtel Ponsardin during the year of the first Clicquot family vintage.

Poor Joséphine—unable to produce an heir and a bit too free with her favors—had been since then unceremoniously dumped, but Nicolas's reward for his hospitality and his zealous support of the new regime was to become the mayor of Reims, not by public election, as one might have expected of a former Jacobin revolutionary, but by the imperial decree of the emperor.

In the spring of 1810, even Barbe-Nicole was caught up in some of the excitement surrounding her father's new position and Napoléon's impending second marriage to the Austrian archduchess Marie Louise—niece to the ill-fated Marie Antoinette and, like her aunt before her, being sent to her future husband as so much checked baggage in a train of magnificent carriages from the east. Her destination was the Château de Compiègne, a grand royal palace some fifty miles northeast of Paris. The road passed very near to Reims. Barbe-Nicole certainly witnessed the arrival in the city of the pretty archduchess and her convoy. Living in the center of Reims, she would have found it hard to miss. But it was especially hard since her father, always a royalist at heart, had personally organized the extravagant celebrations to welcome her.

While more fashionable women like her sister were aflutter with talk of seeing the new empress and of the magnificence of her court, Barbe-Nicole had just one wish. She hoped that this new marriage to one of Napoléon's most powerful sparring partners would buy them some peace. The "marriage of the Archduchess Louise is fixed for the 25 of March at Compiègne [and] she will pass our village," she wrote to Louis Bohne. "If she can give us the peace it will be a great good for the people."

Whatever her father's personal feelings about Napoléon—and personal feelings don't seem to have guided his political allegiances unduly—Barbe-Nicole by now hated the man. She had no patience with his wars any longer, and she and Louis referred to him in their letters simply as "the devil." His open support for her competitor, Jean-Rémy Moët, undoubtedly played some small role in their antagonism.

Her feelings for the brazen emperor were probably not softened when she learned that Napoléon had been spreading his influence further in the vineyards of the Champagne. He awarded another competitor, Memmie Jacquesson, proprietor of Jacquesson and Sons in nearby Châlons-sur-Marne, with a gold medal intended to reflect the emperor's personal appreciation of "the beauty and richness of their cellars." Then, as an additional mark of his favor, Napoléon asked Jacquesson to supply the champagne for his wedding to Archduchess Marie Louise. It was discouraging. These were sales Barbe-Nicole hated to see go to a competitor—especially one who had been in business for just over a decade. In the luxury wine market, she was already learning that name recognition meant everything, and here was another newcomer nurturing a personal relationship with the most powerful man—and purchaser—in all of France.

The biggest change of all for Barbe-Nicole that year was the most obvious one: Against all the odds, she would soon be an independent woman running a well-funded international business. That fact alone makes her an exceptional woman in her era. A surprising number of women—widows especially—ran small companies in order to ensure their family's economic survival, especially in traditionally feminine businesses like dressmaking or innkeeping. But in the entire century, only a handful of women in France owned businesses with the sort of capital that Barbe-Nicole commanded. She was already a pioneer, just by having taken these enormous chances.

On the last day of July, she opened her own new account ledger for the business that she would call, from that moment forward, Veuve Clicquot Ponsardin and Company. Her account book showed on the order of 60,000 bottles of wine in stocks, six dozen additional casks, 10,000 empty bottles, and nearly 125,000 corks. Her father-in-law, Philippe, still prepared to gamble on her ambition and talent, reinvested his 30,000 francs, maintaining a share in the company both were both determined to keep alive.

To hurry the liquidation and settlements, she began sending out announcements that summer to clients, asking for the prompt payment of outstanding accounts. She was anxious to settle the books. On some of these announcements, we see her elegant and carefully looped signature, reading simply: Veuve Clicquot Ponsardin. It is the same distinctive signature reprinted today on every bottle of the yellow label nonvintage champagne that bears her name.

In the cellar and with the direction of the business, she had other new ideas and new plans as well, but they were initiatives she wanted to discuss with Louis Bohne when he returned from his travels. Louis was in love, and he had delayed beginning married life during his long years on the road for the Clicquot family. Now he was engaged to Miss Rheinwald, the daughter of a town councilman. There are no other details about this young woman who captured Louis's heart. All we can guess about her is that, like Louis, she came from a German family. Louis planned to take several months off from work while the liquidation details were arranged. It would be an extended honeymoon, a chance to start a family for a man who had spent much of the past five years far from home.

Barbe-Nicole welcomed the opportunity to have Louis close at hand during the early months of her new solo leadership. The other salesmen would be back on the road immediately, bringing in new orders even as the final business of Veuve Clicquot Fourneaux and Company was resolved. Louis, however, would be able to advise, and she would be at leisure to talk through her plans with this reliable—and undeniably expert—employee, just as she had heard François do in that long summer before his death. A number of important decisions needed to be made that would shape the future of the business profoundly. If Barbe-Nicole had the advantage of seeing things with the fresh eyes of inexperience, she also had the sense to learn from those she trusted.

There was the question of her trademark, but that was simple enough, at least. During her partnership with Alexandre, they had burned the symbol of the anchor into the corks of the wines blended and bottled by the company. It was as close to a trademark as any champagne house had at the turn of the nineteenth century, when wine labels were still virtually unknown. Shipping cases and casks were often labeled with the company initials and with some information to identify the client and the type of wine to avoid things going astray on the crowded docks of wartime Europe, but the colorful marketing of bottles that we know today had not yet been invented.

At this time, once a bottle of wine was unpacked, only the cork and the color of the resin sealing wax around the collar of the bottle distinguished the wine of one house from another. The sealing wax collar, the so-called *goudron*, was often elaborate and pretty, but it was not particularly reliable as a way to distinguish the wines of one vintner from another. Moët colored his caps in brilliant greens flecked with gold or silver. But Philippe Clicquot used exactly the same color scheme. So did Barbe-Nicole after him. Marketing was in its infancy, and at a time when many brokers still purchased their bottled wines ready-made from a variety of local suppliers, few champagne houses or few of their clients thought of particular wines as the distinctive product of an individual company.

Apart from the colorful *goudron*, the only other way to identify a bottle of wine as coming from the cellars of the Widow Clicquot was the symbol branded on the cork. The family had first used the anchor as a company symbol just after her marriage, when Philippe and François started Clicquot-Muiron together, and she was determined to continue the tradition. Perhaps it reminded her of François's presence in the company that they had dreamed of building together. Perhaps it was a nod to the export markets and the ocean trade that François had worked to open. From the beginning, it had always been used because it was the traditional symbol of hope. They had started using it when the future seemed promising, when they could look forward to a life together and to prosperous new directions. She would not give up on it now—and the symbol can still be found today on the labels of a bottle of the Widow's famous bubbly.

Now at the helm of her own company, she had other, more thorny questions to tackle about work in the cellars and the direction of her business in a disastrous economy. With the intensification of the blockades and the unstable currency rates, it was a difficult time to export wine, and Barbe-Nicole could not afford a major financial setback. She was risking her own independence, and the company had been struggling for several years. She retrenched and diversified. Under her new direction, the company began selling more local red wines by the barrel on the domestic French market, rather than going to the unnecessary expense of bottling these wines for an international luxury market that in many cases she could not reach. The largest proportion of these wines was from the grapes raised on her own estates, sold to clients within a few hundred miles of Reims.

When she did export bottled wines, Barbe-Nicole also made a point of including an impressive selection of high-end vintages from other, more fashionable parts of France. The red wines from the Champagne, which had once rivaled the wines of Burgundy in their bouquet and delicacy, were no longer so highly reputed. The exceptions were wines from a handful of renowned villages in the Champagne, villages that most fortuitously included Bouzy, where it was now left to her to manage the Muiron vineyards that she and François had inherited. She could still remember spending the long hours of the early morning watching the crush in the coolness of the pressing room, and she knew that it was excellent land. Involvement in every aspect of the business was to be her hallmark, and the barrels from the Bouzy estate are likely to have been the first wines that Barbe-Nicole could boast of being crafted under her sole direction. By selling them directly to customers, she maximized her slender profits.

She also continued making champagne. The obstacles to international trade made an exclusive focus on sparkling wine impossible for a young broker still establishing her name, and she would have to be prepared for some proportion of her stocks to sit unsold in her cellars for months, perhaps even years. On those long summer nights before the harvest, when François and Louis had dreamed together of vast new markets in Great Britain or in Russia, Barbe-Nicole had been enchanted, and she still believed in their shared vision. Even as she turned to concrete sales in domestic markets, she kept her travelers seeking out new opportunities abroad and keeping up old contacts on the other side of closed borders.

Barbe-Nicole's workday, in the cellars or at her desk, began at seven in the morning, and she rarely set aside her account books and letters until nine or ten in the evening. Running a family business required a staggering amount of work, and she prided herself on quickly and carefully answering the endless correspondence she received. This commitment came at a high personal cost. At some point during her first years of running the business with Alexandre, Barbe-Nicole sent her daughter, Clémentine, away to a convent boarding school in Paris. Since six or seven was the usual age for girls to be enrolled in convents, it is likely the loss of her daughter as a companion coincided with the founding of the joint company in 1806. She had already learned, like so many single mothers, the heartbreaking challenges of raising a child while running a business.

Sending Clémentine away to school in Paris had not been a coldhearted decision. Barbe-Nicole's sister had been sent to school at the same age, and strange as it may seem to modern parents, who would no more send their young children away to a convent than leave them on the side of a busy street unattended, boarding school for young girls was normal. But that did not mean Barbe-Nicole didn't miss her daughter. Her letters show that she was a devoted and pragmatic mother, determined to protect her daughter's future and her happiness but also convinced that Mentine, as the girl was known in the family, had not inherited the same sharp intelligence of her mother or grandfather. Still, Barbe-Nicole knew that the nuns would look after Clémentine and that she would be taught to read and write. Clémentine surely learned, as her mother had done before her, the art of fine needlework and the Catholic catechism, and Barbe-Nicole could rely on her mother's Paris cousins to keep an eye on the girl in the event of something unexpected. There was no doubt, however, about the life that Barbe-Nicole imagined for her daughter. It would not be a future in business. It would be the same life of quiet domesticity and affluent privilege that Barbe-Nicole had rejected.

That summer, Barbe-Nicole had reason to think about that life of luxury and the risks she was taking with the business. She had decided to sell some of her jewelry in order to finance the business. She could have spent her days finding occasions to wear it. Now, much of her capital was tied up in the company, and there must have been cash flow issues. Otherwise, it is unlikely she would have parted with these family assets.

During the first year of the transition, when her affairs were being disentangled from those of Alexandre Fourneaux and when joint holdings were being liquidated, the company would make only a small profit. She owned sizable vineyards and had some excellent stocks in her cellars. None of that was much help in paying the salaries of her cellar workers or settling the inevitable bills, however. By August, Barbe-Nicole had come up with a plan, asking her salesman Charles to sell her jewelry at the royal courts of eastern Europe.

The letters that she wrote about the sale are anxious ones, and worry about the jewelry occupied her mind for much of the autumn. Charles was using all his persuasive charms drumming up orders in Léopol (now Lviv, Ukraine), then part of the Austrian Empire, and Barbe-Nicole hoped he might also find a noble family to buy some jewelry: a large quantity of rose pearl necklaces and a diamond valued at an astonishing 3,000 francs—close to $60,000. By mid-October, Charles had shipped half the necklaces to one of his friends, who had offered to act as an agent. She begged him not to let the diamond out of his sight. "I pray that you will keep it on your person," she wrote him. It would be far too valuable to lose. A month later, the diamond remained unsold, and then it disappears from the account books in the company archives at Veuve Clicquot Ponsardin. Few people had money to spend on extravagances of this sort. Louis wrote from Vienna that the nobility were short of cash. For the working people, it was worse. It had been three years since the wheat harvest had been sold. People couldn't afford to buy even this staple crop. It seems likely that Barbe-Nicole got to keep her diamond, although she needed the capital more.

Much of her energy that autumn was also given over to worrying about technical difficulties in the cellars. Her chief winemaker was now Jacob, the same man who had worked for François and his father at Clicquot-Muiron, and they were in constant communication. Often, Jérôme Fourneaux could be found advising or lending a hand. Cloudy wine or ropey wines still frustrated her, and there were the inevitable disappointments of breakages.

Then there were problems with the bubbles themselves. Sometimes customers complained that they were too big and gassy, with a tendency to froth and leave an unappetizing thick and beady foam on the top of the glass. Barbe-Nicole and Louis referred despairingly to these large bubbles as *yeux de crapaud*—toad's eyes. Louis, quite serious but with a bit of the honeymooner's rakish charm, confessed, "This is a terrible thing that gets up and goes to bed with me: toad's eyes! I like large eyes everywhere except in Champagne wine. May Heaven preserve us from their destructive effect." He and Barbe-Nicole often shared flirtatious little jokes like this. Just because she was a widow and just because she educated her daughter in a convent didn't mean she lived like a nun. But the concern about toad's eyes was not a laughing matter, when it came down to it. The flaw, likely caused by allowing the wine to rest too long in wooden casks in the early stages of production, was a serious obstacle to luxury sales because clarity and *mousse* mattered more to their customers even than taste. And they had no clear idea how to solve the problem.

Unfortunately, the glasses used to drink champagne in the nineteenth century, although not the cause of toad's eyes, would not have helped the problem. Barbe-Nicole drank her sparkling wine from the broad, shallow glasses that we call *coupes* and usually associate with the glamour of the Jazz Age and early Hollywood films. These glasses were first made popular during the seventeenth century, and wine lovers everywhere used them for drinking champagne well into the twentieth century, despite firm instructions to hosts and hostesses after the 1850s to "never use the present round saucer animalcula-catching champagne glasses, but . . . tulip-shaped ones."

Today, the staunch preference is for the tall, slender champagne flute, and if you care about your champagne having the smallest possible bubbles—and many connoisseurs do—the flute is the glass to use. Owing to basic mechanics, the bubbles are smaller and prettier in narrow glasses. Still, more often than not, which glass to choose and the size you like your bubbles comes down to a question of appearance rather than taste. Bigger bubbles do not taste appreciably different from smaller ones. The finest champagnes are celebrated for their small, slow bubbles, which rise with mesmerizing grace to the surface of the glass and leave a light and airy foam. This is because the older a champagne is, the smaller the bubbles become. Because only vintage champagnes are aged extensively, we naturally associate small bubbles with the finest-quality wines.

By December, as Barbe-Nicole was looking forward, perhaps with some trepidation, to her thirty-third birthday, the books had been mostly closed on Veuve Clicquot Fourneaux. The Clicquot family still owned cellars and offices on rue de la Vache, and Barbe-Nicole also owned a country estate outside Oger, in the heart of the Côte des Blancs, just south of the renowned vineyards at Avize and Cramant and on the edge of the great forest that stretched for miles to the west. Although architecturally imposing in the classical French style, with a broad hip roof and big open windows looking onto the fields, the house was her refuge, decorated for comfort, with soft sofas and chairs in the cheerful blue chintz that was then the height of fashion. From the rooms, Barbe-Nicole could watch the progress of her vines, chardonnay grapes destined to become champagne.

Despite the allure of Oger, she spent most of her time in Reims, running the business as often as not from one of the pleasant rooms at home. She still lived in the house she had shared with François before his death, on rue de l'Hôpital, named after the hospital that stood in that part of town. It was a serene and airy place, and the focal point of her private office was a pretty wooden desk, built in the popular style of the Empire period and still on display at the tasting rooms of Champagne Veuve Clicquot in Reims. From here, she maintained the account books and wrote pages and pages of correspondence to her salesmen, clients, and suppliers. It was reassuring to know that the cellars beneath her home connected, in their dark circuitous way, to the cellars underneath her childhood home at the Hôtel Ponsardin.

Less reassuring was the news from ports across Europe. The British had intensified their policing of the blockades, and conditions for international trade were growing steadily worse. Back on the road, Louis was exasperated, and he had nothing nice to say about the British, either. He called them "maritime harpies" and the "assassins of prosperity." More bluntly, he wrote to Barbe-Nicole in a fit of pique, "The more I come to hate the English, the more I wish for the corruption of their morals. That God would give us peace so we could avenge their evil gullets . . . [and] make them addicted to habitual drunkenness." Louis fantasized that drowning the British in the champagne of the Widow Clicquot would be a just retribution. How they would have suffered!

In fact, despite the closed ports, few British wine lovers were feeling very parched. During the holiday season, the British market was one of the strongest in Europe for champagne makers, and Louis himself made some lucky sales there. "Here," he wrote to Barbe-Nicole, "2,000 bottles have been easily sold because of the season . . . on Christmas day all the English . . . drink their champagne wine, it is the day exclusively privileged in their homes for this drink." Jean-Rémy Moët, with his far stronger contacts in Great Britain and his better name recognition in the island nation, was having even greater success. But the seasonal British market could not keep all the champagne makers in the region afloat. The next year they learned that one of their competitors, the firm of Tronsson-Jacquesson, was bankrupt.

By the summer of 1811, Barbe-Nicole could be forgiven for feeling a bit panicked. Despite the slow collapse that year of the French economic blockades, the allied counterblockades had lost none of their sting. That spring, she had orders for fewer than thirty-three thousand bottles. With Napoléon and the czar again at odds, in large part because of Alexander's lackluster support for the French emperor's crippling trade restrictions, the Russian market—where she had once been recognized as an emerging name in the champagne business—was effectively closed, and war on that front again seemed certain. The Russians were building up troops on the distant borders of French territories in the east, and the British ruled the English Channel. Much of Europe was still broke, and the continent was limping along on the brink of fresh economic collapse. All export required licenses, but Barbe-Nicole knew what they really were: heavy war taxes on her wines.

As France began to lose ground, everything seemed to become more vicious. Louis sent back to Barbe-Nicole letters from Austria telling her about the destruction and misery that he saw everywhere. Napoléon controlled Austria, along with Prussia and Denmark, as client states, but the "independence" of these "sister republics" came at a high and often humiliating cost for their citizens, and the very idea of offering to sell a luxury like champagne was offensive to people who had been brutalized by Napoléon's armies. Louis quickly understood that he would not find a warm welcome.

The cash flow problems were becoming increasingly serious, and Barbe-Nicole urged him—and all her travelers—to bring in whatever sales they could. Lower the prices if need be, she wrote to Louis in Holland. By autumn, as he traveled through Belgium in search of clients, he could only report the same problem. He begged and cajoled, he lowered his prices, and still there were no sales. He was lucky if he was not insulted or abused.

Making matters a hundred times worse was something that should have been cause for celebration. The harvest of 1811 was marvelous. As one nineteenth-century tourist in the French wine country observed, "There had never been . . . a grape so ripe, so sugary, and one harvested under such favorable circumstances of weather." Since spring, much of the northern hemisphere had been watching the passage of a great comet, and the vintage that autumn had coincided with its most brilliant appearance in the night sky. As far away as America, "the great comet was attracting all eyes," and one man who saw it later recalled "how many superstitious terrors it gave rise to." Throughout the Champagne, the rural people whispered that it was a portent of great change and of the fall of empire. In homage to a perfect harvest, winemakers abandoned their own trademarks and branded their corks with stars, the mark of the *Vin de la Comète*. Barbe-Nicole was among them.

This abundance meant that prices for wine plummeted. It would be one of the two greatest vintages of the century, but despite the falling prices, few people could afford it. Even barrel wines would go to waste, so Barbe-Nicole did the sensible thing—what winemakers had done throughout the previous century when the market was soft. In the spring, when the cask wines had been racked and clarified, she bottled the wine and turned it into champagne. It would sit, slowly transforming itself, in her cellars for at least a year, and she could buy herself some time. An intelligent plan—but it did nothing to help cash flow.

Once bottled, the champagne of 1811—a vintage year, if ever there was one—would continue to improve for many months. Putting the wine down in bottles was not the catastrophe, least of all for the wines themselves. The problem was the time it would take to realize any money from the sales, at a moment when little ready cash was finding its way to the account books. Normally, Barbe-Nicole would age her champagne for a year or a year and a half, putting it down into the cool cellars before summer and not shipping it until the following autumn. This meant that sparkling wines generally went to market two years after harvest, and the winemaker could then expect to sell it at luxury prices. During these two years, champagne houses had a great deal of their money tied up in stocks; add to this the technical problems in producing a clear champagne and the risks of breakage, and it is easy to understand the attraction of barrel wines, which were ready for sale within months.

If barrel wines could not be sold quickly, their advantages disappeared. Wine in wooden casks might last a few years in ideal cellar conditions, but some slow exposure to oxygen was inevitable, and the wines deteriorated if held too long. The same wine in hermetically sealed glass bottles might age well for a decade or more. Champagne was more delicate. Before disgorgement—the process of removing the spent yeast cells from the bottle after the second fermentation—sparkling wines continue to improve, resting on the lees, for several years. Under French law, vintage champagnes today are aged for a minimum of three years. Some of the finest are aged as long as seven or eight years. After disgorgement, it is a different matter. Champagne rarely improves with additional cellaring, and there is cause to celebrate the expert advice: Drink it promptly.

Nothing improved during the winter of 1812. If anything, the political and economic situation grew worse. Napoléon was preparing for his invasion of Russia, and struggling family businesses were ordered to surrender their property to the army, as requisition orders to fit out the soldiers. Young men were once again forcibly recruited into the military. There were rumors that, soon, older men would be conscripted as well. None of this was good for the champagne business.

Louis spent the spring of 1812 hunting orders in northern France. His wife was expecting the birth of their first child that year. Barbe-Nicole was to be the baby's godmother, and the impending arrival of the new addition to his small family may have played a role in his desire to stay close to home. The collapse of the international markets also made Louis's attention to the domestic market a sensible decision.

Then just when Barbe-Nicole thought the market had reached its nadir came another devastating blow, not just for Barbe-Nicole, but for the entire Champagne region. Napoléon had his heart set on the development of the French wine trade. He commanded ministers of state such as Jean-Antoine Chaptal to encourage the industry with scientific reforms, and he was pushing the development of new sugar sources for winemakers. He had nurtured the career of his favorite winemaker, Jean-Rémy Moët, and had listened when his friend complained about policy—although nothing could persuade Napoléon to lift the crushing trade restrictions that he believed would cripple his European enemies and lead to the greater glory of France. Still, in the midst of conquering much of a continent, he had found time for rest and relaxation in the heart of the Champagne, and the superiority of French wine was the source of pride and satisfaction to this self-made emperor. He wanted the winemakers of the Champagne to succeed in particular, and there was no secret about it.

So when the French invaded Russia that June, the czar issued an immediate decree banning the importation of French wines in bottles. Everyone knew that the target was champagne. It alone could not be transported in barrels; if it was, all the fizz would disappear. It was a small yet calculated and personal retaliation. Napoléon had championed the champagne industry. Russia would destroy it. In Reims, a good deal of the resentment was directed at Napoléon himself. In exasperation, Louis declared the emperor "an infernal genie who has tormented and ruined the world for five or six years."

The borders to the east were now firmly closed, and after a long night spent scouring the account books, filled with mounting despair, Barbe-Nicole knew she had no choice about what she would have to do next. Grim-faced and sorrowful, she broke the news to her salesmen, men who had faced all the discomforts and dangers of the road far from home and, against formidable odds, had brought back a handful of sales even in that dark year. She had no job for them. Only Louis would stay on, and the company of Veuve Clicquot Ponsardin faced an uncertain and unhappy future. As Louis put it that year, "The Good Lord is a joker: eat and you will die, do not eat and you will die, and so patience and perseverance."

By the middle of September, the French army had captured Moscow, but it was not much of a victory. Unable to defeat Napoléon, the czar and his allies had retreated to Saint Petersburg, burning everything in their wake—Moscow included. The streets of the city were deserted. "All the houses of the nobility," wrote a British witness, "all the ware-houses of the merchants, all the shops . . . were fired; and . . . the conflagration raged and rendered Moscow one flaming pile."

Even Napoléon's brother Jérôme saw the handwriting on the wall. Jérôme also had a soft spot for Jean-Rémy Moët and his sparkling wine, and he stopped in Épernay on his way to Rome, apparently keen to pick up a few bottles for the road. After ordering six thousand bottles of champagne, all of the *premier cru*, Jérôme lamented that it was so little. "If circumstances were less sad," he told Jean-Rémy, "I would take double; but I believe the Russians won't let me drink it." When Jean-Rémy asked what he meant about the Russians, Jérôme shared with their old friend a state secret. He predicted that the war with Russia would prove a great misfortune.

Jérôme's prediction was accurate. When Napoléon began marching his troops back to France in the final months of the year, it was a disaster. More than half a million men had been sent to fight in Russia, but only thirty thousand or so made it home. Many died of disease, malnourishment, and the freezing winter temperatures that had made Louis so anxious to avoid a fate in the prison camps of Siberia only a few years before. This meant in 1813 another round of forced recruitments, more taxes, more requisitions.

With Napoléon leading the war abroad, Empress Marie Louise was left to govern France, and when a delegation was sent to offer her the money needed to raise more troops, Nicolas Ponsardin was among them. The reward for his loyalty would be the noble title that he had dreamed of in those long forgotten days before the Revolution. He was awarded that year the honorific of *chevalier,* or knight, and wore proudly the star of the French Legion of Honor. With the help of men like Nicolas, Napoléon had raised another army of half a million war-weary men by midsummer. By October, most of them had been killed in the Battle of Leipzig. This time, the Russians were coming after them. Napoléon crossed the Rhine, within a few days' march of Reims, with a mere sixty thousand men and prepared to defend the nation.

That autumn, looking eastward, her vineyards now harvested and bare, Barbe-Nicole knew that desperate times were on the horizon. Disaster and destruction were coming. By the end of 1813, the citizens of Reims found that war had come to their doorstep, and Barbe-Nicole's family was again faced with negotiating a treacherous and frightening political position. Her father, once a revolutionary and republican, had in new times served a new ruler. He had become mayor of the city and a noble baron by imperial decree. If Napoléon fell, there was every chance of Nicolas falling with him. In the aftermath, Barbe-Nicole's family could lose everything—perhaps even their lives.

Chapter 9

Chapter 9

War and the Widow's Triumph

On the eve of the new year in 1813, Barbe-Nicole certainly had plenty of champagne on hand, but this abundance was part of the reason that she had so little to celebrate.

She was glad to see 1813 fade into history. Sales of her wine had been down again that year—down, as she could not help but recognize, a staggering 80 percent since 1805, the year of François's untimely death and her decision to take up running the business. Travel across the continent had become hopelessly unprofitable and increasingly dangerous, and the business was floundering. There was no way to put a positive spin on it. She must have wondered whether the financial risk that she had taken and all the years of hard work were worth the emotional strain. The company was failing, and she knew that the businessmen of Reims—perhaps even her father—would say that this was why women should not run trading houses.

When the bells of the great cathedral of Notre-Dame de Reims rang in the new year, the bitterness in the winter air matched her mood precisely. For Barbe-Nicole could not have been in high spirits when she considered either the year that was passing or the prospects of what was to come. As everyone in Reims understood, the war was edging closer. Napoléon had once said that the countryside of the Champagne would make a perfect battlefield. In this last desperate year, when he still ruled an empire greater than any since Roman times, he would test that hypothesis.

For Barbe-Nicole, his arrival was particularly unwelcome. Already, one could see evidence of the amassing troops in the countryside. If the conflict dragged on, as it had a way of doing, come spring there would be no regular work in the fields or in the vineyards, a grim prospect for anyone whose hopes and fortunes were invested in a harvest. By January, the distant echo of cannon fire resounded faintly through the cobbled streets of Reims, and shopkeepers sweeping the pavement in the bright air would stop to listen solemnly.

No doubt recollecting her own childhood and the frightening escape from the abbey of Saint-Pierre-les-Dames at the height of the Revolution, she hurriedly fetched Clémentine from her convent school in Paris. Clémentine was now fourteen—only a year or two older than Barbe-Nicole had been when the Revolution began—and Barbe-Nicole remembered watching that earlier political upheaval through the cracks of a shuttered window, in hiding. She knew something of what it meant to live in turbulent times and had no intention of trusting her daughter to the care of strangers or even cousins in the midst of a war.

By the end of January, the echoes of cannon fire and horse hooves were no longer faint, and Barbe-Nicole knew it was only a matter of time before there would be troops of one fashion or another in the streets of Reims, looking for food and supplies and shelter and, she had no doubt, as much wine as they could get their hands on.

If her cellars were looted, she would never be able to recover. It would be the end of her business and of the dream that she and François had shared in those first years of their marriage, when life seemed to hold for her such different possibilities. She was sick with worry over the fate of the wine made in that legendary year of the comet, the 1811 vintage, which tasted like dry honey and was slowly turning a light golden hue in the coolness of her cellars. It was a wine destined for greater things than rough soldiers intent on a night's oblivion. It was a wine destined to make her famous, and Barbe-Nicole had some inkling of it. So, in advance of the troops, she ordered her workmen to begin sealing the entrance to her cellars. The wine would wait out the war in uninterrupted darkness.

The arrival of the troops was indeed a certainty. Napoléon was engaged in a bloody contest with the allied coalition in the countryside that stretched just beyond Reims, and it was in the wet, cold landscape of his familiar boyhood Champagne that an empire was to slip from his grasp at last. He would not relinquish it readily. The French routed the Russian and Prussian armies in the village of Montmirail, and the defeated troops retreated to Reims. As evening came, the streets of the city were filled with the ominous sound of metal striking stone and horses and the footfalls of fifteen thousand cold and weary men, dreaming of their homes to the east. The occupation had begun.

Listening from her offices, Barbe-Nicole could hear the chaos in the streets and the loud voices ringing out and the occasional chorus of martial song with words she could not understand. She was waiting for the knock that she knew would come, the knock demanding that she release cases upon cases of wine. Whether they would pay for it was another matter. She surely knew by now that three hundred thousand allied soldiers had taken up residence in occupied Épernay and immediately looted Jean-Rémy's cellars. Before the war was over, he would lose more than half a million bottles of champagne.

In despair, she told her cousin in Paris, Mademoiselle Gard—to the family, simply Jennie—that she anticipated the worst. "Everything is going badly," Barbe-Nicole lamented. "I have been occupied for many days with walling up my cellars, but I know full well that this will not prevent them from being robbed and pillaged. If so, I am ruined, so it is best to be resigned and work to survive. I would not regret my losses except for my poor child for whom it would have been better if this Misfortune had come five or six years earlier, because then she would never have known any of the pleasures that she will lose, and which will make her miserable. But I will struggle to do without everything, to sacrifice everything, everything, so that she will be less unhappy." There would be devastating losses for the rest of the family as well. Her brother's textile factory at Saint-Brice was destroyed by the invading troops, and much of the industry of Reims was crippled.

When the Russians arrived at last, it still surprised her, but even more surprising was that they were gentlemen. The leaders of the Prussian and Cossack armies gave their troops free rein to loot and pillage. The Russians were more restrained, and they were determined to keep administrative control of Reims. There was an ugly bureaucratic tussle when the Russian prince leading the armies, Serge Alexandrovich Wolkonsky, insisted that there would be no looting and no retributive requisitions. To the Prussians, the prince sent word that his orders came directly from the czar. There would be no pillaging of Reims. And "as for your insolent threat of sending troops to Rheims," he told the Prussian leaders, "I have forces here to receive them."

For Barbe-Nicole, it was a bittersweet irony. Her cellars would not be looted. They would mostly buy her wine. For years, she had struggled to sell her champagne, and Louis had traveled across half the continent in search of customers in regions as remote as Turkey and Albania. Each time, he had come back disappointed and discouraged. Now, here at her doorstep was an army of men all ready to buy her wine, not the prized 1811 vintage, which she guarded jealously, but the accumulated stock—still fine wines in their own right—that she had been unable to move during the long years of the war. The soldiers, eager to believe the war was almost at an end, drank with enthusiasm. Watching them guzzle her wines, Barbe-Nicole was philosophical. "Today they drink," she said. "Tomorrow they will pay!"

More ironically still, although Barbe-Nicole would not have known it, the arrival of the Russians would also prove a brilliant marketing opportunity for winemakers throughout the Champagne. Although she had already made a name for herself in imperial Russia, had already captured a significant market share in the days before the economic collapse of the war and the closing of the borders, that recognition had surely faded in the years that had followed. These new men would never forget her sparkling wines. Watching the destruction of his cellars, Jean-Rémy also saw the potential. "All these officers who ruin me today," he predicted, "will make my fortune tomorrow. All those who drink my wine are salesmen who, on returning to their own country, will make the product" famous. Barbe-Nicole would benefit from these same ambassadors.

The Russians, however, were not the only ones in the winter of 1814 to enjoy the champagne of the Widow Clicquot. In early March, the French army under the leadership of General Corbineau recaptured Reims.

Some joked that Barbe-Nicole and the other wine brokers had done their part for the war effort by supplying the allies with strong local wines. When the French entered Reims, "about a dozen prisoners were made, who had been laid under the table by the first and pacific artillery. At the moment of the attack of the French troops, there remained some drinkers but no soldiers. These, dead drunk, had not heard the sound, 'To horse!'" Of course, the French troops wasted no time in celebrating their victory, either. There is a legend, in fact, that it was during these days that the art of *sabrage*—opening champagne bottles with military sabers— was invented. According to the story, "Madame Clicquot . . . in order to have her land protected, gave Napoléon's officers Champagne and glasses. Being on their horses, they couldn't hold the glass while opening the bottle." So they lopped off the necks of the bottles with their swords, and *sabrage* was born.

These Russian prisoners of war did not suffer long as captives. The French victory was short-lived. A week later, the French were forced to retreat, and the Russians again occupied the town. Finally, in mid-March, a desperate and furious Napoléon vowed that he would sleep that night in Reims, the city that could make kings. In making this vow, Napoléon was confident that he would be graciously welcomed at the Hôtel Ponsardin, where he and Joséphine had stayed before, the guests of the charming Nicolas, in more promising times.

But Nicolas Ponsardin did not need a comet and the superstitious sensibilities of the peasants, who read in it a chilling portent, to know that Napoléon would not be emperor for long. The coalition was closing in on the French, and defeat seemed inevitable. Still, in the past, Napoléon had succeeded despite insurmountable odds. Who was to say that he might not manage to do so again?

Not for the first time in his eventful life, Nicolas found himself in a delicate and dangerous political position, unwilling to offend Napoléon in the event he was victorious but unprepared to align himself too closely to a man who was not likely to remain in power long. Even worse might be the consequences if the city fell to the emperor's enemies. It was Napoléon who had made Nicolas mayor, as a mark of his special favor. If the political winds shifted in a new direction, it would now make him the target of retribution. So when it was hinted that he should leave town, Nicolas prepared to do the sensible thing. Hedging his bet, he wrote Napoléon a letter, promising that the city of Reims and those who governed it were his stauch allies, and then he hightailed it out of town, leaving the emperor to take his chances. Well in advance of Napoléon's arrival, Nicolas called for his carriage, left word with his children, and went out of town on an extended business trip to the remote city of Le Mans. He did not return to Reims until well after the curtain had closed on the final act.

In the small hours of the morning, long before the dawn, Napoléon passed through the triumphal gates of the city, the same gates that once welcomed kings on their way to their coronation. Despite the darkness and the cold, the city was alive with excitement, and great crowds gathered along the route to welcome the emperor with exuberant cries and banners and speeches and all the pomp and circumstance that could be arranged at such short notice and after years of war. It was Barbe-Nicole who greeted the emperor at the door of the Hôtel Ponsardin, which her father had deserted. She assured Napoléon that the family was waiting to welcome him only a short distance away, at the home of her brother, Jean-Baptiste.

What must Napoléon have thought when he learned that the Hôtel Ponsardin was empty? It is hard to imagine that a man as astute as Napoléon failed to understand the lack of confidence the absence implied. Or perhaps it did not much matter. Nicolas had charged his son with meeting his social and political responsibilities, so Napoléon was welcomed as a personal guest of the family into the elegant mansion on rue de Vesle where Jean-Baptiste lived with his wife, Thérèse.

Napoléon stayed with the Ponsardin family for three nights. For Jean-Baptiste and Thérèse these were thrilling days, filled with important visitors and elegant dinners and the excitement of being at the center of world events. They were also stressful days. Entertaining the emperor in the midst of a war he was in the process of losing was a dicey business.

Thérèse was frantic that her hospitality should be graceful and exacting. As was the custom, she herself filled the emperor's pillows with the softest new down. Jean-Baptiste, meanwhile, must have perceived how politically delicate his father's absence was. And despite Barbe-Nicole's disdain for the emperor and for the commercial ruin he had created, she was far too wise to complicate the family's plight by giving any appearance of disrespect. Only their sister, Clémentine, who was one of Reims's reigning socialites, perhaps welcomed the honor without misgiving.

As the Ponsardin family entertained Napoléon during those fading days of the French Empire, he surely drank some of Barbe-Nicole's champagne. Indeed, he must have tasted that divine vintage of 1811. For a guest as powerful as the emperor of France, for a man known for his love of fine champagnes, Barbe-Nicole would have offered nothing less. She would have done it just to prove to him that Jean-Rémy Moët and Memmie Jacquesson were not the only ones who knew how to craft something marvelous.

She is unlikely to have explained to Napoléon the symbolism of the comet insignia branded on the end of each of her corks in that year's vintage, a comet said by those who worked the vineyards and the fields to prophesy the end of his empire. In the weeks and months that were to come, Napoléon must have remembered those days with the Ponsardins and the champagne of the young Widow Clicquot as the last taste of victory itself, for within three weeks, his meteoric career would be at an end, and Napoléon would find himself stripped of power and sent into a forced exile.

First, however, he would see Jean-Rémy. It must have annoyed Barbe-Nicole to no end. When Napoléon left the Ponsardin family home, he headed directly to Épernay, where he visited one last time with his old friend. Despite the champagne that they undoubtedly shared, it was a somber and serious occasion. Napoléon was too experienced in war not to understand the odds he faced.

The story goes that Jean-Rémy found his friend intently studying a map. Looking up to find Jean-Rémy, Napoléon quietly unpinned his own Legion of Honor, the small but ornate five-starred cross that signified noble rank in imperial France. Napoléon then pinned it on his friend's coat, saying only: "If fate intervenes and dashes my hopes, I want at least to be able to reward you for your loyal service and steadfast courage, but above all for the excellent reputation you have achieved, both here and abroad, for the wines of France." Napoléon was a wine lover to the end. And he was loyal to Jean-Rémy, as always.

Napoléon abdicated the throne of France in early April, and the Russians were briefly in Reims again, celebrating the end of the war in boisterous spirits. Barbe-Nicole had reason to celebrate as well. Russian officers toasting the end of the long campaign toasted with her champagne. Everywhere in the city, "Russian officers . . . lifted the champagne glass to their lips. It was said even that many of them preferred the popping of the bottle of Rheims to the cannon of the Emperor." After long years of war, the British were no less exuberant. Lord Byron wrote to his friend Thomas Moore in the second week of April, "We clareted and champagned till two." Already, champagne was on its way to becoming another word for mass-culture celebration.

Barbe-Nicole was simply glad that the war would soon be over and she would soon be free to gratify the Russian love of fine French wines. "At last the time has come," she said, "when, after the sufferings our town has known, we may breathe freely and hope for a general and permanent peace, and consequently for commercial activity which has stagnated for too long. Thank God I have been spared. My properties and cellars are intact, and I am ready to resume business with all the activity that recent changes will allow."

That the Napoleonic Wars should have ended in the Champagne region is mere happenstance, but it was a pivotal moment in the history of this wine, a moment that forged its cultural identity. Champagne wine was already enjoyed as the drink of festivity. It had been since the earliest days of its history. But a hundred little obstacles had impeded its broad commercial appeal. For centuries, it had been the wine only of the wealthiest and most discerning of connoisseurs, and the total production in France at its prewar height had never been more than four hundred thousand bottles. Within decades of Napoléon's defeat, it would multiply more than tenfold, to over five million.

However much Barbe-Nicole despised Napoléon, his support for the industry and nearly fifteen years of reforms, which had changed everything from the laws of Europe to the condition of roads throughout the empire, made a different future—and her own fame—possible. It was the events that took place that spring in the Champagne, the occasion for half a million soldiers and minor British lords to celebrate the end of an empire with sparkling wine, that transformed champagne into an international cultural phenomenon, rich with universal symbolism and meaning.

Still, when the Russian czar Alexander ordered provisions for a banquet meant to fete three hundred thousand troops at Camp Vertus, the champagne came from the cellars of Jean-Rémy. That even the czar favored her competitor must have been irritating. Perhaps this preference was what focused her energies on getting back to business immediately and recapturing her own share of the Russian market that she and Louis—and François before them—had worked so hard to open.

It would take time to work out the political settlements, but when the end of the war finally came, as she now knew it would, it would be a new beginning for her champagne enterprise. She seized the initiative. By the end of April, even before the peace was yet certain, she had opened her cellars and had returned to work, checking the long rows of casks to see how the vintage had fared, making adjustments and taking notes, and beginning the arduous process of disgorging some of the wines.

If the occupation of Reims had not been a boon, it had not been a disaster, either. "Thanks are due to Heaven," she wrote. "I do not have any losses to regret, and I am too fair to grumble about expenses from which no one will be saved." She sent her workmen back to the vineyards in earnest, all with an eye toward the future, when the trade bans on France would finally be lifted and she could begin shipping her wines again.

Barbe-Nicole was not one to wait passively on fortune, however. She had begun almost instantly planning a daring enterprise, the execution of which would prove to be the greatest gamble of her career. She was at the crossroads of her life, and she knew it. The moment the Bourbon kings of France were restored to the throne, and working in absolute secrecy, with only her trusted salesman, Louis, and their Russian distributor, Monsieur Boissonet, as her conspirators, Barbe-Nicole decided to run the blockades one final time, in advance of the formal restoration of international trade.

As she had discovered that spring, the Russians adored her sweeter, fortified champagnes, and if only she could get her wines there before any of her competitors, there was a nation waiting for its first legal taste of French champagne. It was risky and dangerous, and if she failed, this would be the end.

The stakes could not have been higher. It was a large shipment, and she was sending it without permission or security. She was breaking the law and breaking all the rules of common sense. The plan was to deliver several thousand bottles of champagne by chartered ship, first to the open port of Königsberg (present-day Kalingrad, Russia) and then, the instant the trade ban was lifted, immediately onward the short distance to Russia. If the cargo was discovered traveling without a license, it would be confiscated and destroyed—and much of that amazing vintage of 1811 would be lost forever.

Worse, if her local competitors were to learn of her venture, or if they happened to be plotting one of their own simultaneously, the result would be immediate ruin. Nothing would be more infuriating than Jean-Rémy getting the upper hand in Russia once again. As Barbe-Nicole knew, success depended not just on getting her wines to Russia but on getting them there first, weeks before other shipments could arrive, when hers would be the only French champagne available in the ports and markets.

The moment Napoléon abdicated, she began writing letters, trying to charter a ship in secret. In mid-April came the encouraging news from Louis that Monsieur Rondeaux, a shipping merchant in Rouen, could help her. There was a ship ready to load her wines and take them to Russia, if she could get them to Rouen quickly. In the event Russia was still inaccessible, they had devised elaborate contingency plans. The wines could surely be sold at Königsberg or sent on to other ports along the English Channel if needed. She had learned the lessons from Amsterdam well: Never again would she let wines go to waste in warehouses.

Louis would travel with the shipment. Her first plan had been to send six thousand bottles of wine. Then, at the last minute there were maddening delays. Although the foreign troops had left Reims and the wines could travel safely, there were few local men able to help with the cellar work after the long war. "You know," she told Louis, "our wines must be properly cared for and rebottled before being shipped and since I have not enough capable workmen to complete this indispensable operation, I must delay deliveries." Finally, when it came time to load the wines onto the wagon destined for Paris and then on to Rouen, the final count was 10,550 bottles of her finest champagne. The news had just arrived that the blockades on the Baltic ports had been lifted, although bottled French wines were still banned in Russia.

Still, she was sure that the Russians would welcome her wines. Soon, other brokers would also be sending shipments. But it might take them several weeks to arrange a ship, and she had a head start. It was a race for Russia. Jean-Rémy was already writing to Count Tolstoy, the grand marshal of the imperial palace in Saint Petersburg, requesting permission to send the czar thirty thousand bottles of sparkling champagne, and within weeks he would send several thousand bottles to Russia for the open market, simply on the chance they would pass customs unimpeded.

On May 20, Louis and the wines left Reims for Paris, on the way to Rouen and the seacoast. The anxiety was at fever pitch. There was no way of knowing if other competitors had come up with the same idea. Perhaps they were already too late. Perhaps the wines would be lost long before they ever reached Russia, victims of uncertain times and a long sea voyage, undertaken far too late in the warm spring season to make any winemaker confident.

Louis would be traveling for weeks with the wines, in harsh conditions, and in Paris he stopped to purchase provisions for the trip, staples like dried ham and biscuits, tea, and apples. He would also need to arrange for his own bed and personal comforts on the ship. Barbe-Nicole was sympathetic. Among the cases of wine, she had also slyly included a present for Louis—some things to feed his "gullet," she told him. It was a hamper filled with small luxuries: one and a half dozen bottles of excellent red wine from nearby Cumières, half a dozen bottles of cognac to warm the chilly evenings, and a small, leather-bound copy of Miguel de Cervantes's *Don Quixote*, the famous Spanish tale of an adventurous knight determined to fight even the most foolhardy battles. Given the risks they were taking and the recklessness of their own adventure, it was a witty present, just Barbe-Nicole's sort of dry humor.

Finally, at eleven o'clock on the night of June 10, Louis and the shipment set sail on the *Zes Gebroeders*, under the command of Captain Cornelius. The crispness of the night air belied what Louis found belowdecks. The ship was infested with lice and vermin, and he was so anxious for the fate of the fragile and pressurized cases of wine rocking in the hold that he determined to sleep on rough nights with the cargo. It could hardly be worse. As Louis knew only too well, the bottles were prone to breakage, and they could shatter with a remarkable force, destroying an entire case at a time.

For the sleepless Louis, it was a long trip. For Barbe-Nicole back home in Reims, the nights and days were even longer. On July 3, nearly a month later, the *Zes Gebroeders* finally crept into the harbor of Königsberg, a Baltic seaport then in Prussian territory. It had been a rough and increasingly warm crossing, and it might already all be over for them. The wines might have burst. Or the changes in the temperature might have caused the wines to go cloudy and ropey. After years of war and terribly depressed sales, there was no margin of error for the company any longer.

The morning when the wines were unloaded dawned stiflingly hot, and Louis opened the first case with a heavy heart. Amazingly, the first bottles that he drew from the packing baskets were absolutely crystalline, and there had been no breakages. It was the same for the second case and the third. Their condition was perfect, "as strong as the wines of Hungary, as yellow as gold, and as sweet as nectar," he wrote. Best of all, "Our ship is the first, in many years, to travel to the North, and from the port of Rouen, filled with the wine of the Champagne."

Their secret ruse had succeeded. None of Barbe-Nicole's competitors had guessed her plan, and the champagne made by the Widow Clicquot created a frenzied competition among purchasers within days of its arrival. Before Louis could have the shipment forwarded to the imperial city of Saint Petersburg—even before the cases were fully unloaded from the *Zes Gebroeders*—clients besieged him at his hotel, begging to be allowed to purchase just a few bottles. On the docks, wine merchants nearly came to blows as the stock apportioned to Königsberg dwindled. With the cunning business acumen that Barbe-Nicole so admired in him, Louis wrote playfully that he was now deliberately playing hard to get and asking prices that she never would have believed possible—an astonishing 5.5 francs a bottle—the equivalent of more than $100 and equal to what she paid her vineyard laborers for an entire week of their backbreaking work.

Learning of their triumph in the dim light of her office, Barbe-Nicole might have brushed a lock of hair back from her cheek and let herself enjoy a slow, broad smile of satisfaction. In that moment, she must have thought about François and about the long summer days when they rode through the fields of the Champagne to inspect the small vineyards at Bouzy or when they simply stopped to look out over the hills in silence. Making this wine had been his dream, and here in front of her was the proof that her faith in that dream had not been wasted. Even Barbe-Nicole could not have dreamed what else was still to come. On this first evening of her success, when she was only just beginning to understand that she was on the verge of something big, something wonderful, she might have indulged her fancy for a moment. Then she put pen to paper, already planning the immediate departure of another shipment of her glorious champagne.

Chapter 10

A Comet over Russia: The Vintage of 1811

S uccess brought with it new challenges and new opportunities—all of them risky and exhilarating. Like her father, Barbe-Nicole was not a passive idealist, and she was never more levelheaded than in moments of crisis. In an age of social unrest and economic uncertainty, Nicolas Ponsardin was a survivor. His daughter would be that and more.

The first shipment was a stunning victory, her first major coup in almost six years of running the company. It was making her a local celebrity. As word of her daring and foresight reached her competitors in Reims, there were whispers of astonishment and—what a pleasant change—even whispers of professional jealousy. Soon Louis wrote, tongue in cheek, with his fantasies of driving the competitors mad with envy. "I am bored of seeing them leave us in peace taking the money," he wrote. "When the time is right . . . celebrity is the natural result, it is this that I am after for you; better to be envied than pitied; while they backbite, we will fill our pockets, and when we have skimmed the cream of the pot, we will laugh in the corner to watch them grimace in their dens and wring their hands. . . . You [can rest] secure . . . in the exclusive confidence of Russia [and] in your bank account." Indeed, in a matter of weeks she had brought in the equivalent of over $1 million in sales.

Now, Louis could report that they had sold their entire stock of the first 10,550 bottles of the Widow Clicquot's champagne. Some of it he had sold the moment he landed—just enough to recover the costs and make them a small profit, in case of disaster. The rest he had sent on to their distributor in Russia, Monsieur Boissonet, where the prices they commanded were even higher. In both markets, there was a buying frenzy. Barbe-Nicole wrote, breathlessly, "Great God! What a price! How novel! I am over the top with joy and satisfaction. What overwhelming happiness this change will pay out. The Heavens have showered me with blessings, after all the terrible moments I have passed. I owe you a thousand and thousand thanks."

While this news of their financial success was fabulous, even more heartening were the rave reviews. Winemaking was her passion, and Barbe-Nicole knew that she had been a relentless and sometimes even meddlesome employer. She didn't keep to her offices and leave her winemakers to craft the vintage. An unrepentant perfectionist, she had her hand in everything. Now, that vigilance had clearly paid dividends.

Louis reported from Königsberg that when people tasted Barbe-Nicole's wines, the streets of the city buzzed. The Widow Clicquot's 1811 vintage—the wine from the year of the comet—was extraordinary. "I am adored here," Louis told her, "because my wines are adorable . . . what a spectacle." Her champagnes were the toast when the king of Prussia celebrated his birthday, and Louis wrote to tell her that "two-thirds of the high society of Königsberg . . . are at your feet as a result of your nectar. . . . Of all the fine wines that have teased northern heads, none compare to Madame Clicquot's 1811 cuvée. Delicious to taste, it is an assassin, and anyone who wants to make its acquaintance will become well attached to his chair, because after paying his respects to a bottle, he will go looking for crumbs under the tables."

Louis wasn't kidding when he said that people who drank her 1811 champagne were likely to find themselves under the table come dawn. Not only was it delicious, it was powerful. The rich, sugary grapes of that perfect harvest had created a strongly alcoholic wine, with an excellent *mousse* that made the corks come flying out with a pleasant and resounding pop. What those British scientists discovered at the end of the seventeenth century that made the production of champagne possible in the beginning was the simple fact that adding sugar increased *both* alcohol and fizz. During the harvest of 1811, nature needed no assistance, and the result was intoxicating.

In Saint Petersburg, the Widow Clicquot's wine was an even greater sensation, if that were imaginable. It sold for higher prices than she ever could have dreamed. Those same aristocratic officers who had come to love her wine during the occupation of Reims were now prepared to buy her champagne at any price. Soon, Czar Alexander declared that he would drink nothing else. Everywhere one heard the name of the Widow Clicquot and praises of her divine champagne. Knowing that the Russian market was at their feet, Louis laughingly wrote a final letter from Königsberg to tell her that he was even now headed to the shops to buy wine for a farewell dinner. He had sold every last bottle, and he was on his way to Saint Petersburg, eager to take new advance orders. Before long, he wrote: "I have already in my portfolio [orders for] a new assault on your caves." Barbe-Nicole was ready for them. She was ready—and then some.

What came after those first few moments of unimaginable pleasure, rereading Louis's letter with news of her triumph, was a sickening sense of relief. The secret gamble she had taken was far, far bigger than anyone had known, and it was enough to keep even the most hardheaded businessman—or businesswoman—up at night in a panic. Now, it would make her success more stunning than her competitors could imagine.

Before she knew that her champagnes would command an astonishing 5.5 francs a bottle and could be sold from a hotel room—before she even knew that the wines had survived their perilous sea journey in the last days of a war that defined a generation—she had started making plans to send a second, larger shipment. More of that magical vintage of 1811, which those lucky enough to taste it agreed was nothing less than spectacular.

While Louis and the first shipment were still making their uncertain way to Königsberg in the tossing hull of the *Zes Gebroeders*, merchants in Reims had learned that the Russian czar had lifted the ban on bottled French wines. It had been a ban calculated to thwart Napoléon and his dreams of making champagne a distinctive French luxury. Now, Napoléon had been defeated, and all of Saint Petersburg was thirsting for a taste of champagne.

Word of the end of the ban had spread throughout the city's commercial network with a feverish intensity. In the business offices and along the docks of the river, where local wines began the long, slow journey to Paris and the seacoast, all the talk was of the export trade—and of the astonishing prices champagne would bring as all of Europe celebrated the end of an agonizing war. Already cellar work was under way to prepare thousands of bottles for travel.

Barbe-Nicole quickly realized that she faced another agonizing decision. Within weeks, it would be impossible to charter a ship. Throughout France, merchants were rushing to get their products to the export market, and there would not be enough boats to satisfy them all. If Louis was successful and if her wines survived the voyage, there would soon be no way to get more cases to him—unless she acted immediately. The advantage of arriving first, she knew, would soon be lost. And it wasn't a matter just of sales. It was a matter of market share. She did not want to sell just ten thousand bottles of wine. She wanted to conquer the entire market.

The risk of making plans to send the second shipment blind had meant that, should Louis fail in Königsberg, her financial ruin would be compounded terribly—perhaps hopelessly. She would have to make a bargain with a sea captain before she knew exactly how she would pay his bills. It took nerve and determination, but Barbe-Nicole saw that there was no real choice. She had not come this far to lose the first opportunity in years because her courage failed.

Thank goodness she had not flinched. When news reached her competitors that she had beat them all to the international market, when they began scrambling to find ships to carry their wines, she had—for the second glorious time—a head start. Already Monsieur Cléroult, captain of *La Bonne Intention,* was waiting for her in Rouen, ready to deliver another 12,780 bottles of that legendary vintage of 1811. The sea journey would still be treacherous for these delicate wines. This time, no one would sail with them.

Now, her greatest enemy was not a grueling wartime economic climate. It was the summer weather. Extreme temperatures—either hot or cold—would ruin her wines, and there were only two times during the year when a champagne dealer could reliably make shipments. Transporting bottles of champagne in the summer heat was a sure way to end up with shattered glass. Frozen wines fared no better. But during the spring and fall, weather permitting, the wines could be sent by barge, along the broad river that runs through the Champagne region. This second midsummer shipment was being sent much too late.

Even in season, there were perennial problems with the wines arriving in good shape. Barbe-Nicole did not have the advantages of contemporary winemaking technologies or modern transportation. Her bottled sparkling wines had to survive a bumpy and slow journey, packaged only in woven baskets and wooden crates, along the roads and docks of Europe, unprotected from delays, temperature variations, and robbery. Cask wines transported in barrels—barrels that were easy to tap and reseal on the road—were subject to the additional hazards of adulteration, when thirsty handlers siphoned off a bit of the product to ease the journey and replaced the missing volume with water. Or worse.

Amazingly, however, the second shipment also survived. It was victory following on victory. Writing to her cousin Jennie, who was still struggling with wartime shortages in Paris, Barbe-Nicole was reeling from how quickly everything had changed in Reims. "If my business continues as it has gone since the invasion of the allies in France, if my daughter is someday married," she wrote in November, "I will be able to live, if not as one of the rich, at least in affluence, and then my house will always be a safe port, where you can retire, without depending on anyone. We wait together for what divine Providence has planned for us. So we go day by day and do not despair. You remember how last year at this time I was desolate! . . . I didn't have any hope of doing anything [and] the advance of the Russians over the Rhine was the last straw. And now, out of all these misfortunes came the good business I have had, and I dare to hope for more. Maybe for the rest you also have a dose of good luck coming. We can't always be unlucky, in my experience. And so, my dear friend: courage, patience, and resignation."

In truth, her luck was not yet finished. Not even close. These two daring shipments were to make her one of the most famous women in Europe and her wine one of the most highly prized commodities of the nineteenth century. As Louis told her, it was a success born out of "your judicious manner of operating, your excellent wine, and the marvelous similarity of our ideas, which produced the most splendid unity and action and execution—we did it well, and I give a million thanks to the bounty of the divine Providence who saw fit to make me one of his instruments in your future well-being—and no trials in the world would stop me from doing it again, to justify the unlimited confidence you have placed in me, and which has produced such happy results. Certainly you merit all the glory possible after all your misfortunes, your perseverance, and your obvious talents." As Louis recognized, it wasn't the sales figures or the excellent quality of her wines alone that would finally turn her into a business legend. It was the astonishing ruse that got her champagnes to Russia first. The secret advance shipments were a breathtaking one-two knockout punch that turned the Widow Clicquot into a luxury brand name in one of the world's largest—and most fashionable—markets.

Ironically, the celebrity that followed had little to do with Barbe-Nicole the private woman. Like the poet Lord Byron, whose witty travel adventure *Childe Harold's Pilgrimage* became the runaway best seller of 1812, she could say in all truth that she awoke one morning to find herself famous. Unlike that rakish devil-may-care young lord, however, few people who repeated the name of the Widow Clicquot in the first years of her meteoric rise on the world stage knew the story of the woman behind the company. Perhaps this curious manifestation of the public anonymity that should have been her destiny—the same pragmatic kind of self-effacement signaled by her decision to wear the black widow's weeds permanently—was part of the reason a woman-owned business was able to flourish in an increasingly conservative postwar Europe.

At the same time, it is also worth considering, even if only in passing, what it was about the first few decades of the nineteenth century that was so special. It was during these years that the champagne industry, like so many other industries in postrevolutionary Europe, went from being the craft of rural artisans to big business. The family-run wine brokerages of the late eighteenth century were on the brink of becoming large commercial companies—or they were on the brink of disappearing. A generation earlier, the actual winemaking had been in the hands of the rural growers, who raised the grapes, made the wines, and, especially with champagne, bottled them. François had been part of the small group of wine distributors who cautiously began to take this last stage of the wine-making process out of the hands of the farmers, and he had occasion to wonder sometimes if the new risks were worth the increased profits. What François had begun, Barbe-Nicole had embraced with a singular sense of mission, and it was because of this that she was poised to become an important figure in the evolution of champagne.

Champagne, after all, was not going to be an artisan family affair for long: The future was in a manufacturing model of doing business. A boom was coming in the champagne industry, and those who bene-fited from it were the entrepreneurs who were starting to take control of the production process. Barbe-Nicole, who had always found pleasure in watching the harvest and learning the cellar work, was at the vanguard of this movement. She not only bottled the vast proportion of her own wines but she committed herself to blending and aging them. Thinking like the daughter of a manufacturer, she hounded her suppliers mercilessly. In the company archives in Reims, there are pages and pages of scolding cor-respondence where she writes about the shape of the bottles she needed delivered or the quality of the corks she wanted cut. The manufacturers soon learned that she would come to complain in person if it was the only way to get what she required. Before long, she would also begin buying new vineyards, in order to supply more of her own grapes.

The world of business was changing, and the wine industry was changing with it. It seems obvious now, but at the beginning of the nine-teenth century, capitalism was still a relatively new idea. "The world market which was slowly coming into existence acted as the engine of proto-industrial growth" in France, and mass culture emerged with it. In this quickly changing business climate, Barbe-Nicole was lucky—not so much in her choice of husband, but in Philippe and her father. Their creative engagement with the early industrialization of the textile indus-try and with the new economy of a peacetime Europe, combined with an old-fashioned willingness to entertain the possibility of a entrepreneurial daughter, at precisely that moment when this was becoming socially un-acceptable, meant that Barbe-Nicole had a chance. A few years later, it

was harder for a woman to enter the world of commerce. A few years earlier, and she wouldn't have learned how the world of commerce was being
transformed. The old model of the bourgeois family businesswoman was
doomed, and what is truly astonishing about her story is that Barbe-Nicole
was uniquely positioned to invent a new model.

If she had tried to run an eighteenth-century company, no one today
would remember the Widow Clicquot. I've never yet found the local who
could tell me the story of the Widow Blanc or the Widow Robert, even in
the coziest country bistro. Ironically, the rise of capitalism and the end of
the bourgeois family businesswoman went hand in hand. As one scholar
puts it, "Most gender historians, and even business historians, agree that
those women would have disappeared between the end of the eighteenth
and the middle of the nineteenth century, pushed out by the combined
impact of the separate spheres ideology and of structural changes, such
as industrialization, the use of extra-familial capital, and the 'managerial
revolution.'" If Barbe-Nicole had clung to the old model of women in the
commercial sphere, she might have struggled by. But she would never
have become one of the most famous businesswomen of her century.

Instead of clinging to the old ways and retreating to the safety of a
modest, outdated, but still tacitly acceptable entrepreneurial role for
women, Barbe-Nicole became an ardent industrialist. She was not just
the first woman to build a commercial champagne house founded on new
mercantilist principles; she was one of only a handful of entrepreneurs to
do it at all. She wasn't amazing just as a businesswoman. She was amazing at business. When we look at the names of the famous champagnes
on our grocery store shelves, the so-called *grandes marques*, it should come
as no surprise that these are the names of Barbe-Nicole's nineteenth-
century competitors. Jean-Rémy Moët and his son-in-law Pierre-Gabriel
Chandon. Jules Mumm. Louis Roederer. Charles Heidsieck. Her grandmother's family, the pioneering Ruinarts. A small group of entrepreneurs
modernized the champagne industry and made vast fortunes in the process. The Widow Clicquot was among them from the start.

Chapter 11

The Industrialist's Daughter

By the time she was in her late thirties, Barbe-Nicole had achieved something spectacular. When the summer of 1815 began, she was at the helm of an internationally renowned commercial empire— and she was one of the first women in modern history to do it. The odds against her had been genuinely staggering. There was not just a glass ceiling; there was an industrial culture that increasingly told women they had no place in the public world of business and economics, no foothold even on the first rung of the corporate ladder.

Sadly, women like Barbe-Nicole are still a rarity in the modern world of winemaking. They are a rarity in the world of champagne especially. In France, a handful of women run wine estates—prestigious, wonderful places like Château Margaux or Château Mouton Rothschild. Still, they are not champagne houses. Only at Champagne Veuve Clicquot Ponsardin is there a woman at the helm today, and even that is a relatively recent development.

But Barbe-Nicole did more than just run the boardroom of a world-renowned champagne business; she also took a central role in crafting the sparkling wines that carried her name. Today, in all of Europe, there is not a single woman who does both. If one wants to find the modern equivalent of the Widow Clicquot, the best place to look is not the Champagne but the still emergent wine country of Northern California, in those golden oak–covered hills of Napa and Sonoma counties. The collapse of the California wine industry in the 1970s and 1980s had the same effect as the Champagne crisis of the 1780s and 1790s: An "industry in retreat" opened doors for new entrepreneurs and especially for women winemakers.

In my own journey to find the Widow Clicquot—to discover what it must have been like for Barbe-Nicole in her first decade of running her own wine company—I sought out some of these modern champagne women. What amazed me most was that they displayed the same steely charm and no-nonsense style that were Barbe-Nicole's personal hallmark. One of the most charming is Eileen Crane, president and winemaker of Napa's Domaine Carneros, whom I first visited because of a curious bit of company history. Domaine Carneros was founded in the 1980s by the champagne house once run by Barbe-Nicole's first business partner, Alexandre Fourneaux—now known as Champagne Taittinger.

I visited Domaine Carneros on a warm, clear October afternoon. Until you drive through the vineyards of wine country in the weeks after the crush, it is easy to forget that this corner of California has foliage to rival the back lanes of my native New England. In the days before the rains come to soak the dry chalk hills, the grapevines slowly turn orange and red. The estates at Domaine Carneros are set against this leafy canvas, a great French château rising out of the fields—or at least an imitation of one.

It is a building that Barbe-Nicole would have recognized instantly. Here, in the midst of the rugged American West, the champagne company has raised a replica of the Château de la Marquetterie, which still stands in the southern village of Pierry in the heart of the Champagne. Barbe-Nicole passed it every autumn, on her way to the vineyards in the southern Côte des Blancs, renowned for its chardonnay grapes. Built in the 1750s on the site of the ancient estate of the monks of Saint-Pierre aux Monts de Châlons, the château was named after its famous vineyards, where the local black pinot noir and white chardonnay grapes were laid out in a playful checkerboard fashion—like a piece of the inlaid veneer woodwork known as "marquetry." In the first days of the revolutionary terror, when Barbe-Nicole's family was caught up in the dangerous turmoil of Jacobin politics, the château's owner was among the thousands who fell victim to the guillotine in 1793. But already the château was renowned for the role it had played in the history of champagne. It was here, only a few miles from Hautvillers, that the seventeenth-century monk Jean Oudart—one of Dom Pérignon's lay brothers and probably another of his local collaborators—conducted some of the earliest but least remembered experiments with that sparkling wine once known simply as *vin mousseux*.

Barbe-Nicole would also have recognized Eileen Crane, I think. We sit in her office overlooking the veranda of Domaine Carneros, where visitors enjoy her sparkling wine at café tables, and she talks with passion about winemaking. About making champagne not just something for the rich and famous but something for ordinary middle-class people ready to celebrate little luxuries as wonderful and as simple as the beginning of a weekend. Barbe-Nicole had the same vision. People still worry, Crane says, about champagne: how to open it, how to serve it. They worry that they have to wear a tuxedo and use the right glasses. The truth is, champagne is great with pizza and a bubble bath. Even the legendary wine connoisseur Hugh Johnson tells us—and who could possibly dispute such transparent wisdom—"Any big glass is good for champagne." Barbe-Nicole, with her disdain for all things fussy and her love of champagne, would agree.

Ironically, the glasses we use to drink our champagne today also owe a great deal to Barbe-Nicole's legacy as a winemaker. This is because Barbe-Nicole was not just a brilliant businesswoman, she was also one of the most important technical innovators in the commercial history of sparkling wine. I ask Eileen Crane which glasses she prefers for drinking champagne, and with a laugh she tells me that her sister has a collection of dozens of unique and mismatched champagne glasses, some modern and some antiques, that she uses at parties. Each guest chooses whatever strikes his or her fancy, and that, she says, is the best method. But, more soberly, she also reminds me that in the early days of champagne, before the Widow Clicquot came on the scene, before even the stylish rounded *coupes* of the mid-eighteenth century, the first champagne glasses looked like miniature versions of the V-shaped stemware that we use today for drinking pilsner beer, and they were made of frosted glass. This was the custom because for a long time champagne was served just like pilsner beer—carbonated and a bit clouded. Barbe-Nicole became obsessed with producing clear wine that sparkled like mineral water. Without her single-minded devotion to this element of craft, champagne would never have become a luxury product accessible to the middle-class market.

Barbe-Nicole today is credited with three achievements: "internationalizing the Champagne market," "establishing brand identification," and developing the process known in French as *remuage sur pupitre*—literally "moving by desk." In 1815, with her triumph in Königsberg already the topic of business legend, no one doubted her international prowess. In early pamphlets trumpeting her accomplishments, it was said that she had conquered Russia with her champagne—and from a commercial and cultural perspective, it's not much of an exaggeration. In the first years of her fame, the Widow Clicquot had already become synonymous with sparkling wine throughout much of Europe. Before long, young playboys in the clubs of London were calling simply for "a bottle of the Widow" when they were low on bubbly. In Russia, she was known as Klikoskaya, and her name was celebrated in some of the greatest nineteenth-century works of Russian literature. But it's the last achievement that makes Barbe-Nicole most famous in winemaking history. Without her discovery of *remuage*—an efficient system for clearing champagne of the yeasty debris trapped in the bottle after secondary fermentation—champagne could never have become the world's most famous wine.

After her stunning coup in Russia, Barbe-Nicole discovered that she had a new set of problems. Increasingly, it was production that worried her. With Louis in Saint Petersburg capitalizing on their success, the orders were rolling in. The problem was how she was ever going to fill them. "It is cruel," Louis wrote, "to have to refuse orders, as I am going to have to start doing, when I am easily able to place twenty or thirty thousand bottles."

The weather was not cooperating. The harvest in the autumn of 1815 was dismal, which was sure to lead to a supply crunch when the bottles came to market in 1817. More immediate for the local peasantry, crop failure meant the distinct possibility of starvation. The situation was so grave that Barbe-Nicole's father led a fund-raising charity campaign among the local businessmen to help feed the poor, raising 60,000 francs—well over $1 million. The local entrepreneurs had good reason to pay attention to the workers' plight, Barbe-Nicole in particular. Winemaking was a labor-intensive undertaking. By winter, grain was impossible to come by in the markets, and the countryside had become dangerous. She knew there would be problems in the fields again in the spring. Her problems were small compared with those faced by her vignerons, of course. But for her they were troublesome enough, because by the beginning of 1816 there simply wasn't any finished champagne left in the cellars. She had sold all her reserves. After years of struggling just to stay in business, nothing was more frustrating than having to turn away orders. Worse, without champagne to send, Barbe-Nicole knew that she risked losing all the customers her daring adventures had won her, just at the moment when her sparkling wine was becoming a recognized luxury product in the world market. She needed champagne—excellent champagne—and she needed it fast.

But there is no hurrying the birth of a great wine. Standing grim-faced in the dim light of her cellars, Barbe-Nicole knew that her only real hope was in finding a way to solve the worst production bottleneck: the tedious delays in disgorging the wines. During the secondary fermentation, when sugar and yeast were added to the bottle to make the wine sparkle, the new champagne was left with a layer of sedimentary gunk. All the traditional methods of removing the debris had drawbacks. *Transvasage*—pouring the wine from one bottle to another—destroyed some of the sparkle and wasted too much good wine. Meanwhile, the elaborate techniques of disgorging bottles that had been stored on their sides by tilting and shaking them, however gently, was costing her a fortune in labor, and—worst of all—it took forever. Filtering with a *colle* spoiled the quality of the champagne, and in the hands of some winemakers it was positively dangerous. As Robert Tomes tells the story in *The Champagne Country* (1867), "The old way, which involved knocking the bottles upside down to settle the sediment, used drugs and clarifiers that could be poisonous, [and] took many months."

Surely there was a better way of clearing the wines, a faster way that would allow her to produce the best-quality wines, in large numbers, at a nice price. In the cellars, she tried to urge her workers to speed the process, but they told her it couldn't be done.

"You only have fifty thousand bottles ready," she told them, "I asked for double!"

"Madame," they replied, "you can't ship muddy wines."

"No, I want to ship very clear wines and in sufficient quantity."

"You will never get it," the workers assured her. "No one knows any other method besides the one we are using."

"I will find one," she promised.

But her cellar workers just laughed, leaving Barbe-Nicole annoyed and determined.

Before long, Barbe-Nicole was mulling over a new and astonishingly simple idea. Perhaps storing the bottles not on their sides, but on their necks—*sur pointe*—would allow the debris to settle into the neck of the bottle more efficiently and thoroughly. When she told the cellar workers about her plan, they laughed again. It would never work. She would just end up having to do all the work twice, they predicted. "Great advance," they whispered. "Is this going to make the wine settle any faster? Take a look at this stupidity. It is still muddy, and now we have to wait for the deposit to fall back to the bottom again. A mess. It's a complete mess."

But Barbe-Nicole was determined to find a solution to her new business crisis. Secretly, she had her sturdy kitchen table moved into the cellars and ordered that it be riddled with slanted holes just large enough to hold the neck of a champagne bottle at an angle. Working with her cellar master and collaborator, Antoine Müller, she stubbornly conducted her experiments; "slipping quietly into the cellar day after day, while all the workmen were at dinner, she moved herself some hundreds of bottles in the rack" and began slowly turning and tapping the bottles each day, coaxing the sediment onto the cork. After only six weeks, Barbe-Nicole was amazed—and gratified—to discover that with a quick flick of the cork, all the residue came shooting out, without any harm to the wine and without all the tedious work. With this new system, she would be able to accelerate her production and keep her hard-won share of the export market. Above all, she knew that what it meant was growth—and a devastating advantage if she could keep it out of the hands of her competitors.

There was one competitor Barbe-Nicole particularly looked forward to devastating: Jean-Rémy Moët. In Russia, Moët was her greatest competitor, and the satisfaction of beating him to the opening of the Saint Petersburg market had been profound. She knew that he had already been working with the talented inventor and wine lover André Jullien to find a way to perfect the process of *transvasage*. There was word of preliminary cellar experiments with siphons, "rigid tubes fitted with a tap" that would prevent winemakers from losing the prized sparkle when moving champagne from one bottle to another, and Jean-Rémy was experimenting with new botanical *colles*. The industry was poised on the brink of transformation, but it needed new innovations to flourish. Now that the market for champagne was exploding, it was a question of whether winemakers could discover new techniques for mass-producing this delicate wine—and a question of who would discover it first.

With the success of their experiments, Barbe-Nicole brought all the work in her cellars to a halt. Immediately, they would change over to her new way of disgorging the wines. There was grumbling still. And she pleaded with her workers not to reveal what she already knew would be a crucial company secret, as important to the future of her business as those stealthy plans that got her wines to Russia before any of her competitors. It is a sign of the loyalty she inspired—and the effects of a generous profit-sharing system with some of her key employees—that *remuage* remained a secret for the better part of a decade.

What she and Antoine Müller discovered changed the way champagne is finished to this day. In his book *A History of Champagne* (1882), the wine aficionado Henry Vizetelly describes *remuage* as he saw it done in the nineteenth century. A "loose brown sediment," he writes, "has been forming . . . to get rid of which is a delicate and tedious task. As the time approaches for preparing the wine for shipment, the bottles are placed *sur pointe*." Then it is left to the cellar workers known as *riddlers* to slowly twist and turn the bottle, "sharply turned in one direction every day for at least a month or six weeks" until the sediment "forms a kind of muddy ball . . . finally expelled with a bang when the temporary cork is removed." In Barbe-Nicole's cellars, the cork was released with a small hooked knife, the debris flying free. They topped off the bottle with a bit of wine—the so-called *liquor d'expédition*—and sealed it again with her trademark branded corks using a tool they wryly called the guillotine, "from which tragic instrument," Robert Tomes tells us, "the idea was derived." Barbe-Nicole could still remember images of those from her revolutionary childhood.

Today, the system of riddling that Barbe-Nicole used in her cellars is still practiced in many champagne houses, although in recent years there has been a move by the large commercial producers to mechanized rotation in crates known as *giropalettes*. An expert cellar worker, it is said, can turn as many as fifty thousand bottles in a day, and these skilled employees carry on the tradition when making vintage champagne in France. But, of course, champagne houses no longer use kitchen tables. By the 1830s, winemakers throughout the Champagne turned instead to standing A-frame racks called *pupitres*. The word means "desk," but in fact they look more like old-fashioned childhood easels. They can be found in cellars and antique shops in any part of the world where sparkling wine is crafted.

Within months of her discovery, Barbe-Nicole had the pleasure of knowing that they would be able to produce clear champagnes in increasingly greater numbers. Perhaps she also had the pleasure of hearing before too long that Jean-Rémy was frantic. "We must wrack our brains to obtain as good a result" as the Widow Clicquot, he wrote in one letter during the years to come. Her brilliantly clear wines were maddening. Unfortunately, the intense competitive environment also brought out some equally spirited—but less attractive—feelings in Jean-Rémy. His letters reveal a bitter condemnation of Barbe-Nicole that hints at the powerful gender stereotypes she continued to face as a businesswoman. "The adventure of Madame Clicquot," wrote Jean-Rémy, "is infamous." It was an infamous adventure for a woman, perhaps. And, as Jean-Rémy's biographer puts it, these letters are "sufficiently eloquent to show the rivalry that existed between Jean-Rémy Moët and the Widow Clicquot. . . . A climate of imitation that flirted with espionage reigned between the two houses."

The climate of espionage aside, Jean-Rémy would not discover her secret any time soon and adopted her technique only in 1832. In the meantime, the discovery of *remuage* in her cellars gave Barbe-Nicole the edge she needed in a burgeoning industry to become—and remain—a major international player. During the second decade of the nineteenth century, champagne went from being a regional curiosity, known only at the royal courts of Europe, to becoming the world's most recognizable wine and an iconic symbol of celebration and style. Writing in the 1860s, Robert Tomes noted, "It is only within the last fifty years that the trade in champagne has become important. . . . Its origin hardly dates beyond the eighteenth century, and it was still, even in the middle of that century, so rare that only a few rich and privileged amateurs tasted it. Moët and Chandon in 1780 . . . thought it a bold venture to have made six thousand bottles in a year." In the year following the legendary vintage of 1811, Barbe-Nicole was scraping by on sales of under 20,000. By the 1820s, industry leaders like Barbe-Nicole and Jean-Rémy were exporting upward of 175,000 bottles a year. Champagne never looked back. But for Barbe-Nicole, it would not always be such clear sailing.

Chapter 12

The Wine Aristocrats

As her gaze took in the assembled guests of the small family party on this winter evening, Barbe-Nicole caught the twinkling, knowing eye of her father across the room and she smiled back at him wryly. She knew what he was thinking; she was watching the tension in the far corner of the parlor mount with the same sense of gentle amusement. Two eligible bachelors were vying for the attentions of her daughter, Clémentine, seventeen years old and just home from her convent education in Paris.

The one, sitting at Clémentine's side showing her card tricks, seemed to be winning, but perhaps only for the moment. Barbe-Nicole had already heard him confess that he would have to leave town in the morning and miss the chance to dance with her at some ball or another next week. Probably it was the ball hosted by their neighbor Marie Andrieux that the young man had in mind. Barbe-Nicole knew Marie well and could even say that she was a friend. They had known each other for years. But sometimes it was Marie's husband, Florent Simon, whose company and talk Barbe-Nicole most enjoyed. A man with political ambitions, he was her father's deputy mayor. He was also a businessman, and his business was champagne. Marie, meanwhile, occupied herself with hosting one of the most stylish salons in the city, and there were always balls and parties being planned. Clémentine—never graceful and confident in social situations—was already in a state of anxiety about this upcoming dance, as she was about all dances. Even a simple game of cards like whist could leave the girl in tears at bedtime, ashamed of her own awkwardness. "Don't cry, Mentine," her mother had told her only recently, "I'll buy you wit when I marry you off." Clémentine had only sniffled more quietly.

Glowering nearby stood the young man Barbe-Nicole thought of simply as Clémentine's subprefect. The assistant chief of the Reims police had been courting Clémentine steadily for weeks. It was pleasant to see him set back on his heels a bit, because regardless of how many suitors charmed Clémentine, the decision about whom her daughter would marry—and for how much money—was one that Barbe-Nicole fully intended to make. The anxious subprefect didn't have a chance.

But neither did this charming young man at her daughter's side, she was afraid. He was fabulously rich, and when he had asked for Clémentine's hand in marriage, she had proposed the generous dowry of 100,000 francs—more than $2 million—in cash as a wedding gift. His family was bargaining for three times that amount, despite knowing that Clémentine would eventually inherit another sizable fortune from Nicolas and her mother, who had made her their heiress, in addition to her being her mother's only child. Barbe-Nicole had countered by offering the income from another 100,000 francs a year, but it seemed clear this was not going to be enough. Already, in a moment of frustration, she had protested at the indignity of selling girls "like cabbages in the market."

Indignity aside, however, Barbe-Nicole knew that marriage was a marketplace. Her own wedding to François had been the result of similar negotiations. Still, to her cousin Jennie, Barbe-Nicole confessed that it was making her anxious. "All this marriage talk," she wrote to Mademoiselle Gard, "for a month has been making my head spin, so much so that I cannot sleep." All that spring, Barbe-Nicole chaperoned Clémentine to one party after another, waiting for the girl to catch the eye of a likely suitor. For young women like Clémentine, the stakes were high. Girls were expected to catch a husband their first year out of the convent—especially if they were the heiress to a grand champagne fortune. Anything else would be an embarrassment. At party after party, however, Clémentine seemed to have no luck.

Then, one evening, quite unexpectedly, Barbe-Nicole discovered a new prospect. He was sitting in her drawing room. For a young man of his class, he had slender means, and men of slender means did not often frequent the imposing Clicquot home. But this was no ordinary young man. His name was Louis Marie-Joseph Chevigné —the Count of Chevigné. Her father, Nicolas, was giddy at the prospect. Since those long years before the Revolution, he had dreamed of power and the aristocracy. Now that the empire of Napoléon was also a thing of memory, Nicolas had been relieved to learn that King Louis XVIII had reconfirmed his title as Baron Ponsardin. A baron was nothing next to a count, however, and Nicolas—like all the rest of the extended Clicquot-Ponsardin family—took an immediate liking to this twenty-four-year-old nobleman with flowing dark hair and flamboyant sexuality.

Barbe-Nicole took a liking to him, too. In fact, it may be that she took a bit too much of a liking to Louis de Chevigné. He certainly understood that Clémentine's hand depended, as much as anything else, on his wooing her mother. According to at least one account of the family legend, Barbe-Nicole "was infatuated." Letters from his friends show that Louis had a calculating side in the whole business. He set out to marry Clémentine because he wanted the riches that came with it: "easy living for the time being, and opulence in the future," as one of his friends summed it up. It is hard to imagine that anyone who knew him believed that he would ever make a faithful, steady husband, either. But he was charming—so charming that very little else seemed to matter either to the awkward young Clémentine or to the famously hardheaded Barbe-Nicole—a woman who had turned down far wealthier suitors before this struggling young count arrived in Reims.

Perhaps it was the tragedy of Louis's life story that Barbe-Nicole found so compelling. It reminded her of her own childhood during the Revolution and of the terrors that might have been their fate, were it not for her father's keen political sense of timing. While the enterprising Ponsardin family had not only survived the Revolution, but flourished, Louis's family had been destroyed. In 1793, the year of the most violent purges, his parents disdained the republican mobs. They lived a life of unimaginable splendor and privilege. Louis's beautiful mother spent her nights "assisting at the balls of Marie Antoinette, [and] being invited to the theatre at Versailles." His father, the count, spent his days "riding in the carriages of Louis XVI, and . . . accompanying his majesty to the hunt." They had been born to rule France and to protect their king. His father joined the royalist forces fighting to put down the democratic insurrection, not knowing that his wife—like so many other noblemen and -women in that year of frenzied horror—would spend her final days in a foul prison, half-starved and brutalized.

Louis was only a few months old when the arrest order came. In those days, they were sudden, capricious, and violent. Revolutionaries arrived at the doorstep, dragged their victims into hay carts, and paraded them through the streets, where they were taunted and often much, much worse. An Englishwoman who witnessed such arrests was horrified. "It was not uncommon," she wrote, "for a mandate of arrest to direct the taking of 'Citizen Such-a-one, and all persons found in his house.' A grand-daughter of [one aristocrat] was arrested in the night, put in an open cart, without any regard to her age, her sex, or her infirmities, though the rain fell in torrents; and, after sleeping on straw in different prisons on the road, was deposited here [where] our holy mother Guillotine is at work. Within these three days she has shaved eleven priests, one *ci-devant* [former] noble, a nun, a general, and a superb Englishman, six feet high, and as he was too tall by a head, we have put that into the sack!"

When they came for Louis's mother and for her sister, the Countess de Marmande, all five of the Chevigné children—Louis and his four elder sisters—were taken to prison as well, where they would await trial for treason against the state and the almost inevitable execution in the public squares that came with it. But before the guillotine, celebrated in this year of frenzy as an instrument of rationality and justice, could take them, Louis's mother, aunt, and three of his sisters were dead from the crippling diseases that spread throughout the unsanitary cells. In the final hours of her life, his mother made a heartbreaking decision. She begged a woman passing through the halls to take her two surviving children—the baby Louis and his nine-year-old sister, Marie-Pélagie. Perhaps she hoped that they would be reunited with their father. But he would die, too, before the summer was out, and the children were left orphans, dependent on the charity of strangers. Luckily, two wealthy women in the town of Nantes stepped forward quietly to take them. Madame Andigné adopted his sister, and Madame de Rouillon promised to care for the baby Louis, now heir to the abolished title of count and in great danger if discovered, until his family could come for him—if any of them escaped the guillotine.

In the end, both Louis and Marie-Pélagie, along with their uncle, the Count of Chaffault, came through those dangerous years alive. As a young woman, Marie-Pélagie was married and became Madame Urvoy de Saint-Bedan, while at thirteen Louis, now under the care of his uncle, was sent to an imperial boarding school in Nantes, where he would be trained for an officer's position in the military guard. While he served Napoléon, however, in his heart he was a royalist. In the last days of the empire, when Bonaparte returned from exile to fight his final battle at Waterloo, the twenty-two-year-old Louis fought for the restoration of the kings of France. As his reward, Louis XVIII returned to the young count all his titles—but no one could restore the family fortunes. Louis, a dispossessed young lord with the less than princely annual income of some 8,000 francs (a not quite impoverished $160,000 a year), retired to his uncle's small estate in Boursault, a mountainous village on the south banks of the river Marne, in the heart of the Champagne wine country.

Now, Louis found himself in the drawing rooms of one of the richest families in Reims, proposing to marry its only daughter. Nearly forty, Barbe-Nicole was as enamored with the dream of power and aristocratic connections as her father, Nicolas, had ever been. Ironically, this fiercely independent woman never considered the possibility of her daughter following in her footsteps. There was no question of Clémentine remaining single and taking over the helm of this feminine commercial empire. There was no question even of Clémentine marrying a wealthy entrepreneur who might let her listen quietly at the sidelines in silent partnership, as Barbe-Nicole had done in the first years of her marriage to François—not now that there was the chance of making her a countess or of marrying her to a man with the magnetic charisma of Louis de Chevigné. But Barbe-Nicole was not completely head over heels. Making her daughter a countess was also going to be very good for business. During the boom years of the champagne industry, "obtaining noble titles was a shrewd marketing strategy," adding to the glamour and allure of the company name—and profits to the company coffers.

The marriage was at its heart a business deal, and it is a sign of Barbe-Nicole's own attraction to Louis that he managed to get the better half of it. She had refused to budge from a dowry of 100,000 francs in order to marry Clémentine to a man with an astounding fortune. The landless Louis bemoaned the same number publicly—though privately he knew that "a mother with an only daughter will do for friendship what she might not promise on paper." In the letters flying between Louis and his friends during the negotiations, no one doubted that the more Barbe-Nicole saw of Louis, "the less she will be able to refuse."

They were right. At first, Barbe-Nicole had balked at the negotiations. Some say that the timid Clémentine, perhaps tired of this parade of suitors, for once insisted and threatened to enter her Paris convent permanently. Already, Barbe-Nicole could not say "no" to this intoxicating young count. She had fumed the last time that anything more than 100,000 francs would jeopardize her own decidedly comfortable lifestyle. "I won't make myself destitute," she wrote her cousins, "it would be too hard to have to go begging to one's children." Now, she offered Louis 200,000 francs and an annual income of another 20,000—plus free accommodation with her in the family home on rue de l'Hôpital for years to come. It was expected, of course, that the young couple would live in the family home. And Louis knew that when Barbe-Nicole died, there would be more money. One of his friends rather callously reminded him that it was worth "awaiting the rest of the inheritance—which shouldn't take long."

The engagement was formally announced in July, and plans were soon under way for an elaborate wedding in the nearby cathedral. In the elegant invitations, copies of which can still be found in one of the Clicquot family genealogies, Barbe-Nicole announced that the wedding was planned in Reims on the tenth of September. As was befitting Monsieur le Comte, Louis started complaining almost immediately that Clémentine's dresses were not sophisticated or grand enough to impress his aristocratic friends. Soon Barbe-Nicole had given her future son-in-law control even over Clémentine's wedding gown—and the generous budget that went with it. Her cousin in Paris was placing many of the orders for lace and silks, and Barbe-Nicole quickly threw up her hands and handed over the bankbook. "Arrange as you like with Monsieur de Chevigné about the trousseau," she wrote. "I know little about such things [except that] usually it's money thrown away."

Then, just as the wedding plans were working themselves into fever pitch, came terrible news. In August, just weeks before the ceremony, Barbe-Nicole's brother, Jean-Baptiste, was found dead, from causes that were never recorded. There was no longer any question of the sumptuous wedding that Louis de Chevigné was so eagerly and expensively planning. The entire family was in mourning, and convention demanded a respectful show of restraint and sobriety for months to come. Instead of the social event of the season, Clémentine was married—like her mother before her—in a quiet family mass.

Although she would never have wished for something so terrible to happen to her uncle or her aunt Thérèse, Clémentine must have been secretly relieved that she would not have to stand up to the rigors of a grand social occasion. She was a modestly pretty girl, but a convent education and a domineering mother had formed her into an obedient and awkwardly innocent young woman, always anxious about behaving properly. Her new husband was naturally gracious and fashionable—and was very particular that his wife should have the same appearance.

Her convent education also could not have prepared her for sex, and there was no question about Louis being a lusty sort. It's hard not to feel for poor Clémentine. After her wedding night, the girl was embarrassed. It was weeks before Barbe-Nicole could report that "Clémentine is no longer shy with her husband, she *tutoies* him." That Clémentine began her marriage using the formal form of French address rather than the familiar *tu* is a sad testament to how little influence she had in her choice of husband and to how little experience she had of men at all. Barbe-Nicole, made pragmatic by her experience of marriage and her years of struggling in the business world, was not exactly brimming with concern.

How much more embarrassed Clémentine would have been in the first year of her marriage had she known of the other letters Louis was soon writing and receiving. His self-congratulatory rakish charm is more boorish than endearing. Clémentine became pregnant immediately, and before long there were locker-room references from his friend Richard Castel to the countess's "pretty 'bushel of wheat'" and to his conquests in the bedroom. That was nothing compared with what she had to look forward to. These raunchy references to their intimate life were merely a prelude to the risqué erotic tales that Louis would publish in the years to come. Perhaps he was already gathering materials. As one visitor to Reims who met Louis observed, "The Comte de Chevigné, who had not yet written his [erotic] fables, [was] perhaps still engaged in living them."

Clémentine and Louis were married just at the peak of the harvest season, and the three of them—the young couple and Barbe-Nicole—spent the first two weeks of their honeymoon together living at the family farm in Bouzy, where they could watch the *vendange* and visit the little pressing room where, years before, Barbe-Nicole first had learned some of the secrets of winemaking. Here, at last, Barbe-Nicole drew the line. Louis imagined that he would take a hand in the champagne business, and he began touring her vineyards and quizzing her growers. However much Barbe-Nicole adored her son-in-law, however willing she was to indulge all his whims, even the expensive ones, she wasn't about to let him take over her company. In the beginning, it was their one source of tension. Soon, there would be others.

Those new tensions would always be about money. Louis, it transpired, was not just a playboy but also a gambler, and in those days, men of fashion played for shockingly high stakes. In London, the Duchess of Devonshire—ancestress to Great Britain's late princess Diana—lost millions at the faro tables, and her husband was forced to mortgage family estates that had been safeguarded for generations. Even the lowly sandwich was a sign of the times. It was invented when Lord Sandwich, determined to ruin himself in a gambling "hell," as the rooms were then called, refused to break the game for dinner. The servants brought him meat between slices of bread instead. Some people have suggested that gambling "was a protest against bourgeois and capitalist modernity." If so, Louis's rebellion was part of his own assertion of aristocratic identity—identity complicated by his marriage to a middle-class heiress. Oddly enough, the pragmatic and steely Barbe-Nicole found men who took risks exhilarating and attractive. Perhaps it was an inclination formed in her girlhood, when the secrets of the Ponsardin family and her father's political ambitions created an atmosphere of danger and excitement.

Soon, Louis wanted a grand house for his society entertainments and trips to Paris. The couple was still living with Barbe-Nicole, and after Clémentine's baby, a little girl named Marie-Clémentine, was born in the autumn of 1818, they started spending winters at a new house in the capital. Barbe-Nicole, who hadn't visited Paris since her own girlhood, now sometimes went with them. Then, unable to refuse this son-in-law any of his costly whims, she also bought a country house near his uncle's estate in the Marne River valley—a small château perched at the top of a rocky outcrop in Boursault, where Louis would throw lavish dinner parties and begin dreaming of new, expensive plans for renovation and expansion.

Today, Barbe-Nicole's estates at Boursault are firmly closed to the public, but visitors to the small hillside town can get a glimpse of the original house by visiting the small winery that the owners run from the grounds. The champagne made at the Château de Boursault won't set the wine world on fire—although the little restaurant across the street from the village church, practically the only show in town, is one of the undiscovered gems of home-style French country cooking. But the Boursault bubbly is one of the few wines in the region that are still 100 percent estate grown, and it's nice to think that it is made from grapes that Barbe-Nicole once tended. Surrounded by ominously tall stone walls, the house is an imposing gray pile with quaint round turrets and a large gravel courtyard. Acres of quiet gardens spill out behind. Above all, the castle had the distinct advantage of being set squarely in the middle of the Moët family vineyards. Here at last was a chance to lord it over Jean-Rémy. Literally.

Caught up in living this aristocratic lifestyle and proud of her family's public prominence now that her father was the mayor of Reims and her daughter was a countess, Barbe-Nicole didn't begrudge the expenses exactly. But even with the business now selling almost $12 million worth of champagne a year, she had still sacrificed some of her personal financial security to give Louis his extravagant dowry. Louis, for his part, had always planned to bargain for more. Perhaps unsurprisingly, it was during these first years of her daughter's marriage to Louis that Barbe-Nicole began to entertain the idea of turning over the business to someone else—someone she could trust to manage it.

Suddenly, thinking about the future like this seemed urgent. Philippe Clicquot, who had supported her since the early days of her enterprise, died in the final months of 1819 at the family home on rue de la Vache. Almost precisely a year later, after a long and painful illness, her father, Nicolas, passed away at seventy-three years old. And just like that, she was left without two of her closest advisers and without the company of two men on whom she knew she could depend. A solemn procession of town worthies and National Guardsmen followed her father's casket to the grave, and he was remembered with remarkable frankness as a man who was "pliable and pragmatic in his beliefs . . . of great intelligence, with a taste for authority and power." But he was also honest, decent, and, as one of his biographers put it, "skillful in his acquaintances."

Barbe-Nicole now unexpectedly became heir to the family compound at the Hôtel Ponsardin. It had always been understood that it would be Jean-Baptiste's inheritance, as the only son. But Jean-Baptiste was dead. After her father's passing, the family home—and the social responsibilities that came with owning one of the city's great estates—belonged to her.

Someday, this mansion would also belong to Louis and Clémentine, along with Barbe-Nicole's home on rue de l'Hôpital, the country estates at Oger and Bouzy, their little home in Paris, and the castle on the hill in Boursault. But by 1821, Louis was needling her for a country estate of his own, where he could indulge his gentlemanly hobbies of gardening and botany. She finally relented and bought them another large property to the north of Reims, in Villiers-en-Prayères. By then, Barbe-Nicole had already made up her mind about the company. She was determined that Clémentine and Louis would never get near it.

Louis Bohne would have been the obvious candidate for running the company in her old age. Together they had built Veuve Clicquot Ponsardin and Company into the world-renowned business that it was, and some of this fabulous luxury she owed to him and his sharp business instincts as a salesman. She knew that he cared about the legacy of her champagne with a passion that matched her own. But she was still coming to grips with the sudden news of his death that winter as well. After all those years crossing a war-torn continent, after the dangers he had faced as a suspected spy in Russia at the height of the conflict, he had ended up dying in the most mundane fashion: He slipped off an icy bridge.

So she turned instead to another of her employees, a fast-talking dreamer named George Christian von Kessler. He had been one of her salesmen during those lean years before the Russian triumph, and since 1815 he had been a junior partner of sorts in managing the business. In December, she shocked her staff and her family by announcing that in three years' time, at little more than forty, she intended to retire—and to give George the entire business as a gift.

A decision this extraordinary makes it easy to wonder if there was something more to Barbe-Nicole's relationship with George von Kessler. There is no concrete evidence that there was. Then again, in this new era of the domestic angel and the good mother, there wouldn't be, and it's pretty difficult to imagine that Barbe-Nicole threw off all thoughts of sexuality at the age of twenty-seven. Besides, George was recently widowed, and grief has a way of helping people find each other. Or perhaps it's simpler still. The local gossip suggests that Barbe-Nicole had a habitual weakness for handsome young men, and who can blame her? Rich men have often made a life's work of seducing secretaries, and Barbe-Nicole at least was doggedly loyal to the men she admired.

Still, a promotion was one thing. Giving away the family company was astonishing. Almost equally unbelievable was the idea that Barbe-Nicole was considering retirement at this particular moment. At the beginning of the century, when she and François were first experimenting with the commercial production of sparkling wine, there were ten champagne houses. In 1821—largely as a result of her success and the success of her early competitors—there were more than fifty, all struggling to make enough wine to meet the fabulous demand created for this new luxury product. Already there were signs that a vast new market was learning to love champagne as well. Americans were beginning to clamor for bubbly by the 1820s, and as Charles Heidsieck put it, "There is no country where you can make a fortune so easily just by sending a product that pleases people and sells well."

Barbe-Nicole already had her fortune, of course, and the pressures of running an increasingly complex and demanding business were real. Her outlook complicated by grief and depression—and by emotional entanglements as well, if there was any truth to the talk—she was struggling with the shape of her future. There had been great personal losses, enough to leave anyone reeling. But it wasn't long before she reconsidered her rash decision. In the summer of 1822, less than a year after her announcement, Barbe-Nicole abruptly revoked her promise to give George the business. It was only more cause for tongue wagging in the commercial offices of Reims. The gossips noticed, not coincidentially, perhaps, that a new young man had joined the business team of the Widow Clicquot as a clerk. He was a handsome twenty-year-old German named Matthieu-Édouard Werler, who soon changed his name to the more francophone Édouard Werlé.

Writing the history of champagne at the end of the nineteenth century, the American author Robert Tomes summed up the situation neatly: "Werler . . . came a poor boy to Rheims from the Duchy of Nassau. Taken into the employ of the Widow Clicquot as a lad of all work, with a mere pittance of two dollars or so a week for wages, his intelligent activity won for him rapid advancement. The gossips of Rheims assert that the blue eyes, ruddy face, and broad shoulders of the youth, finding favor with the hitherto disconsolate widow, caused a livelier appreciation of his moral and intellectual qualities in the counting-house, and gave an irresistible impulse to his progress." Before long, he was her constant companion in the cellars, and she had given him responsibility for her vast vineyards and for choosing the wines. Someday, she would tap him as her successor. For now, reenergized, she had given up any idea of retiring soon.

We can only imagine what George von Kessler thought of this change of fortune and the gossip circulating in Reims about Barbe-Nicole and her fancy for this strapping young man. Considering he lost out on the gift of a major international company, it's easy to guess he was feeling a bit desperate. He certainly didn't quit his job. Instead, along with Louis de Chevigné, he began encouraging Barbe-Nicole to expand the business in new directions. Perhaps it was already clear to both Louis and von Kessler that the champagne business was lost to Édouard Werlé. Perhaps von Kessler preferred the idea of heading up a different line of business, and Barbe-Nicole thought he would be best suited somewhere other than in her cellars. Perhaps she thought she owed it to him. Whatever the case, in the summer of 1822, Barbe-Nicole took up two new commercial enterprises. She returned to the textile industry that had made the Ponsardin and Clicquot fortunes. And in June she opened the Veuve Clicquot Ponsardin and Company Bank. It would prove far and away the most disastrous business decision of her life.

Chapter 13

Flirting with Disaster

I t was an unlucky time for Barbe-Nicole to be making so many important decisions. Still disoriented by the death of her father and
the unexpected demise of Louis Bohne, she was unmoored. And
perhaps, after almost a decade of one fabulous success after another, she
had been lulled into the dangerous belief that nothing could go seriously
wrong. Eager to take some definitive action about the future, she started
by making Édouard cellar master in the summer of 1822. Antoine Müller
was leaving the company, and Barbe-Nicole was determined to give the
promotion to Édouard—despite the fact that this young clerk, the son
of a postmaster, had worked with her for only a year and had almost no
experience making champagne.

Barbe-Nicole also went on a spending spree that summer. With her
refinements to the *remuage* system, the house of Veuve Clicquot Ponsardin
was running efficiently, and she had succeeded in turning a small family
sideline into an industrial powerhouse. By hiring George, she had even
led the way in embracing the managerial revolution, boosting her profits
but, ironically, helping to bring an end to the old tradition of family-run
businesses and, especially, to the tradition of the family businesswoman.
The result of it all was vast profits. Barbe-Nicole was already among
the wealthiest industrialists in the Champagne—and one of the richest
middle-class women in all of France.

She was mostly interested in buying property. The house that she and François had inherited on rue de l'Hôpital was an affluent bourgeois home, certainly spacious and elegant enough for her small family: Clémentine, Louis, and baby Marie-Clémentine. The Count and Countess of Chevigné—as Louis and Clémentine were now styled—spent most winters in Paris and much of the summer at the turreted château in Boursault or the estates in Villiers-en-Prayères anyhow. Barbe-Nicole's new plan was to turn the family home into the business offices for the fledgling Veuve Clicquot Ponsardin and Company Bank. Her personal residence would now be the palatial home known in Reims as the Hôtel le Vergeur, a sprawling building with three pitched roofs and a timber-beamed facade. Inside, it was a carnivalesque wonder reminiscent of the nearby grand cathedral. In one room, the ceiling was decorated with sculpted figures emerging from the beams—images of contorted faces, monkeys, even dragons. The fourteenth-century original mansion was destroyed during the World War I, but the reconstructed building is now home to a local history museum. Committed to this plan of business expansion, she also found new offices for the wine company on rue du Temple, not far from her childhood home. Today, these buildings, tucked discreetly behind iron gates and a shady gravel courtyard, are the corporate world offices of the company that bears her name.

One thing still has not changed in the world of business: More solid companies are destroyed by overreaching expansion than almost anything else. And Barbe-Nicole was not just building her business, she was starting two new ones in the space of a summer. The temptation is easy to understand. Modern commercial banking was also in its infancy at the beginning of the Industrial Revolution, and for years Barbe-Nicole and Louis Bohne had been forced to rely on a complicated line of credit from bankers as far away as Paris. Making champagne required all the big houses to tie up huge amounts of capital in the cellars, sometimes for a period of years, and foreign payments could take almost as long to clear the books.

Most important, banking was another major step toward vertical integration for the company, an idea at the heart of her manufacturing-style model. Already, in fact, "bankers played a secondary role . . . in the production cycle" of champagne. Without a line of credit, it was sometimes impossible to raise enough money to keep making new champagne when the old stocks were still aging in the cellars, and she had already been acting as her own banker for years. Her employees, willingly or not, had also been some of her first clients. A *voyageur* (traveling salesman) or a *commis voyageur* (traveling clerk) was typically required to loan his personal savings to his employer, in exchange for a 5 percent return in interest. It was part of his commitment to the business. Men like Louis—forerunners of the modern corporate manager—earned salaries and a share of the company's profits, but they also had to invest in the companies they helped to build. Opening a bank to serve the other winemakers in the Champagne was a logical extension of the practice. Jean-Rémy Moët started self-financing his production costs as early as 1819, and Barbe-Nicole was determined to do him one better. Taking control of the financing side of the wine trade—especially if it could be turned to additional profit—seemed like an obvious next step.

Her decision to pick up the textile trade must have seemed even more obvious. After all, with the death of her father and her only brother before him, there were lucrative family interests in cloth manufacturing that would otherwise just disappear. With the mechanization of the textile industry and the rise of what the poet William Blake called its "dark satanic mills," there was a great deal of money to be made, and Barbe-Nicole was bursting with confidence. It was a confidence that George was feeding with his enthusiasm.

At first, there was no reason for Barbe-Nicole to question her entrepreneurial instincts or her charmed future. The champagne business had made her immensely rich, and she was already one of the most famous entrepreneurs of her day. Her home was also among the most splendid in Reims—so splendid that in 1825, when Charles X was crowned king in the cathedral of Reims, following the ancient traditions of France, one member of the royal family stayed as her houseguest: Louis-Philippe, the Duke of Orléans, a man with republican sympathies who would soon become the last king of France.

When the bank opened, deposits and business rolled in. With George as both partner and professional manager, they started expanding the textile company as well, buying new mills in Germany and funding the purchases with large loans from the bank. From there, it is a familiar story. George wasn't gambling with his own money so much as with hers, after all, and soon there were bad investments. By 1825, three years into this financial adventure, it was time to face facts. The champagne business was still going strong, but the out-of-town textile mills were struggling terribly. Soon the losses were dragging down the bank as well.

Sitting up late looking at the books and worrying over the figures left her with a pounding headache. She must have been shaken by self-doubt, too. In the space of just a few short years, Barbe-Nicole was almost $14 million in the red. It wasn't her own skill as a businesswoman that she questioned. If those mills had been in Reims—somewhere she could march into and set to rights—the venture could still have been salvaged. But they were in far-off places, where she had to rely on someone else to handle her business. A woman, even a matronly widow, did not take journeys without some male relative at her side, and there is no evidence that Barbe-Nicole ever traveled beyond her native France. The fact that she ran an international business for decades and conquered markets that she never visited makes her story that much more astonishing.

Instead, Barbe-Nicole now had to question her personal judgment. As long as she could keep her heart from getting involved, she was an excellent judge of character. But she had a soft side and a generosity that could get the better of her. That was the essence of the story with Louis de Chevigné. She found it painful disappointing him when his heart was set on some new extravagance. So she didn't. Everyone knew it was the same in the offices. It was part of her charm. When a tearful and frightened young lad was sent to deliver a defective load of glass bottles that had come from the factory misshapen and useless, everyone knew that Barbe-Nicole wouldn't have the heart to refuse the shipment. Sure enough, the crates were unloaded. They were sent back to the suppliers the next day with a sharp note, of course, but she hadn't wanted to see the boy cry.

Something about George and her relationship with him had prevented her from approaching these investments coolly. She would pay a high price for this indulgence. Like Louis de Chevigné, George had an enthusiasm for spending his way out of a problem, and for months he and

Barbe-Nicole had been arguing about the investments. Édouard was after her to stop the financial hemorrhaging at the bank, and Barbe-Nicole knew that it was time to make a painful decision. In the spring of 1826, she decided to stop throwing good money after bad. She and George would have to split. In fact, a lot of things came to an end that year, and the financial losses were only just beginning.

The worst of the year's losses were personal. There was another death in the family, this time a terrible one. The image haunted her for years. Her twenty-four-year-old nephew, Adrien, was killed in the vicious attack of a rabid dog in May, leaving the family to grieve over his savaged body and over the horror of his death. Her brother's widow was disconsolate. In the space of a decade, poor Thérèse had lost her husband and her child, and because there were no other sons, it was the end of the Ponsardin family line.

The other losses were far smaller but no less real. That summer was Édouard's wedding to a young woman named Louise-Émilie Boisseau. The new Madame Werlé was the near relation of one of their competitors at Champagne Roederer, and Édouard—who was not ashamed of preferring the finer things in life—had married with all the instincts of a keen businessman. Barbe-Nicole had seen him at work, where he ruled over the employees with an iron hand, and she could have guessed that Louise-Émilie would have a rough bargain of it. But if she and Édouard had been enjoying, as the gossips of Reims said, a flirtation, things were suddenly far more complicated.

Of course, there was also the collapse of her relationship with George. After all their months of arguing about the business and money, after the decision to part ways, there was not much of their earlier warm friendship left. Now, he was engaged to marry the daughter of an important state official back in Germany, and there was little chance she would ever see him again. In the liquidation of their partnership, George agreed to take the foreign mills and disappeared to start a new life. Flush with a bit of family capital, he ran the mills and before long founded his own sparkling wine business—never more than a modest success in the nineteenth century, but now Germany's oldest and most prestigious producer of sparkling wine.

In Reims, Barbe-Nicole was left with the bank. It turned out that closing down a bank was rather more difficult than opening one, and she offered Édouard a share in the company's profits in exchange for his taking on some of the complex management. By now, Barbe-Nicole was running a large operation: The champagne company alone had, at different times of the year, hundreds of employees. While the liquidation of the bank was slowly beginning, Barbe-Nicole also had other business worries. The champagne industry was changing rapidly, and it was a constant struggle to stay ahead of new developments and to keep the competitive edge that made her one of the big players in the business.

Most irritating were the new problems with impostors using her name in Russia to sell cheap champagne at her luxury prices and damaging the one thing that kept the sales coming in: her reputation. It was in part the steep costs of a bottle of the Widow Clicquot's wines that had established what one enthusiast called "the superiority of her brand." Barbe-Nicole knew what historian Kolleen Guy has recently discovered: "The price of the wine [of the Champagne] depend[ed] principally on the reputation of its manufacturer; wine with marks and labels of a well-known or celebrated maker [sold] for double the price of the same wine with an unknown brand." The difficulty was that, impostors and fraud aside, the only way a customer could recognize a bottle of the Widow Clicquot's champagne was by the brand burned into the cork. Consider what buying a bottle of wine would be like today if the only marketing were on the ends of the corks. Then, consider that most corks are actually covered with aluminum sleeves. Those sleeves are meant to imitate the wax seals used to protect the necks of wine bottles in the early days. Barbe-Nicole used them regularly.

Buying wine in the 1820s had something of the blind tasting party about it. Wine labels—*étiquettes* in French—were only beginning to become familiar sights in the cellars in the 1820s. Barbe-Nicole had first sent bottles with labels in 1814, when customers were still willing to pay outlandish prices for the legendary 1811 vintage of her Bouzy red but were also increasingly suspicious about what was really in their expensive bottles. Plain white labels, with just the date and the location of the vineyard and a few floral swirls for a bit of prettiness, served as inexpensive reassurance. She was still labeling the bottles only when customers requested it, and it would be almost another decade before *étiquettes* were common either in her cellars or in the Champagne—but increasingly, Barbe-Nicole began to wonder if it might not be a good idea to protect her good name a bit more aggressively. So, to combat the fraud and with an eye toward the future, she went through the trouble of registering her trademark comet cork with the local officials.

The manufacturing of champagne was also becoming increasingly mechanical by the end of the 1820s, and Barbe-Nicole knew that her new system of *remuage*—just beginning to appear in other cellars across the Champagne, as the secret of her technique leaked out—had played a role in increasing the rate of production. Now that she could no longer count on the competitive advantage of her secret method, there was the real possibility of falling behind. Already, the bottles used by champagne makers were being mass-produced in factories, made by machine in more regular shapes and sizes. Suddenly, it was possible to stack more bottles in the cellars safely.

André Jullien had been working in Jean-Rémy's cellars for over a decade trying to find new equipment able to speed the disgorging process, too, and now in 1825, the first mechanical bottling machines appeared in the French wine country. Two years later, there was the announcement of an industrial instrument for corking the bottles. By the 1830s, Cyrus Redding's monumental *History and Description of Modern Wines* (1833) was touting new, modern winepresses with "two wooden cylinders, turning in opposite directions." In the 1840s, Adolphe Jacquesson—son of Napoléon's favored purveyor, Memmie—patented the wire cork cage for sparkling wines still known as the *muselet* and the little metal cork caps called *capsulets.* Jean-Baptiste François revolutionized the champagne industry by discovering how to measure residual sugar, leading to better control of the *mousse* and fewer breakages, and Dr. Jules Guyot changed the landscape of vineyards around the world when he showed winemakers the advantages of planting grapes in the familiar rows we see today, rather than the traditional circular clumps. Everyone in the industry knew that the race was on for the final stage in the industrialization of champagne—a wine famous for being handcrafted and a wine that, even today, can never be made simply by machine.

Just as Barbe-Nicole was faced with these new capital costs and with having to decide how fully to invest in the mechanization of her cellars, the other shoe dropped in the financial world. By 1827, France was in the middle of a painful recession. Two years later—when Édouard was still in the process of extricating her from her investments in the Veuve Clicquot Ponsardin and Company Bank—it had turned into a full-blown depression. There were massive crop failures across France, causing misery for count-less working families. In industrial centers like Lyons and Reims, even the looms were grinding to a halt as the textile industry struggled. Barbe-Nicole had risked too much capital on the Clicquot banking enterprise, and she knew in the back of her mind that there was a dangerous exposure.

Barbe-Nicole went out of town for several weeks that winter, to spend time with Clémentine and Louis at his uncle's estates in the Vendée. Sud-denly, while she was too far away to do anything about it, disaster struck. They had been depositing much of the Clicquot bank's capital reserves with the large and well-established firm of Poupart de Neuflize, a financial institution with long-standing ties to the French woolen trade. What they didn't know was that Poupart de Neuflize—like many banks in Europe that winter—was on the edge of failure. As the company went into a credit meltdown, its accounts were frozen, and the investors panicked. Within hours, Édouard was besieged with customers demanding their deposits, and they were in the middle of a run on the Widow Clicquot's bank. It was certain to destroy Barbe-Nicole financially.

Knowing that Barbe-Nicole and her company were facing ruin, Éd-ouard made a gutsy decision. He would risk his own fortune to save hers. Thanks to his share of the company profits and a prudent marriage, that fortune was now considerable. After gathering up the deeds to his proper-ties, he raced out of town to Paris. It was ninety miles to the capital, hours of travel in his carriage along the dusty roads of post–Napoleonic France, and as he passed through acres of vineyards on his way out of Reims, Édouard must have thought how foolish it was to have played such a high-stakes game with an otherwise uncomplicated future. As the countryside of the Champagne slowly gave way to the lower plains of the Paris basin, his thoughts turned to what he would say when he reached his destination: the offices of an old business associate, Rougemont de Lowenberg, a banker who specialized in offering lines of credit to wine merchants. He needed to persuade this careful financier to give him as much as 2 million francs in cash—the equivalent of $44 million. Louis would need to ride with it back to Reims that night. Otherwise, Barbe-Nicole would be forced into complete liquidation, and the champagne of the Widow Clicquot would be a thing of the past.

Édouard, of course, succeeded. He exuded good sense and self-discipline. The bank loaned the company 1 million francs in cash and opened an immediate line of credit for the second million Édouard would need to save the business. By the time Barbe-Nicole got the message telling her the heart-stopping news, a tired and resolute Édouard was already standing in the open offices of the bank, prepared to pay out the deposits of any client. Now that investors were reassured their money was safe, the run on the bank quietly ended, and Barbe-Nicole—who sustained total losses of almost $5.5 million—was still in business.

Once she learned of her narrow escape, Barbe-Nicole was determined not to be in the banking business for long. It would take more than another decade to extricate her finances fully from this foolhardy venture, but there was now no question about her new company strategy. She would focus on one thing and one thing only: champagne. As she famously announced, they would make only the best. She had risked everything and overextended her resources, and she had nearly lost it all—her palatial home in the Hôtel le Vergeur, the country estate at Oger with its cheerful broad windows overlooking acres of vines. Gone would have been the château at Boursault and the grand lifestyle that she was still bankrolling for Clémentine and the spendthrift Count of Chevigné. Gone the hopes of a grand marriage someday not too distant for the eleven-year-old Marie-Clémentine.

She had weathered the storm, and all thanks to Édouard. Still, the business had sustained a blow to its financial health. Above all, the dissipation of her energies meant that the house of the Widow Clicquot, for the first time since its great triumph over the Russian market in 1814, was falling behind its competitors. In 1821, she had sold an astonishing 280,000 bottles of champagne; now, exactly ten years later, her total sales were down to fewer than 145,000 bottles—far less than Jean-Rémy could boast at any time in the 1820s. If she wanted to recoup her losses and continue at the head of one of the world's great champagne houses, Barbe-Nicole would have to work to recapture her position. Now, she would have to begin rebuilding the business, once again, in the midst of political turmoil.

The economic crisis of 1829, which nearly brought down the Clicquot bank, was merely a symptom of larger problems, and just as in the years preceding the bloody Revolution of 1789, desperate economic circumstances were leading to anger and action. The weather in July 1830 was hot and dusty, and with the final defeat of Napoléon in 1815, the Bourbon princes once again ruled over France. King Charles X, thinking he would take advantage of the summer vacation that had left much of Paris quiet, announced new repressive reforms, limiting the freedoms of the press, restricting voting rights only to the richest citizens, and—most infuriating of all—barring the affluent middle classes from holding the highest public offices.

The result was middle-class fury. The businessmen and bankers shut down the city. They closed offices and factories, knowing it would bring the staggering economy to a grinding halt, and the journalists responded by blaming it all on the king. Compared with the bloody events of 1789, it was a restrained and pointedly economic protest, but it set off a firestorm. Soon, it was not a middle-class protest at all. Already in Paris, more than half the population was living in squalid poverty. That July, in a city of 755,000, an astonishing 227,000 families had applied for bread cards—vouchers allowing the destitute to purchase food at a small discount. After years of struggling with high unemployment, thousands more workers and day laborers found themselves without jobs, and the result was another revolution.

For three days—known in France still as Les Trois Glorieuses, or the Three Glorious Ones—the streets of Paris were riotous. Arriving in the city, François-René de Chateaubriand described the scene. The boy driving Chateaubriand's carriage "had already abandoned his jacket with its [royal] fleur-de-lis buttons." The old tricolor flag of the Revolution was once again fluttering sharply in the breeze, hung from windows and roof-tops. "Clouds of white smoke rose here and there among the houses," Chateaubriand recalled, and "cannon-shot and the sound of muskets blended with the noise of the alarm-bells. . . . I was watching the ancient Louvre fall." Within hours, the king, remembering too well the fate of his Bourbon forebearers, was beating a hasty retreat out of the country.

Barbe-Nicole was worried, too—and with good reason. If the working-class battles in the streets of Paris spread to the great commercial centers like Reims, this time there would be no finessing it. Already in nearby Épernay, the vignerons were rioting and the town hall had been sacked. In these eastern provinces of France, the dislike of the Bourbon kings—and their supporters—was especially intense. Her father had thrived during that earlier revolution, still so vivid in her memory, by disguising the fam-ily's royalist allegiances, but Louis de Chevigné's aristocratic family had not survived. Now Barbe-Nicole knew that they were once again on the brink of a peasant revolt. And her daughter was a countess. Bourgeois roots alone would not be enough to save them. The only safeguard was to declare their support for the protesters, and Louis de Chevigné did his best. The Count of Chevigné—whose mother had danced at the balls of Marie Antoinette—declared himself to be a populist and a liberal.

For a man of his class, it was not an easy decision to make. It was going to be a harder one to live with. At that moment in French politi-cal history, it was not a choice between a monarchy and a republic. If it had been, Louis would almost certainly have supported the king. All his family ties bound him to the nobility. Instead, it was a choice in 1830 be-tween two kinds of kings—the autocratic and splendid aristocracy of the ancien régime and its hereditary heirs or a new vision of a modern king, one with bourgeois values.

More simply, for Louis, it was a choice between two parts of the ex-tended family that made up the ruling classes of France, the "legitimist" but repressive Bourbons or the radical—even revolutionary—Louis-Philippe, Duke of Orléans, whom Barbe-Nicole and her family had wel-comed into their home less than a decade earlier. Louis-Philippe had led a life right out of a romance, and it was hard not to find this dashing nobleman endearing. During the turbulent years of the Revolution, he was an ardent supporter of reform and liberty, even going so far as to join the radical Jacobins and—shockingly—to vote in support of the execution of Louis XVI. Soon, it was his own neck on the line, however, and at nineteen the young duke fled into an impoverished and dangerous exile. Forced to live in disguise, sometimes passing as a tramp and later finding employment as an underpaid schoolteacher, first in Switzerland and then in America, he traveled the world until Napoléon's fall from power made it safe for him to return to France—more than twenty years later. Now again at the forefront of the aristocracy and able to regale his hosts with fabulous stories, the duke charmed Barbe-Nicole and her family during his stay, and he had charmed the people of France as well. He had the support of the middle classes, and he was the darling of the working people. Already, some were saying that he should be king.

Knowing that to some of his family it would seem like a betrayal, the Count of Chevigné came out in support of the Orléanist revolution. When the National Guard was revived to fight for the democratic rights of the people, Louis was among them, waving the tricolor flag of an earlier, more radical, generation. But, as he confessed to his old friend Richard Castel, it was complicated. "My feelings are divided," he wrote, "but I regret more than anything the family ties; [still,] I have found ample reward in the days of July and in the tokens of affection that have been given to me."

If Louis struggled with his decision, Barbe-Nicole did not. Nicolas Ponsardin was not the only steely pragmatist in the family. In this revolution, as in the last, her family would prosper. In fact, the years to come would be the golden age of the entrepreneurial upper classes in France. Louis-Philippe, the Duke of Orléans, would come to be known as the "bourgeois king," and in the words of one historian, "The reign of Louis-Philippe was a business régime," whose motto was *Enrichissez-vous*—"Get rich." Although the working people of France fought this second revolution in the streets, there was a reason the middle classes had started it, and they would be its primary beneficiaries. As king, Louis-Philippe would rule France in relative tranquillity for nearly twenty years, the vast majority of them a new economic boom time, and with a now single-minded vision, Barbe-Nicole would dedicate herself, once again, to rebuilding one of Europe's business legends.

Chapter 14

The Champagne Empire

I t is lucky that Barbe-Nicole refocused her energies when she did. There was a small window of opportunity, and it was quickly closing. The champagne industry—aided by the support of Louis-Philippe— changed dramatically over the course of the next few decades. Most of the world's famous champagne houses today established themselves as fierce competitors with a global reach during the middle years of the nineteenth century. As early as the summer of 1831, when the vines were ripening in the fields and the cellars were quiet, the new king made his first visit to the Champagne wine country, and soon there would be many more. In his passion for sparkling wine, Louis-Philippe would rival Napoléon. Champagne had always been the drink of kings. Sensing new growth in the industry, Barbe-Nicole decided to take on another business partner. To restore the fortunes of her company, she would need help. For a second time, she would cut Louis and Clémentine out of the world of commerce and industry. For an investment of 100,000 livres—a mere $2 million— she gave Édouard Werlé a 50 percent share in the champagne business. Like the financial marriage it was, the company from that moment forward added his name to that of the Widow Clicquot.

With Édouard now a full partner in the champagne business that Barbe-Nicole had already turned into a household name in much of the world, Louis, the Count of Chevigné, was out of luck. Édouard had en-

couraged her to turn off the tap when the textile investments were drain-
ing her resources, and he offered her the same advice for dealing with
her charming son-in-law. But Barbe-Nicole could refuse Louis nothing,
and there were constant requests. He wanted to remodel the vast gardens
at the château in Villiers-en-Prayères. He needed more cash to support
his aristocratic lifestyle. And, of course, he was always looking to pay his
gambling debts, a point of honor among gentlemen. Before long, Édouard
took up the habit of dealing with Louis's most exorbitant demands.

Her hard work had created a world of privilege and ease for the Count
and Countess of Chevigné. While Barbe-Nicole, now in her fifties, was
still putting in fourteen-hour days from dawn to dark, trying to assure
a strong company footing after the banking catastrophe, Louis and Clémentine were free to dance until dawn and sleep until noon. They lived
the charmed life of rich aristocrats in the dazzling age of industrialism.

Still, it must have stung a bit to be so abruptly and determinedly cut out
of the business. In making her partnership with Édouard, Barbe-Nicole
had effectively given away half of an immensely lucrative family business
to a man who had started out in her offices as a handsome and clever
clerk. There were some people who still remembered the rumors about
what was at the root of his meteoric rise, and perhaps there was some
emotional element to the decision as well. Certainly, as a simple matter of
numbers, if Barbe-Nicole wanted to cash out and retire, she could have
sold the business for far more than Édouard's modest investment. But
Barbe-Nicole knew that Édouard had been more than just a loyal employee over the course of the past decade. In him, she had found a fellow
entrepreneur on whom she could rely unhesitatingly. She also did not
forget that he had saved her. Without his intervention in those precarious
first hours of the bank run, there wouldn't have been much of a company
to consider passing on. Having come so close to losing everything, Barbe-
Nicole had found her second wind as an entrepreneur, and she had also
found a new partner. She was filled with ambition and competitive drive,
and she was going to lead the way in shaping the business models of the
nineteenth century as well.

Always alert to the changing commercial climate, Barbe-Nicole was
once again ahead of emerging trends. It was part of what made her a

legend. In the years to come, the manufacturing model of business would require thinking like a corporation and not like a family unit, and with it came what historians call "the managerial revolution"—the rise of the salaried businessmen and company executives we know today. Ironically, it was this new model of the professional managerial class that, more than anything else, signaled the end of the traditional opportunities for untrained bourgeois women in family businesses. Barbe-Nicole was making the savviest decisions she could to stay competitive in a changing marketplace, and she needed someone willing to put in the same crushing hours that she demanded of herself. That would never be the style of the handsome count. Bringing Édouard into the business, first as a professional director with a share of the profits and later as a full-fledged executive partner, was one step on the way to turning the wine company of the Widow Clicquot into a legacy company. She was smart to do it. The cold facts are that "by the mid-1840s, [even] personally managed enterprises . . . had become specialized, usually handling a single function and a single product." The economics of industrialization demanded it, and soon it demanded full-time management staff as well. These would be professional men able to lead large companies. Ironically, however, Barbe-Nicole was helping to establish a trend that would close the door on other talented and untested young women looking for a chance to enter the business world.

During the next decade, Barbe-Nicole dedicated herself to rebuilding her champagne empire. She had almost let it slip from her grasp, and now she was determined to secure its future. It was a critical moment in the history of the company. Had she fallen behind at this juncture, the wines of the Widow Clicquot might easily have shared the same fate as those of the Widow Binet, who was once listed by the city of Reims as a leading champagne maker. Nothing of the Widow Binet's story—or of her business—remains. In the late 1830s, the commercial world was changing rapidly. Success meant walking a fine line between craft and industrialization. Already, the first railroad tracks were being laid in France, and improvements were under way in the Champagne to modernize the

canal system that linked the province to the capital. Soon, the steam loco-
motive would change the business climate and landscape of Europe. The
first train wouldn't reach Reims for more than another decade, and for
now Barbe-Nicole and Édouard had to rely on the old-fashioned means
of transportation: wagons and barges carrying her delicate wines to sea-
ports and Paris. But the coming railroads already meant the growth of
mass markets—and the need to advertise in them. The result in the years
to come would be the rise of the champagne label. Until then, Édouard
would take to the road, bringing in clients for the company, as Louis
Bohne had done before him. He would do it with the same talent. Soon
the company sales had doubled.

Barbe-Nicole worked with a furious intensity, and even if she was not
like the other grandmothers of her generation, family was always very
much on her mind. She thought a great deal about motherhood, especially. Her mother, Jeanne-Clémentine, passed away quietly in 1837, at
seventy-seven, leaving Barbe-Nicole and her sister orphaned and no less
bereft for being in their adulthood. Barbe-Nicole knew that it was the end
of an old way of life, the end of her own bourgeois roots. She had grown
up in a world different from the one her daughter now inhabited. And
she was glad. In those uncertain days before the occupation of Reims,
her greatest worry had been for the luxuries and the life that Clémentine
would lose. Now, she still believed that the business—if she could restore
it—would be a guarantee of her family's comfort. Left in the hands of Édouard, it could become a hedge against futurity, a silent source of riches.

In the summer of 1839, those same riches gave rise to new celebrations
and more thoughts of family. Her granddaughter, Marie-Clémentine,
now twenty-one years old, was married with great ceremony. Listening
to the eager preparations all winter, Barbe-Nicole could smile to think
how pleased her father, Nicolas, would have been. For Marie was not
only the daughter of a count; she was marrying one: the pious and proper
Louis Samuel Victorien de Rochechouart de Mortemart, a member of
one of the most famous noble families in all of France. In his portraits, he
sits ramrod straight, surrounded by the splendor that was his fortunate
birthright. He was also a gentle man possessed of an artistic sensibility,
with a passion for growing rare and beautiful orchids and a remarkable

skill as an amateur artist. After the solemn ceremony in the cathedral, a long train of carriages wound up the hillside to Boursault for a lavish celebration, with case upon case of the Widow's finest champagnes. As a wedding present, Barbe-Nicole gave the young couple a magnificent gift: the very castle itself.

The sober Count de Mortemart was a sensible match for stout little Marie, who soon gave him a little girl named Pauline, Barbe-Nicole's first great-grandchild. By 1841, Marie had also given birth to a little boy, unimaginatively named Paul. Eventually, there would be another little girl named Anne, on whom Barbe-Nicole doted. The champagne house of the Widow Clicquot—for that was how it was always known, despite Édouard's name on the company books—was back on solid footing. It had taken a decade of careful management and hard work, but more than just recovering, the company flourished. It was once again firmly established as one of the region's—and, therefore, one of the world's—most important champagne houses. Now, the company profits were making Barbe-Nicole rich all over again. It was clear that the only option was to continue to expand the company and bring in more managerial staff.

It was also clear to Barbe-Nicole that Édouard didn't need her there every day to do it. She would never be ready to let go entirely of the business she had created, and she wasn't even remotely prepared to sell out. But in 1841, at sixty-four, the Widow Clicquot retired. It was time. From Épernay came word that her old competitor Jean-Rémy Moët had died, and it was the passing of a generation. Her generation. Jean-Rémy had left the company in the capable hands of his son Victor and his aristocratic son-in-law, Pierre-Gabriel Chandon de Briailles, who famously did business together under the name Moët et Chandon. She knew that before long, she would have to trust the business entirely to Édouard, one way or the other.

Now, she decided not to wait, at least not formally. Still, it wasn't much of a retirement in the end. Barbe-Nicole was a workaholic and intent on keeping a guiding hand in the business to which she had dedicated her life. Retirement simply meant that she would be able to spend more time at Boursault, and by the 1840s she was spending only the winter months in Reims. She might have felt old at sixty-four, but if Louis de Chevigné had been thinking he would come into his inheritance anytime soon, he was sadly mistaken. Contrary to all expectations and at a time when the average woman in France lived fewer than forty-five years, Barbe-Nicole still had a long life ahead of her. The champagne company she had transformed from a small family business into one of the world's great commercial empires would still be at the center of it. Years later, the traveler Robert Tomes remembered "Madame Clicquot [as] a dwarfish, withered old woman of eighty-nine years, whose whole soul was in business, scanning over each day to her last the ledger of the commercial house to which she had given her name."

Even so, Barbe-Nicole did now agree to let Édouard take over as director of the company, and she approved bringing two new partners into the business. Monsieur Dejonge became the early equivalent of company chief financial officer and was the CFO responsible for the increasingly complex account books. Then, with Édouard's own promotion to what we would now think of as CEO, there was an opening for a new cellar master, in charge of overseeing the winemaking operations. That job—and the new partnership—went to Monsieur de Sachs. Surrounded by all these counts and barons and eager to be treated with the same grand dignity, the new cellar master soon remembered a noble ancestor in Germany of his own. As one visitor to Reims put it: "He is also a German, and a nephew, it is believed, of [Édouard] Werler. Although boasting a German title, he was not better provided for in his youth than his poor and adventurous uncle."

In this company organization, Barbe-Nicole was a one-woman board of directors. Internationally, she had already become an icon—although too often it was an icon without a face. She was quickly becoming purely a name in the eyes of the world, even if it was a famous and elegant one. By 1842, it wasn't simply that the word *Clicquot* had become synonymous with champagne. A "bottle of the Widow" was beginning to take on a larger cultural role. The Clicquot champagne was already appearing in some of the century's greatest works of literature. But with her retirement, Barbe-Nicole the woman was disappearing from public view. While her partners dedicated themselves to the continued expansion of her company, which soon had sales figures topping four hundred thousand bottles of champagne a year, Barbe-Nicole tried to enjoy the role of grandmama. "Here I have my grandchildren and great-grandchildren around me," she wrote to her cousin that year. "It is a reminder to me that I am not young and will be thinking about packing up soon and saying good-bye, which I shall do as late as possible." She was as good as her word on that score.

However much she tried to fit into the nineteenth-century model of the domestic grandmother, however, Barbe-Nicole could never manage it. After a lifetime of twelve-hour workdays, she needed more than lively children to occupy her mind. Louis de Chevigné had thrown himself into garden designs and writing bad poetry. Barbe-Nicole resumed her passion for buying—and decorating—houses. With the revitalized champagne firm of Veuve Clicquot Ponsardin and Werlé now bringing in annual sales of more than $30 million a year, money was no object. And to save the Count and Countess of Mortemart the humiliation of just a small country château, she offered to build the family an immense new one.

Now firmly ensconced among the noble families of France, the Chevigné and Mortemart families ran in the most splendid circles, and Barbe-Nicole enjoyed the festive and elaborate family parties that Louis, in particular, relished arranging. On the feast of her namesake, Saint Barbara, in early December each year, there were lavish birthday celebrations that he arranged to please her, and he would improvise flattering poems to amuse her and her noble admirers. Like her father and, more recently, like Édouard Werlé, she was taken with all the trappings of aristocracy. "I am making preparations," Barbe-Nicole wrote, "for my removal to the country and M[onsieur] de Mortemart . . . is coming down with one of his friends and his brother-in-law, the Marquis d'Avaray. Since my old château is so small, I cannot receive too many visitors at a time, but we are building a new one which will be able to house up to twenty guests and as many servants, which should save me much embarrassment and allow me to put up many more people without giving up my own bed."

The new mansion was years—and hundreds of thousands of francs—in the making. Paying for the new construction meant that Barbe-Nicole had a free hand to indulge her fancy. She had always been drawn to the Renaissance style in particular. Her home at the Hôtel le Vergeur was built with a classical facade. But this wouldn't be the impressive house of a rich merchant like her home in Reims. She wanted a palace and with the architect, Jean-Jacques Arveuf-Fransquin, hit on a plan to design a château that would imitate—and rival—the famous castles of the Loire Valley. Built of a warm golden stone and topped with airy towers, it is delicate and ethereal.

In the nineteenth century, an amusing story of its construction was told among the locals. "Not content . . . with the old-fashioned house at the bottom," Barbe-Nicole, it was said, "raised an imposing structure at the top of the hill. This . . . is [as] much like a veritable château, with pepperbox turrets, as the imagination of the aspiring architect, aided by all the wealth of the Clicquots, could make it. Its grandiose spaciousness and luxurious appurtenances make it the wonder of every Parisan *badaud* [sightseer] and rustic visitor. Among its other attractions is a dining room, adorned with elaborate armorial carvings in wood, with which are inter-twined the initials of C. and M., of the noble names of Chevigné and Mortemart. On one occasion a party of the neighboring farmers paid a visit to the château. . . . On reaching the dining room, he pointed, with conscious pride at serving such a distinguished master, to the carved armorial shields surmounted with a double crown, and bearing in gold the initials C. and M.

"'You see,' said the *cicerone* [guide] . . . 'those letters mean *Chevigné-Mortemart.*'

"'Bah!' replied one of the knowing country-men. . . . 'They mean, I tell you, *Champagne Mousseux*. Wasn't that the making of their fortune?'" She might be the mother of a countess these days, but the locals never let anyone forget that Barbe-Nicole and her family had entrepreneurial roots. They knew perfectly well that it was champagne that bought all this splendor and not ancient family titles.

More than a century later, one of her ancestors remembered growing up at Boursault: "It was a grand château, all white, clinging to the side of a wooded hillside . . . in the middle of a vast park with the scents of fresh water, gooseberries, honey, and flowers." Another visitor described the "dining-room . . . adorned with modern tapestries and richly sculptured panels . . . a monumental chimney-piece of Burgundy stone." Her niece Juliette recalled how the drawing room "opened onto a library placed in a turret," a testament to Barbe-Nicole's enduring love of books and their world of chivalric romance.

Today, getting a glimpse of Barbe-Nicole's château can be done only from a distance, over the height of a stone wall at a point where the enclosed park dips low and the narrow country road that skirts it on the south clings conveniently to the higher hill. Or it means taking one's chances with the proprietor of the winery now set just inside the gates of the park—a pleasant and handsome man, dressed impeccably in cashmere, who is quite determined to protect the privacy of the current owners. After pleading my obsession late one afternoon, we were finally rewarded with the briefest of visits: ten minutes in the grounds to look at the house and peek in the windows. The château emerges dramatically from the woodland parks that surround the estate. As the eye is drawn along the sweeping pathway to the grand front entrance, a simple Latin inscription that she had added is still visible: *Natis Mater*, Mother to Her Children. She was generous to a fault. But Barbe-Nicole was also a domineering and insistent mother.

Barbe-Nicole had already been playing the matriarch for years, slowly moving her family from the affluent bourgeoisie to the ruling classes. Ironically, it was in part her rejection of the stereotypes of her day that gave her this domestic stature and power. Of course, there were some things she could not control, and it would seem young Marie-Clémentine's love life was among them. No one knows if it was a thwarted affair of the heart or just a one-sided obsession. But today there is one other way to get a good look at the Château de Boursault. Marie's lovesick admirer, the great industrialist and railway innovator Adalbert Deganne, whom the family had turned down as a suitor back in 1839 after four years of devoted courtship, built an exact replica of it in the southwest of France, on the beach of the spa town of Arcachon. Deganne's castle—an extravagant mark of his devotion to the now matronly Marie—is today preserved as one of the town's splendid casinos. Inside, amid the dizzy whizzing of the slot machines, it is hard to imagine many similarities between this château and the rural hush of Boursault, but from the quiet distance of a café table on a summer's evening, over a couple of staggeringly expensive cocktails, it is quite enchanting.

Oddly enough, the other thing no one could control was Louis de Chevigné's spending habits or his sexuality. Still gambling, he was always in debt. Considering he was a rich man, with a mother-in-law who bankrolled his lifestyle, he must have been reliably unlucky. Louis was undoubtedly still smarting under his mother-in-law's decision to cut him out of the family economic engine. With his tighter control of the company purse strings, Édouard was also cramping his style. Louis knew he could count on his charm with *chère Mama* up to a point. He was beginning to wonder if perhaps that point hadn't been reached. The problem was, he seemed always to owe someone money. Not the kinds of debts she was likely to pay—extra costs for the country gardens, something elegant for Clémentine or Marie—but debts for gambling. And there were debts for the other kinds of dubious evening entertainments that a dashing aristocrat could easily find himself drawn into after a few drinks too many.

What was an idle aristocrat to do but turn his passions to account? Apart from gambling, he had three: wearing fancy clothes, writing bad poetry, and acting the playboy. Charles Monselet visited the family at Boursault and recalled that "the Comte de Chevigné . . . was the very image of the dandy, he had the obvious good-looks of the man of fashion, the plumpness of riches. . . . His wealth had allowed him to indulge in the pleasures of poetry." Trimming his expenses with the tailor was unthinkable. But his translations of some classical Latin poems had been politely received, and he knew that his friends found his bawdy verses very witty. Impromptu poetic toasts were one of his social hallmarks, and he had been privately collecting some of his better little compositions. Increasingly, those pleasures were in poetry with a naughty twist. In the first years of his marriage to Clémentine, he had regaled his friends with private details—and they had written to ask for more. Already, he had turned his hand to writing erotic verse, which was meant to be philosophical and rakish.

Sadly, Louis was not much of a poet. But lack of talent never stopped a rich man from publishing. In 1836, Louis had first published some of his erotic poems with a press in Paris, in a volume called *Les contes rémois*, or *The Tales of Reims*. One review sums up his talents quite eloquently: These "imitations of Boccaccio and Lafontaine . . . have none of the wit and grace, but all the grossness, of those authors." For Clémentine it was embarrassing. Even if Louis had not put his name on the title page, everyone in her social circle knew the count was the author. He was proud of the accomplishment. The worldly but conservative Barbe-Nicole was not amused, but she must have hoped that this small edition would disappear quietly. It might have, if Louis had not found himself needing cash again.

Just as construction of the new château at Boursault was beginning in 1843, Louis announced a second and larger edition of his tales. In 1858, he would publish a third, with illustrations. These would be only the first of many editions, and it meant embarrassment for the family for years to come. Rather than take Louis to task, Barbe-Nicole soon turned to what she thought would be a simple solution. Every time a new edition was released—and there were dozens in the next twenty years—Barbe-Nicole bought up as much of the print run as she could find. It was a good strategy, but she was not very successful at keeping Louis's titillating poems out of circulation. Even today, nineteenth-century copies of *Les contes rémois* can be found in antique bookshops without much difficulty and at surprisingly modest prices. Louis may never have suspected that his mother-in-law was behind the excellent sales of each new edition, but publishing the book was still a kind of complex emotional blackmail, and it kept him in ready cash for years to come.

Chapter 15

La Grande Dame

During the first quarter century of Barbe-Nicole's life, there are scant details that reflect the woman behind the name. In the last quarter of her life, it is very much the same. When she retired and became once again a mother and a grandmother, a woman who built houses and decorated them, who threw lovely parties and enjoyed her family, and who turned to charity and good works, she returned, at least in outward appearances, to the traditional role of the nineteenth-century lady. With this departure from the public sphere of business, her life—as extraordinary and celebrated as it had been—fades back into the shadowy realms of unrecorded history. The name, of course, continued. Everyone still knew the wine of the Widow Clicquot. But there were few who recorded their intimate impressions of the woman.

Still, even the most basic historical facts show that the years after 1850 in the Clicquot-Mortemart household were sad ones. At the beginning of that year, Marie-Clémentine was the mother of three small children. By the end, she had buried her first—ten-year-old Pauline. The family was consumed with the fear of losing the others. Before long, those fears were realized. Just three years later, the little girl's brother, Paul, fell sick with what the doctors then called a cerebral congestion, possibly a result of the cholera pandemic that swept through Europe in the 1840s and 1850s. The boy—only twelve—suffered horribly for several days, racked with seizures and infection, and his baby sister, Anne, who had been born in 1847, later recorded in her memoirs the details of brother's death.

"I was already six when my brother Paul fell ill," she wrote, and "I loved my brother Paul so much that, breaking the rules, I went into his bedroom . . . and hid behind the furniture." When the family found the frightened little girl, her heartbroken father had to carry her from the room by force, as she cried and pleaded. "Paul *wants* me to stay," she begged. She remembered her brother's last words, telling her to go. The danger of the infection was simply too great, and no one could bear the thought of losing both children. The next morning, she woke to find her parents standing at the end of her bed, weeping silently. They had come to tell her that Paul was dead. And they had undoubtedly come just to be sure that their last child was still breathing. Soon, they had reason to worry even about that. Within days, everyone knew Anne, too, had contracted the illness, and for a time, it looked as though she would not survive. Downstairs in the empty, cavernous sitting rooms, Barbe-Nicole, Louis, and Clémentine kept a sad vigil in a silent house.

Anne recovered from the illness, but her family would never be the same. After the death of Paul, life in the château at Boursault was isolated and lonely. Barbe-Nicole had been determined and resilent in the face of tragedy before, but now there was nothing she could do to assuage her granddaughter's grief and consuming anxiety. Marie-Clémentine and the Count of Mortemart were terrified that disease or illness would take their last remaining child, and the world beyond the walled gardens of Boursault suddenly seemed like a dangerous place. With a continued outbreak of cholera in 1854, they delayed leaving for their usual visits to more distant country estates. With so many dying everywhere in France of the epidemic, the parties and houseguests were over, and traveling seemed an invitation to disaster. When they did move, it was only farther north and farther into the country, to the family retreat at Villiers-en-Prayères, with its sprawling gardens and even larger rural park. It was a protected existence for a young girl whose fragile life was at the heart of a family's worst fears.

Anne remembered a solemn childhood, raised "by sad parents and aged grandparents," without any playmates her own age and, increasingly, in a house full of tensions. The two men, especially, did not get along. The Count of Mortemart was a sober and religious man, and he was bound to clash with Louis de Chevigné, who had always delighted in playing the role of the witty and irreverent libertine. Their politics did not agree, either. Marie-Clémentine, a timid woman in the best of circumstances, collapsed under the pressure into aimless fretting; "My dear mother had such a weak character," Anne wrote, "that I thought of her more as a child in my charge," and "life was not always easy." Her grandmother Clémentine was likewise a shy and nervous woman. Barbe-Nicole, of course, was not. But she still adored Louis de Chevigné, and that cannot have helped ease the family tensions. Too often, "animosity reigned."

Perhaps this domestic unhappiness is why the portrait made of Barbe-Nicole sometime in the 1850s doesn't show even the hint of a smile. It is a famous image of the Widow Clicquot, done by the French artist Léon Cogniet and reproduced in the only contemporary biography of her life, Victor Fiévet's *Madame Veuve Clicquot (née Ponsardin), son histoire et celle de sa famille* (1865). It was copied again for English-speaking audiences in Henry Vizetelly's beautifully illustrated *Facts About Champagne and Other Sparkling Wines, Collected During Numerous Visits to the Champagne and Other Viticultural Districts of France . . . with One Hundred and Twelve Illustrations* (1879). Today, both are exceptionally rare volumes, and additional lithographs of the portrait are nearly as scarce.

Somewhere along the way, as part of my search for the Widow, I paid an unspeakable sum for a large and lovely one, and Barbe-Nicole looks out of it and, I like to think, out of the past. She sits sternly in a large and imposing armchair, and the grim solemnity of those years is captured in the set of her broad, square jaw. The eyes are intelligent but hard, and maybe a little tired, and it is the look of a woman who is not to be trifled with. There is still a fierce sparkle in her eyes, and in the original painting, her auburn hair retains those same reddish highlights that her girlhood citizen papers called an ardent blond, even now without a trace of gray—at least in the artist's idealized vision of her. She wears the white lace cap of a genteel French widow and a monumental black robe, lined with crimson sleeves, that looks more like the costume of my sober

Puritan ancestors than the dress of a woman who gave the world its most glamorous wine. This is what surprises me most.

All her wealth and newfound aristocratic privilege are set to the side, and despite the luxury she sold and the luxury she enjoyed, it is the portrait of a bourgeois woman. She holds on her lap just one object, an open book, and she has been caught midgesture, placing a ribboned marker between its folds. Perhaps, as the dapper man who sold me the lithograph in a little antiquarian bookshop on the Right Bank in Paris likes to believe, it is a book on the craft of winemaking. I rather think that it is one of those epic stories she had always loved, a *Don Quixote* or an early novel by Victor Hugo. Perhaps, if she was feeling serious and scholarly, it is *Histoire des Girondins* (1847) by Alphonse Marie Louise de Lamartine—the bourgeois revolutionary who for a brief time ruled over the republican government that once again wrested control of France and forced the abdication of King Louis-Philippe and the end of his so-called July Monarchy in 1848. For a short while, there was a second republic in France, with Charles Louis-Napoléon Bonaparte, nephew of the famous conqueror, its president. But by the time this portrait was made, that republic had ended with a palace coup d'état, and Louis-Napoléon now held the title of Emperor Napoléon III.

Ironically, the revolution of 1848 had working women at its center. In the words of one historian, "Working women had emerged as a locus of tension and debate in the preceding years." Girls were flocking to new low-wage jobs in factories as the Industrial Revolution picked up steam, and popular culture railed against even these advances. "Woman," one journalist wrote, "was not made to manufacture our products or to occupy our factories. She must devote herself to the education of her children, to the cares of her household." Not made to occupy our factories? If Barbe-Nicole read the newspapers, she must have wondered wryly what this journalist would think about a woman running one.

Whatever the book in her portrait is, we can be certain that it wasn't Louis de Chevigné's *Les contes rémois*. But the painting might easily have also coincided with the publication of a third edition of Louis's poems in 1858, a stunt hardly calculated to smooth over the domestic conflict with his straitlaced son-in-law. If Louis's poetic antics were another low point—and another cause of domestic tensions at Boursault—the harvest that year was one of the highlights in a mournful decade: 1858 was one of the rare grand vintages of the nineteenth century and a wine to rival even that "sweetest of assassins," the champagne made in 1811, during the year of the comet.

Since those long-ago days of her marriage to François, Barbe-Nicole had found pleasure in watching the work of the harvest and looking out over the rolling fields of low vines, rising as a verdant haze in the early morning hours. From Boursault she could watch the harvest from her upstairs windows. There were the sounds of low voices in the distance and the creaking wheels of donkey carts, as small baskets of sugary grapes were hauled through the fields to the *vendangeoir*, or crushing room. She could smell wood and fruit and dry summer grasses. This much was the same as it had always been. In the hills to the east, at Bouzy, there was still the old wooden press, the same broad open oak beams and cool stone floors, and she remembered those autumns when she had learned the secrets of her craft.

Now, it was also different. This was no longer a small business but a vast commercial enterprise. In an increasingly industrial age, champagne was (and remains) a manufacturing contradiction—a handcrafted luxury wine, supplied to the world in mass-market quantities. One of the Clicquot-Werlé crushing rooms now had eight presses, capable of processing a thousand barrels of wine at a harvest. In the sprawling cellars beneath the rue du Temple in Reims, where the cuvée was blended, new mechanical cranes lifted up dozens of barrels from the *caves,* and the wine was perfected in vats large enough to supply the international market with hundreds of thousands of bottles of her famous champagne. Yet every grape was picked carefully by hand. In the Champagne today, it is still a time-honored tradition.

Of course, the wine made from this extraordinary harvest would not be making its way to the export market anytime soon. Vintage wines waited years in Barbe-Nicole's cellars. There was no question in her mind that they would someday be something delicious. This had been a rare harvest, and throughout the region, wines made during 1858 would be known as "Consular Seal" champagne—a bit of advertising glamour reminiscent of that earlier vintage made in the year of the comet.

What made this new marketing possible were labels. Barbe-Nicole had been one of the first winemakers to use labels on her bottles in 1814, as a bit of reassurance directed at fussy clients. But it was not a sales device she had yet perfected. She had hardly exploited it at all, in fact. Until the 1850s, no one really had. Then, when the railroads arrived at last in Épernay and Reims, the speed and efficiency of this new modern form of transportation changed commercial culture. Suddenly, the market for business was truly international, and even delicate products like champagne could find their way, without clients having ordered them particularly, to store shelves and suppliers around the globe. What those shoppers needed, of course, was advertising to help them make their decisions along the way. Something that would draw them, in greater numbers than ever before, to life's little luxuries.

The result was an explosion of wine labels. At Clicquot-Werlé headquarters, everyone knew that the best marketing device of all was an obvious one: the Widow's name. Early labels simply read, "Veuve Clicquot Ponsardin, Reims." Édouard and the other partners wisely traded on the basic fact that already, when it came to champagne, she was *the* Widow. And the Widow *was* champagne. By 1860, her label was as familiar around the world as her name. "Many have doubtless noticed the word RHEIMS printed conspicuously on the labels of a bottle of *Clicquot* or *Consular Seal*, or upon any other of the numerous but less noted brands of champagne wine," one loyal wine lover noted. But it was not yet the yellow label known around the world as the trademark of Champagne Veuve Clicquot Ponsardin. That would wait just another few years, for another of the most important changes in the history of this sparkling wine and for the story of champagne's other great widow.

Barbe-Nicole's story was slowly drawing to a close: In 1858, she was eighty-one. She had seen her wines take their place as one of the world's great champagnes, and the business that she had shepherded through the beginnings of the French Industrial Revolution had made her wealthy almost beyond imagining. In just a few decades as her partner, Édouard

Werlé had become "the richest man in Rheims, and one of the richest in France, having, it is said, accumulated a fortune of four or five millions of dollars"—the equivalent of between $8 billion and $10 billion in today's economy. Barbe-Nicole was worth considerably more. At a time when few women commanded powerful commercial empires, she was among the richest in the world.

Always generous to her family, she was also civic-minded. In her last decades, although she never held public office or wielded the sort of influence of the men around her, she was unstinting in her donations to good causes. She gave 80,000 francs—more than $1.6 million in modern figures—to establish a home for poor children, and she intervened to save the ancient Roman triumphal arch in the city of Reims from destruction. As the author Prosper Mérimée reported to a friend, "It is a business of 30 or 40 thousand francs. . . . Madame Clicquot . . . is queen of Reims and . . . has made her highest employee mayor. . . . If she deigns to say a word the arch is saved." Most famously, she donated a fountain to the city of Épernay. The public water supply for the city had run unaccountably dry, and on her nearby property in Vauciennes, tucked in the forestland between Boursault and the celebrated champagne city to the east, she owned an important spring. She gave it as a gift to the townspeople, and knowing that her competitors would also use it to rinse their champagne bottles, she joked, "I have aided you in your work and industry. Don't ever accuse me of being jealous!" The locals responded, with typical dry French wit, by spreading the word that the Widow Clicquot was so generous, she even gave Monsieur Moët a drink. And although it's pleasant to think that Barbe-Nicole was not just a hard-nosed businesswoman but also a kindhearted lady, the truth is that this generosity also helped establish her as a legend and an institution, the grande dame of the Champagne.

Édouard was also now an important man in Reims, and his success is a pointed reminder of the political power that Barbe-Nicole could never wield as a woman—even as a great industrialist. Following in her father's footsteps, Édouard was appointed mayor of Reims, a position that he would hold for nearly two decades. Like most of the French ruling industrial classes, he was "an ardent imperialist," and he enthusiastically supported the reign of Napoléon III. Like Jean-Rémy Moët before him, he became a personal friend of the new emperor, and Louis-Napoléon returned the favor. Before long, Édouard proudly wore the red ribbon of imperial distinction, and like so many of the entrepreneurs at the head of the region's great champagne houses—Barbe-Nicole not least among them—Édouard had arranged splendid political marriages for his children.

But there was one thing the emperor would not do even for his friend Monsieur Werlé—and it was something that jeopardized the future of their company. "The Emperor," everyone said, "will do anything for his favorite wine-merchant but drink his champagne." Louis-Napoléon didn't like it. He had lived in England, and he wanted dry champagne. The problem was, in the words of contemporary observers, that although "the wealthy Veuve Clicquot [had been] by far the shrewdest manipulator of the sparkling products of Aÿ and Bouzy of her day," now "the Clicquot wine is made to suit the Russian taste, which likes a sweet and strong champagne . . . and although doubtless generally . . . good wine, its qualities, whatever they may be, are entirely smothered in the sweetness. Unlike other houses, that of the Widow Clicquot never varies its wine to suit varying tastes. The Clicquot wine is fast losing prestige, and will before too long become obsolete, if not adapted to the more discriminating taste of modern drinkers."

Once again, they were faced with having to adapt in order to survive—although survival now meant something more than a modest middle-class existence. And they delayed. It just didn't seem possible that the British market could matter. It was a tiny part of their annual sales—perhaps a few thousand bottles a year. Barbe-Nicole, in particular, could never forget how even Louis Bohne had failed to sell their wines in London during that disastrous expedition of 1801.

While the directors at Clicquot-Werlé hemmed and hawed and made halfhearted efforts to look beyond the vast Russian market that had made their fortunes, another young woman—only just widowed herself and left with two small children to raise—seized the opportunity. It was an opportunity that Barbe-Nicole's own career in the wine business had inspired. Jeanne Alexandrine Louise Pommery (*née* Mélin) was thirty-nine years old in 1858, and the new widow certainly knew Madame Clicquot.

The Widow Clicquot—one of the nineteenth century's premier brand names—was among the most famous women of her century, even if few of the consumers who celebrated her wines knew much about the woman behind the label. Faced with the same decision that Barbe-Nicole had confronted half a century earlier, after the death of François, and despite a culture that actively discouraged the ambitions of budding young businesswomen, Louise came to very much the same conclusion. She would run the family wine company. Her determination to capture the British market was matched only by Barbe-Nicole's passion for conquering Russia. The decision to sell sparkling wine in mass quantities to the British would make her the second of her century's great "champagne widows" and—more than the shy and domestic Clémentine had ever been—Barbe-Nicole's cultural heir.

Like Barbe-Nicole, Louise Pommery did not inherit either a big business or an established champagne house. In this respect, these two women are unique in the history of champagne. Also like Barbe-Nicole, Louise came to the winemaking business with remarkably little firsthand experience. In fact, her husband, Alexandre, another of Reims's dabbling wool merchants, had become a partner with Narcisse Greno, a traveling wine salesman, in a company that specialized in local still wines only two years earlier. The company offices, tucked in a small street in the shadow of the great cathedral, were not far from the Hôtel Ponsardin or from the cellars of the Widow Clicquot. Alexandre may have been new to the wine trade, but he owned large vineyards in the hills beyond Reims and had invested in this new enterprise substantially—so substantially that when he died, it was left to Louise to run the business or to liquidate.

And run it she did. Louise took control of the Pommery and Greno wine company with enthusiasm. Approaching retirement, Narcisse stepped happily to the sidelines, and with her new *voyageur* and sales director, Henri Vasnier, the brother of an old school chum, Louise turned her attention to mass-market production of the finest champagne. It was a large investment, and becoming a major player in a market then dominated by a handful of companies was a dicey business. But Louise was skilled in the arts of marketing and self-promotion, and she had a decisive air of authority. As one of her contemporaries put it, "She was just as equipped to run a government as a business." Certainly, there could be no doubting her entrepreneurial talents or her sharp intelligence. In just over a decade, she turned the house of Veuve Pommery and Company into an immensely profitable and important business, with annual sales soon exceeding one million bottles of sparkling wine a year—more bottles than were produced even in the busy cellars of the Widow Clicquot.

Madame Pommery's success was founded upon innovation, and one of her commercial discoveries would change how the world drank champagne. Half a century earlier, at the beginning of the Industrial Revolution, Barbe-Nicole had turned her company into one of Europe's most widely celebrated businesses by leading the way toward the mass production of champagne. In the process, she had helped to create a new model for the modern businesswoman. By the 1850s, it was advertising that was poised to transform the champagne industry again, and Louise was prepared to lead the way in mass marketing. She set off for Great Britain to assess the possibilities and came back knowing that there were clients, but they were clients who wanted something entirely different: a crisp, dry champagne. She had her future direction. In 1860, she "invented" champagne in the style we still enjoy today as brut: sparkling wine without the syrupy sweetness that had been the fashion for so long. Today, it is this light style of wine, perfect before dinner as an aperitif or in a summer picnic basket, that signifies the ideal champagne for many of its most devoted admirers.

In just over a decade, Madame Pommery captured an astonishing share of the growing champagne market, and it all happened with the same sudden intensity that Barbe-Nicole had enjoyed earlier in the century. Like Barbe-Nicole, Louise wasted no time building a magnificent château or marrying her daughter into the aristocracy. The Pommery château, however, anticipated today's enthusiasm for wine tourism. In fact, it was during the next twenty years in France that wine tourism, as we know it today, was first developed. Her *domaine* was built not in imitation of the great châteaus of the Loire but in the style of the noble British estates, a strategic nod to the market that had made her fortune. In a sign of the changing times, it was built not out in the country overlooking the vineyards and harvest, but in the heart of commercial Reims, an extravagant and fanciful champagne factory. Even the cellars of this woman with her flair for marketing were named after the great cities to which she shipped—London, Manchester, Leeds, and, before long, dozens of other places around the world. Soon, those cellars were also adorned with great works of art in carved stone. Visitors flocked to the Pommery estates to see the sights and, of course, to buy her champagne.

Louise Pommery—who followed so self-consciously in the footsteps of Barbe-Nicole—was the last generation of women this powerful in champagne. Only the widowed Lily Bollinger in the 1940s would so famously lead one of the great champagne houses in the twentieth century, and she did it brilliantly. But she did not build the company that she inherited. By the 1880s, Champagne Bollinger was already one of the industry giants, with a royal warrant to supply sparkling wine to Great Britain's queen Victoria. The Widow Bollinger was the steward of a family corporation that was already a legacy. Barbe-Nicole and Louise raised theirs to spectacular heights from modest beginnings.

But if Louise was the last woman to build a commercial empire in champagne and one of only two in her century to achieve not just international fame but also dominant roles in the industry they had helped market to the world, there *were* other women winemakers in the nineteenth century. Conditions did not encourage women in business, and astonishingly few middle-class entrepreneurs were able to keep pace with industrialization and the era of big business. But after the fairy-tale success of Barbe-Nicole, there were bourgeois women who tried.

In 1808, a woman named Apolline, the widow of Nicolas-Simon Henriot, founded another small champagne house. It was never more than a modest success. But unusually in the French wine country, seven generations later, her ancestors still run Champagne Henriot as a flourishing boutique winery. After the death of Louis Roederer in 1880, his sister, Madame Jacques Olry, headed for a time one of the region's oldest and most successful champagne houses. Many believe that it was, by the 1860s, "the largest and wealthiest of all" the local companies. Unfortunately, Madame Olry was either not as lucky or perhaps not as talented as Barbe-Nicole and Louise. Despite inheriting one of the jewels of the champagne industry, business declined under her leadership. And in the closing years of the century, Mathilde Emile Laurent-Perrier, after the death of her husband, Eugène, continued to run his family's large champagne business under the name Veuve Laurent-Perrier and Company. She, too, made a fortune selling the brut champagne that Louise Pommery had invented, and she prospered until World War I. But by the 1920s, she was on the brink of bankruptcy, and her successor—the Widow Nonancourt—struggled for decades.

Champagne had always been a difficult business. By 1858, it had become big business as well. Those who succeeded in the second part of this century were by and large wealthy industrialists and the men—and just occasionally the women—who had had the foresight and perseverance to enter the contracting market in wine decades earlier. Now, with the rise of modern advertising and reliable transportation, with industrialization and technologies of mass production from the cellars to the vineyards, the challenge was staying at the forefront of a booming market that was changing almost as quickly as the world around it. Eventually, Édouard and Barbe-Nicole saw that their way of doing business would have to change as well. Within the next decade, the house of the Widow Clicquot would break with tradition and follow where Louise Pommery had led. Its brut champagne, aimed at "the high-class English buyer [who] demands a dry champagne," was advertised with a bright yellow label. Today, this label—the "color of the egg yolks of the famous corn-fed hens of Bresse" and a company trademark—is immediately recognizable to wine lovers everywhere as the mark of the Widow Clicquot.

Chapter 16

The Queen of Reims

S itting motionless and stiff, Barbe-Nicole could see a bit of sky out in the distance beyond the broad windows. Around her were the distant sounds of the household and her staff going about its daily routine and the quiet rustle of her great-granddaughter, Anne, now fourteen, growing restless at her feet.

This would be her last portrait. In the 1860s, Léon Cogniet had returned to create a second likeness of the celebrated Widow Clicquot, dressed in plain gray silk, embroidery in hand, child at her feet. Although surely painted indoors, before some sunny window and surrounded by the cultivated wealth and splendid luxury that were the spoils of her champagne empire, it is the image of a modest domestic lady, sitting on a small terrace, surrounded by rolling hills. The only hint of her great fortune and the business that built it is the wispy view of the Château de Boursault off in the distance.

Barbe-Nicole knew, however, that the picture was more fanciful than real. The painter had an *alfresco* vision, but she was too old to sit for hours outdoors while he dawdled with his brushes. Indeed, she was too old to sit in such a prim fashion for long at all. And however much this man might like to imagine her as the retiring grandmama, however much she might sometimes try to act the part, her whole heart had been in business. It still was. A great deal had changed these last fifty-odd years since she had said good-bye to François and embarked on her own adventure. But her devotion to the business had never faltered. She had made Édouard and herself millionaires many times over. She had seen France transformed into an industrial nation, now crossed by railroad lines and manufacturing centers. Above all, she had seen a lot of life and more than her fair share of early death—her husband, a brother, a father, even two of her great-grandchildren in the space of a few years. Yet she still pored over her account books, still came alive again when Édouard told her of his plans for the company and its future. He told her, too, about his political ambitions and his campaign that year for a seat in the legislature of his friend Louis-Napoléon. How like her father he was.

Now an old woman who had lived decades beyond the age when illness or accident claimed most of her peers, Barbe-Nicole knew her time would not be long. Those around her were passing away steadily, and sometimes it was difficult even to imagine who would carry on the family tradition. Her sister, Clémentine, soldiered on, and sometimes the two sisters sat together and remembered all the changes they had witnessed and all that they had shared in eight decades of living. But already, Barbe-Nicole saw that the health of her daughter, Clémentine, the Countess of Chevigné, was failing. Within the year, she was dead. By 1863, having buried her only child, Barbe-Nicole turned her thoughts to Anne—a pretty brown-haired adolescent on the brink of womanhood and, before long, inevitably, marriage. Anne and her older cousins brought laughter to the formal rooms of Boursault, and now that the young girl was old enough to take part in adult society, there were once again parties and elegant houseguests at Boursault. Anne, after all, was the sole heir to one of France's greatest fortunes, and there was unrestrained curiosity to see "the little Mortemart."

People also came from around the world to see the Widow Clicquot. According to the man who wrote her biography in 1865, "Strangers and visitors were welcomed with an open hospitality, with polite grace and a worldly spirit. . . . All the world was met by the hosts without reserve." With the railways, more friends from Paris showed up for more parties. Then there were curious tourists as well. Boursault offered splendid views of the picturesque scenery of the wine country, and the railroad ran just at the foot of the stone outcrop on which the castle was perched. Nothing was easier than making a pilgrimage to see the Widow Clicquot, and for vacationers and wine lovers, "the Château de Boursault was a must see on their list." It really was the world at her table. Or so it must have seemed.

Writers and artists, princes and politicians, all found their way to the hilltop castle, where they were entertained splendidly. Barbe-Nicole laughingly told them that she was a tyrant in just one thing: They could drink only champagne. The autocratic Louis XIV had announced, *"L'état, c'est moi"*—"I am the state." She quipped, in her sternest manner, *"Le vin, c'est moi."* She found in her midst few revolutionaries. As the writer Charles Monselet remembered, visiting her salons, it was easy to believe that the Widow Clicquot was the exclusive supplier to "every prince, czar, archduke, Roman cardinal, nabob, or lord mayor" in the world. During her pleasant reign, they had all vowed never to drink anything other than her champagne.

And although she was old, Barbe-Nicole was still vitally alive. Victor Fiévet described her as having "delicate features and full of energy . . . underneath the flaws of age and the weakening of the body, her spirit remained mistress and queen. . . . The lively intelligence and the prodigious activity of Madame Clicquot never let her rest. In the calm hours of the evening, if she took up a needle and did some embroidery or sewing, her active and penetrating eye was never fixed on her work; the head moved around, the thoughts wandered, and the spirit was somewhere else."

Barbe-Nicole recognized some of this same ungovernable spirit in Anne. There had been a reason Barbe-Nicole never remarried, and it was that she could never bear to have anyone cosset and restrain her. She had wanted a life in the world. She could imagine the same for her great-granddaughter. Now of a marriageable age, Anne was stubbornly refusing her suitors. Marriage, she thought, didn't suit her, and there was a trail of broken hearts and frustrated aristocratic mothers in her wake. Half the dukes of France and the king of Serbia were vying for her hand. Anne was stonewalling them all. Barbe-Nicole looked on, if not quite with approval, at least with a hearty dose of admiration.

The archival record of Barbe-Nicole's life rests in a small stone building just at the entrance to the Champagne Veuve Clicquot Ponsardin company offices in Reims. Inside, an entire room is filled with the details of the business she ran and the vineyards she purchased. Every shipment of bottles, every wage paid, every order filled, is recorded for posterity, and sometimes, in the midst of all this record keeping, Barbe-Nicole's own voice shines through. Mostly, however, the archivists confess that it does not. So her rare personal letters are that much more important, and in the last years of her life, she wrote one to Anne that speaks more clearly than any other document to the woman Barbe-Nicole was and to how she wished to be remembered. It is her own account of her life, stripped to its essence.

"My dear," she writes to her last surviving great-grandchild,

> I am going to tell you a secret. . . . You more than anyone re-semble me, you who have such audacity. It is a precious quality that has been very useful to me in the course of my long life . . . to dare things before others. . . . I am called today the Grand Lady of Champagne! Look around you, this château, these unfaltering hills, I can be bolder than you realize. The world is in perpetual motion, and we must invent the things of tomorrow. One must go before others, be determined and exacting, and let your intelligence direct your life. Act with audacity. Perhaps you too will be famous . . . !!

This is the heart of Barbe-Nicole's story. A woman who lived with audacity and intelligence, who could look forward to the future and grasp the reins of her own destiny at a moment in her life when the natural thing to do would have been to retreat into grief and misery and a paralysis of inaction. Anne did go on to be immensely fashionable, if perhaps not quite as famous as her legendary great-grandmother. By 1867, she found herself unexpectedly in love, after a frightening accident, with one of her hunting companions, Emmanuel de Crussol. That summer she married Emmanuel, who was also the Duke of Uzès and head of the most hon-ored noble family in all of France. It was a magnificent, even fairy-tale, event, with liveried valets in powdered wigs and golden carriages rolling through the streets.

But Barbe-Nicole was not there to see any of it. In the last days of July, just a year before, in 1866, when the gardens at Boursault were sending forth their intoxicating blooms and the grapes were beginning to grow heavy on the vines that clung to the hillside below the château, the Widow Clicquot breathed her last. She was eighty-nine years old, and she almost alone of her family did not bear an aristocratic title. But she was remembered in death, regardless, as the uncrowned queen of Reims.

Barbe-Nicole had flourished during the long decades of the nineteenth century—as a woman and as an entrepreneur—by embracing the future. Now, that future was left for others to negotiate. Almost immediately, it would be down to her great-granddaughter, Anne, and to her old friend Édouard. Barbe-Nicole also did not live to see the death of her sister, Clémentine, in 1867, and she could not have known that before the end of the next decade, nearly the entire family would be gone.

After her death, Louis, the widowed Count de Chevigné, at last came into the fortune that his friend had so confidently predicted would be his, before long, back in 1817. Now, he did inherit Barbe-Nicole's share of the company assets. There were family vineyards, commercial offices, and the real estate that her immense wealth had collected, along with the now quiet Hôtel Ponsardin. The decision to cut Louis and Clémentine out of the management of the business had been made years earlier. The company was Édouard's to run. What began as a modest family business had been transformed, carefully and deliberately, into a modern commercial enterprise. In truth, Louis was not a young man any longer, either, and so late in life would not have had the skills or, perhaps, the energy to take control of such a large and complex business. The count, after all, was seventy-four the summer that Anne was married.

Ironically, the last years of Louis's life would not be spent in peaceful retirement, amid his poems and beloved gardens. The Count de Chevigné had entered the world in the midst of one revolution, and political events would come to his doorstep again in the 1870s. He was one of only a small group of people who could truthfully say that they had witnessed France's struggle to become a modern republic on four occasions—in the

Revolution of 1793 that had cost him much of his family, in the three glorious days of the July rebellion in 1830, in the summer uprising of 1848, as a middle-aged man of leisure, and now, in the autumn of 1870, when Napoléon III, along with a hundred thousand of his men, was captured not far from the ancient province of the Champagne in the Battle of Sedan. It would mark the end of the second Bonaparte empire and the beginning of the so-called Third Republic in France. It would also come close to costing the Count de Chevigné his life.

The events of 1870 and 1871 came to be known in history as the Franco-Prussian War, and the conflict had been a long time brewing. Ever since the coup d'état of 1851, Napoléon III had been politically besieged from all sides. In France, national politics were torn between agitators who wanted more democratic rights and imperialists who wanted greater prestige for France on the world stage—and new territories. Abroad, there were regimes that looked forward to the restoration of the Bourbon dynasty and the end of the upstart Bonaparte rule. In the end, Napoléon had tried to silence his critics through military power, but it was a gamble he had lost. The emperor retreated to a comfortable exile in Great Britain. The battle for political leadership continued, however, and, in a prelude to the tensions of the World War I, the Prussians and Germans occupied much of central and eastern France—the Champagne included. Édouard Werlé, as the mayor of Reims, was imprisoned. Louis was about to face something worse. The château at Boursault was perched on a steep hill, with a sweeping prospect of the surrounding countryside, and an important railway ran just below the outcrop in a low valley. That November, after a deadly act of sabotage on the tracks just beyond his doorstep, Louis found the military police at his door demanding nearly $10 million in damages. If he did not pay, they would arrest him. And they would see to it that Boursault and all that he loved was destroyed.

At that moment, Louis must have thought back to his mother's courage in the face of certain death in a filthy prison. There was all that his sister Marie-Pélagie and his uncle had endured. There were his own years of embarrassing dependence, and perhaps he remembered Barbe-Nicole, too. In the face of all her challenges, she had remained unflinching. "I am an old man," he told their commander, Count Blücher, "and my life is not worth that sum." Whatever his human weakness—his airs, his crudity, his dissipation, the gambling and self-indulgence—Louis had also proved himself on many occasions to be a man of honor and bravery. Some might even say he showed foolhardy courage, because he was, of course, promptly arrested. After two weeks, when he still refused to meet the Prussian demands, he was told that he would be executed. There was no escaping the irony: He had survived one revolution as an infant only to be murdered in another as an old man. When they came for him with the news, he was unmovable. He asked only for time to write a farewell letter to his granddaughter, Anne. It was a letter she kept always, full of dignity and heroism. Unknowingly, Louis's courage had called the Prussian's bluff. Impressed with the stoic resolve of the aging count, the commander set him free. Louis wisely disappeared into exile to wait out the war.

It was the last dramatic event of Louis's life. In fact, except for Anne, it was the last dramatic event in the lives of anyone in the Chevigné-Mortemart family. In 1873, his son-in-law, the Count of Mortemart, passed away in his early sixties. Just three years later, the Count of Chevigné was also dead at eighty-three. He passed away quietly that autumn in the Hôtel Ponsardin. In his will, perhaps remembering that dark decade of the 1850s and how precious Anne's life had been to them all, he wrote his last good-bye to the young woman. "I thank my granddaughter," he wrote, "for the joy that she brought to the family." Now, only Marie-Clémentine and Anne remained of the family that Barbe-Nicole had shepherded for decades. The following year, with the death of Marie at just fifty-five, it was only Anne.

Like her great-grandmother, the countess was destined to be a widow as a young woman. Emmanuel, the Duke of Uzès, died in 1878, leaving her with four small children and a vast inheritance—an inheritance that included all her great-grandmother's property. Unlike Barbe-Nicole, however, Anne would make her mark in a different way, as a talented and sophisticated aristocrat, with no inclination to rule a champagne empire. She certainly had no inclination to play the part of a bourgeois capitalist. Leaving the care of her stake in the company to agents, the Duchess of Uzès retired to country estates in the south of France and Paris. Boursault fell into disrepair, and the Hôtel Ponsardin was sold to the city of Reims.

The Clicquot family vineyards and the properties that Barbe-Nicole had slowly collected passed into the hands of Édouard, and it would be Édouard and his descendants—his son Alfred and the sons and sons-in-law who came after him—to guide the wines of the Widow Clicquot into the twentieth century, through the phylloxera outbreak in the French wine country and the two world wars that made the region again a battlefield, through the Russian Revolution and the collapse of the market that had made their fortunes. For more than 130 years, no woman would lead the champagne house that Barbe-Nicole had built from its origins as a family business to one of the world's great commercial legends. But even as she placed her company in the hands of the men with whom she surrounded herself, Barbe-Nicole—perhaps unwittingly—opened the road for new generations of women in the marketplace.

Afterword

Today in the *Oxford English Dictionary*, one of the definitions of the word *widow* is still champagne. Yet the short entry also tells a larger story than it intends. The entry reads, "the widow: champagne. From 'Veuve Clicquot,' the name of a firm of wine merchants." Today, for some, perhaps it *is* just the name of a company. In the official history of the English language—in this linguistic testament to her celebrity and accomplishments—Barbe-Nicole Clicquot Ponsardin is nowhere to be found. But when parched young lords in the gambling dens of nineteenth-century London called for a bottle of the Widow, she was still a woman. By the end of the century, of course, that had changed. The story of the Widow has become the story of a company and not the story of the businesswoman whose name it bears. But it's an astonishing thing. Barbe-Nicole lived a life that was, by any standards, quite amazing. Yet my search for the richness and intensity of that life and for the woman behind the label has been spent, more often than I care to admit, staring blindly at street corners and winding country lanes. The other part has been spent under the flicker of fluorescent lights in libraries.

The work in those libraries was not of the straightforward kind. Her personal letters, it would seem, did not survive. The company archives in Reims, though filled with treasures for economists and historians of business, offered up few secrets of the kind I was searching for. Perusal of the early biographies was the matter of an afternoon, although I had to travel five thousand miles to find a single copy of the earliest one—a short account of Barbe-Nicole's life, published in 1865 by a local historian. One of Édouard Werlé's distinguished descendants and the wife of the company president wrote the second in the 1950s, a pamphlet of fifty-three pages. The only biographical sketch in print today is part of a coffee table book on the history of the company, entitled simply *Veuve Clicquot: La grande dame de la Champagne.* I am indebted to them all, of course.

It is a surprisingly thin biographical record, considering Barbe-Nicole's celebrity and accomplishments, and writing this book has been an exercise in the oblique. I have found myself becoming a scavenger of uncollected details about her life and the world in which she lived. I said at the outset that what I wanted to find, more than anything else, was the experience of the woman whose story was printed on a tiny bit of card stock, tucked inside a box of vintage champagne. I wanted to discover not just what she did and when she lived, but how she was able to imagine for herself a different future and how she was able to negotiate those familiar crossroads of grief, despair, and opportunity. It sometimes took considerable imagination. The facts in this story are true—as true as history can make them. I don't mean that. But telling the story of another woman's life, I have learned, is as much a matter of sympathy as scholarship.

The dilemma for any curious historian is a simple one: Without this sympathy, there is silence. Much of Barbe-Nicole's things have been carefully preserved—her homes, her furniture, her property, and, of course, her business. There is even a record of the books in the Clicquot family library, which were sold at an auction in Paris in 1843, just as construction was beginning on her château at Boursault. But what happened to the record of her innermost thoughts and midnight worries over nearly ninety years of living? In the early morning hours, before the streets of Reims were filled with voices and the sounds of bustling industry, it is easy to imagine Barbe-Nicole bending over a small diary. Here, the daily appointments and to-do lists of a busy entrepreneur gave way to private reflection. Loneliness and resolve and ambition jostled for their place alongside household accounts and dress measurements; there were dinner party menus and shopping lists alongside the titles of books she had enjoyed, books she hoped to read, addresses for letters she would send. To her cousin in Paris, she wrote more news, chatty accounts of family life and new babies. There were worries over wedding gowns, anniversary gifts, and, later, over sickness and domestic tensions.

And when she died, who would have thought to save a little book of notes and private musings? By the 1850s, what could be the value of long outdated family news, shared in letters between two old women? There was nothing literary about them, and Barbe-Nicole had no pretensions. Perhaps for a time after her death, they found their way to a dusty box in an unused dresser drawer. Somebody once might have meant to save them. Then the house was sold or the war came. Finally, the papers ended up lining a trunk or lighting a fire. The letters and diaries of remarkably few women ever found their way into the archives, and Barbe-Nicole's were not among them.

But if our books and biographies tell only the personal stories that are richly documented in the archives, it is a strange history that emerges. People with interesting lives and inspiring characters have not always been kings and queens and famous poets. They have not always burned the midnight candle recording their intimate thoughts for posterity. Sometimes they were just too busy or too tired. Perhaps nowhere is this more likely than in the history of women in business. Barbe-Nicole—as exceptional as she was as a person—was not really an exception; she was one of hundreds and perhaps thousands of middle-class female entrepreneurs who found in the commercial world an expression of their talents and dreams. She was far more talented and successful than almost any one of them, of course. In that sense she was unique, and her story is singularly inspiring. But she was not alone.

As one account of women's history written in the late 1860s reminds us, "In Paris, and indeed on the continent of Europe generally, some of the largest commercial houses have women at their head. The name of the Veuve Clicquot, one of the largest manufacturers of champagne, will occur to many readers." But there was also the now unremembered Mrs. Hart, who ran a printing empire. Angela Burdett-Coutts, heiress to one of the world's great fortunes, was at the head of England's most exclusive bank. Great Britain's king Edward VII remembered Burdett-Coutts as "after my mother the most remarkable woman in the country." His mother was none other than Queen Victoria. And, of course, there was the celebrated Madame Louise Pommery, whose biography remains to be written.

In fact, by the end of the century that she helped to define, Barbe-Nicole was simply at the pinnacle and forefront of a fledgling cultural movement in late-nineteenth-century Europe and America: the slow and quiet rise of the modern businesswoman. The first fifty years of the Industrial Revolution had been unkind to women entrepreneurs, and it would take them much of the twentieth century to climb the corporate ladder in large numbers. But by the closing decades of the belle époque, women with determination, intelligence, and a bit of luck were finding their first footholds on that ladder, and they worked in the shadows of the business world for the next century. In the Baker Library at the Harvard Business School, there are records of hundreds of American women who made their way in the world of business. "Despite . . . stereotypes," the curator reminds us, "many women in the eighteenth and nineteenth centuries participated in commerce, both as merchants and as manufacturers." They ran plantations in the South and textile mills in the North. Most often, of course, they prospered in businesses with a feminine touch—fashion houses and dressmaking shops, family remedies and flower gardens. A rare few, like catalog seed merchant Carrie Lippincott or medicinal purveyor Lydia Pinkham, made their fortunes during the 1880s and 1890s. They were unusually adventurous women who defied contemporary gender roles. And like their European counterparts, they often remained invisible; no eager historian ever thought to document the complexity of their lives.

Barbe-Nicole's distinction is to have been the first celebrity businesswoman among them. Some say, in fact, that she is the first woman in history to run an international commercial empire at all. Certainly, she was the first woman—and to this day, one of only a few—to lead one of the world's great champagne houses. Entering the commercial world just as the first rumblings of the Industrial Revolution were reshaping life in nineteenth-century France, she brought the values of the family businesswoman to the age of manufacturing. Barbe-Nicole was not just an extraordinary woman, she was an extraordinary entrepreneur.

In fact, in this era of the great industrialists, Barbe-Nicole was one of the robber barons. By the 1870s, champagne was on its way to becoming the legal monopoly that it remains today, controlled largely by this new breed of wine aristocrat. Barbe-Nicole not only was among them, she had helped to create the phenomenon—one that would make it all but impossible in the twentieth century for enterprising young upstarts like herself to make new fortunes in champagne. By limiting where the grapes could be grown and how they could be harvested, by controlling who could use the word and at what price, the great houses at the end of the nineteenth century—and the men who increasingly ran them—had established an elegant and exclusive cartel. As early as 1880, British wine historian Charles Tovey was protesting against it. "Of all monopolies existing," he wrote, "no single one has led to so much mischief as that of certain houses in champagne manufacture which are the fortunate possessors of reputed brands. It is really and truly the monopoly of these brands which enables the proprietors to add year by year to their already largely accumulated gains. . . . Fortunes, the accumulation of enormous profits, are evidenced by the palatial residences, as well as large possessions, belonging to the magnates of Rheims and Épernay. Nor is their immense wealth their only advantage; they are the plutocracy—the wine aristocrats . . . heroes, celebrated in song, and immortalised in history. If my readers are sceptical, let them refer to the published life of Mons[ieur] J. R. Moët, and his successors, or to that of Madame Clicquot." Barbe-Nicole was not, of course, immortalized in history at all—only the company that she created and the name she made famous survived beyond the end of the nineteenth century. I hope that here, at least, she has been the heroine of her own story.

Acknowledgments

Writing this book has been a labor of love, and I want to thank all of the many friends who joined me so enthusiastically in the extensive "primary" research, with a bottle of the Widow in hand. But in the more sober moments, you also offered much more than good company. I would like to thank Abby Laukka, Jon Hardy, and Erica Mazzeo for coming so far to share the adventure and Bill Hare for his fearless charm, which opened so many doors in France. Jeremy and Paula Lowe were, as always, stalwart supporters of improbable schemes, and Jeffery McLain and Jérémie Fant offered wine wisdom, hearty laughs, and expert tasting adventures. My love to J. J. Wilson for the midmorning walks that kept me writing and to my parents, who in listening to early drafts helped to spin a good yarn, stitch by stitch. Ianthe Brautigan, Anna-Lisa Cox, Adrian Blevins, and Noelle Oxenhandler shared their far greater talents with reckless generosity, and the far-flung Cockneys—as in all things—worked their merry magic at crucial moments. Stacey Glick and Genoveva Llosa made it all possible, and a heartfelt thanks to my fabulous editors at HarperCollins, Toni Sciarra and Matt Inman. And, then, there aren't enough words to properly thank either Thaine Stearns or Noelle Baker and Roberta Maguire: You were the only reasons to drink champagne in that last winter of discontent, and this book has always been for you.

Without the help of many librarians, archivists, and winemakers, this book never could have been written, and I am particularly grateful to the staff at the Sonoma County Wine Library Collection in Healdsburg, the Bibliothèque Carnegie in Reims, the Médiathèque d'Épernay, the Napa Valley Wine Library Collection in Saint Helena, the University of Cambridge Library, the University of Edinburgh Library, the British Library, the Colby College Library, Eileen Crane of Napa's Domaine Carneros, Philippe Bienvenue of Champagne Cattier, the kind staff in the resource library at Champagne Moët et Chandon and in the tasting rooms at Champagne Pommery, and, above all, to the generous people in the Historical Resources Department at Champagne Veuve Clicquot Ponsardin, especially Fabienne Huttaux and Isabelle Pierre.

Notes

PROLOGUE

xiii *This is the story of French champagne*: Champagne is, of course, both a sparkling wine and a region in France. To distinguish between the two, *champagne* refers to the wine and *Champagne* to the historical province. The ancient provinces of France were converted to modern départements in 1790, so that the Champagne now includes the departments of the Ardennes, Aube, Marne, and Haut-Marne, as well as parts of the Aisne, Meuse, Seine-sur-Marne, and Yonne.

xvi *lobster salad and champagne*: George Gordon, Lord Byron, *Byron's Letters and Journals*, ed. Leslie A. Marchand, 10 vols. (Cambridge: Harvard University Press, 1974), vol. 2; letter of September 25, 1812: "A woman should never be seen eating or drinking, unless it be lobster salad and Champagne, the only true feminine & becoming viands."

xvi *Madame de Pompadour*: "Champagne is the only wine that leaves a woman beautiful after drinking it," quoted in Don and Petie Kladstrup, *Champagne: How the World's Most Glamorous Wine Triumphed over War and Hard Times* (New York: William Morrow, 2005), p. 50.

xvi *Madame Cécile Bonnefond*: According to wine expert Tom Stevenson, in an article on Bonnefond's assuming the directorship, "It is the first time that any LVMH house—or indeed any *grande marque*—has hired a woman CEO." *Harper's*, December 20, 2000, available at www.

harpers.co.uk. Today, Champagne Veuve Clicquot is owned by the luxury conglomerate LVMH (Moët Hennessy Louis Vuitton, acquired 1987), which also owns Champagne Moët et Chandon.

xvii   *popular song as "Champagne Charlie"*: The history of the dance-hall tune "Champagne Charlie" is a curious bit of wine marketing. The song was first made famous in the late 1860s by singer George Leybourne, who had been commissioned by the firm of Moët and Chandon to create a popular jingle for their brand. Soon, Leybourne's competitor Alfred Vance had worked out a deal with the Widow Clicquot to write a dueling tune in her honor. The result was a runaway stage battle that helped to spread the popularity of champagne in Great Britain at the end of the decade. However, many believe that Charles Camille Heidsieck was the original model for the "Champagne Charlie" phenomenon. During his sales tours of the United States in the 1850s, it was a popular nickname for the gregarious wine merchant, who used the celebrity to generate massive sales and brand recognition. For many years, Heidsieck also marketed vintage champagne known as "Champagne Charlie," and the song is most closely associated with the firm in the cultural imagination. The best account of the history is available on the official website of the Union des Maisons de Champagne, www.maisons-champagne.com; see also Marcel and Patrick Heidsieck, *Vie de Charles Heidsieck* (Reims: Société Charles Heidsieck, 1962); and Eric Glatre and Jaqueline Roubinet, *Charles Heidsieck: Un pionnier et un homme d'honneur* (Paris: Stock, 1995).

xvii   *"noted drinker of* fizz": "The name of a song that appeared in 1868. . . . The original *Charley* is said to have been a wine-merchant, who was in the habit of making presents of bottles of *champagne* to all his friends." *Oxford English Dictionary*, "Champagne Charlie."

xvii   *less than 85,000 total acres of vines*: Gérard Liger-Belair, *Uncorked: The Science of Champagne* (Princeton, NJ: Princeton University Press, 2004), p. 19. Traditionally limited to 34,000 hectares (83,980 acres), approval for the addition of forty new *communes* to the appellation is pending. See Henry Samuel, "Champagne Producers Have Nominated 40 Villages in Northeastern France That May Be Allowed to Produce Sparkling Wine," *Daily Telegraph*, October 15, 2007, www.telegraph. co.uk/news/main.jhtml?xml=/news/2007/20/13/wchampagne113.xml.

xviii   *registered by the estates of Moët and Chandon*: The company purchased the vineyards at Hautvillers in 1794 but began commercial
production of the Dom Pérignon vintage only in the 1930s; company
promotional materials.

xviii   *All that changed in the first decades of the nineteenth century*: Kladstrup,
for example, reports that at the beginning of the nineteenth century,
there were ten firms and by the 1860s three hundred; Kladstrup, p. 79.

xviii   *even before the Jazz Age*: Statistics from Thomas Brennan,
Burgundy to Champagne: The Wine Trade in Early Modern France (Baltimore:
Johns Hopkins University Press, 1997), p. 272.

xix   *the era when feminism was born*: Although the word *feminism* in
English dates to the 1890s (*OED*), "It is generally held that the first
expression of modern feminism is Mary Wollstonecraft's *Vindication of
the Rights of Women*, published in 1792"; Lea Campos Boralevi, *Bentham
and the Oppressed* (New York: Walter de Gruyter, 1984), p. 23. In France,
similar ideas found expression in the work of Olympe de Gouges,
whose *Declaration of the Rights of Woman and the Female Citizen* was published in 1791.

xxi   *"no business in the world [has] been as much influenced by the female
sex"*: Anthony Rhodes, *Prince of Grapes* (London: Weidenfeld & Nicholson, 1975), p. 8, quoted in Ann B. Matasar, *Women of Wine: The Rise
of Women in the Global Wine Industry* (Berkeley: University of California
Press, 2006), pp. 25–26.

CHAPTER ONE: CHILD OF THE REVOLUTION, CHILD OF THE CHAMPAGNE

1   *angry mobs calling for liberty and equality*: The familiar slogan
Liberté, égalité, et fraternité ("Liberty, equality, and fraternity") was advo-
cated by Maximilien Robespierre during the Revolution of the 1790s,
but it became popularized only during the rebellion of 1848 in France;
see Tristram Hunt, "A National Motto?: That's the Last Thing Britain
Needs," *The Guardian*, October 18, 2007, p. 32.

1   *town of perhaps thirty thousand inhabitants*: Augustin Marie de
Paul de Saint-Marceaux, *Notes et documents pour servir à l'histoire de la ville
de Reims pendant les quinze années de 1830 à 1845* (Reims: Brissart-Binet,

1853), p. 44. Saint-Marceaux, the mayor of Reims from 1832 to 1837 and 1839 to 1845, estimates twenty-seven thousand to thirty thousand inhabitants in 1793. All translations from French sources, unless otherwise noted, are by the author. In translating personal correspondence, particularly, the emphasis has been on retaining the spirit and tone of the original expression rather than on literal transcription.

2   *stories from Paris of nuns being raped and the rich being murdered*: See, for example, Mita Choudhury, *Convents and Nuns in Eighteenth-Century French Politics and Culture* (Ithaca, NY: Cornell University Press, 2004). Hippolyte Taine offered an early indictment of revolutionary excesses in his ten-volume study *Origines de la France contemporaine,* first published in the 1870s.

2   *educated with the daughters of feudal lords and princes*: A detail repeated in various accounts of Barbe-Nicole's early life; the most complete commentary is Michel Etienne, *Veuve Clicquot Ponsardin, aux origines d'un grand vin de Champagne* (Paris: Economica, 1994), p. 22. For more on the abbey of Saint-Pierre-les-Dames, see *Rheims and Battles for Its Possession* (Paris: Michelin, 1919), pp. 98–99.

3   *first steps in the coarse wooden shoes*: Details repeated in Jean, Princesse de Carmaran-Chimay, *Madame Veuve Clicquot Ponsardin: Her Life and Times* (Reims: Debar, 1956), p. 2; also Patrick de Gmeline, *La Duchesse d'Uzès* (Paris: Librairie Académique Perrin, 1986), p. 15.

3   *Phrygian caps . . . military marches*: See, for example, the anonymous *A Residence in France, During the Years 1792, 1793, 1794, and 1795; Described in a Series of Letters from an English Lady,* ed. John Gifford (London: T. N. Longman, 1797).

4   *central legend of Barbe-Nicole's childhood*: In most detail, Chimay, p. 2. Frédérique Crestin-Billet claims that it was Barbe-Nicole's sister; Crestin-Billet, *Veuve Clicquot: La grande dame de la Champagne* (Paris: Editions Glénat, 1992), p. 15.

5   *the crops had failed throughout France*: This and other details of the weather during that year from Brian Fagan, *The Little Ice Age: How Climate Made History* (New York: Basic Books, 2000), p. 155.

5   *might easily pay more than 40 percent in taxes*: Roderick Phillips, *A Short History of Wine* (New York: HarperCollins, 2000), p. 21; Kladstrup,

p. 59. See also François Furet, *Revolutionary France 1770–1880* (Oxford: Blackwells, 2000); and Brennan. Taxes on the rural commoners in prerevolutionary France were crushing and included a 10 percent tithe to the church, the 5 percent *vingtième* income tax, sales taxes, occupancy taxes, local taxes, *banalités* imposed for the use of public facilities such as mills, ovens, and winepresses, and even a tax paid in forced labor known as the *corvée*.

6   *Nicolas was "the town's largest employer of textile workers"*: Lynn Hunt, "Local Elites and the End of the Old Regime: Troyes and Reims, 1750–1789," *French Historical Studies* 9, no. 3 (Spring 1976): 379–399, 385.

6   *the equivalent of perhaps $800,000 a year*: Crestin-Billet offers a figure of 40,000 French francs, p. 11. On the complexity of comparing historical values to modern currency, see the discussion on pp. 72–73.

6   *coronation of King Louis XVI*: Victor Fiévet, *Madame Veuve Clic-quot*, née *Ponsardin* (Paris: E. Dentu, 1865), p. 21; see also Elise Whitlock Rose, *Cathedrals and Cloisters of the Isle de France: Including Bourges, Troyes, Reims, and Rouen* (New York: G. P. Putnam's Sons, 1910).

6   *Today, the imposing structure houses . . . the local Chamber of Commerce*: 10, rue Cérès; Jacques-Louis Delpal, *Merveilles de Champagne* (Paris: Éditions de La Martinière, 1993), p. 33.

7   *his eldest daughter who captured a special place in his heart*: Patrick de Gmeline writes: "She was always his favorite," p. 14.

8   *The fabled vineyards at Hautvillers were among those confiscated and returned to the people*: Brennan, p. 11.

9–10   *Nicolas is said to have planted one of these trees himself*: Gmeline, p. 14.

10   *with a simple word on their foreheads: LIBERTY*: Details of the Revolution in Reims and the festivals celebrating it from the anonymous pamphlet *Description de la fête patriotique: Célébrée à Rethel le 14 Juillet 1790, & jours suivants* (Reims: Jeunehomme, Imprimeurs du Rois, 1790); Gustave Laurent, *Reims et la region rémoise a la veille de la Révolution* (Reims: Imprimerie Matot-Braine, 1930); Arthur Barbat de Bignicourt, *Les massacres à Reims en 1792 après des documents authentiques* (n.p.: V. Geoffrey, 1872); and the anonymous *A Residence in France, During the Years 1792, 1793, 1794, and 1795*, electronic edition, without pagination, available at www.gutenberg.org/etext/11995.

The author of *A Residence in France* describes how in November 1793, "Mademoiselle Maillard of the Grand Opera, in white robe and blue cap, represented the goddess of Reason. On men's shoulders she was carried from the church to the convention." She also adds, "In many places, valuable paintings and statues were burnt or disfigured"; "The greater part of the attendants looked on in silent terror and astonishment; whilst others, intoxicated, or probably paid to act this scandalous farce, danced round the flames with an appearance of frantic and savage mirth"; and nuns in hospitals who "were accused of bestowing a more tender solicitude on their aristocratic patients than on the wounded volunteers and republicans; and, upon these curious charges, they have been heaped into carts, without a single necessary, almost without covering, sent from one department to another, and distributed in different prisons, where they are perishing with cold, sickness, and want!"

CHAPTER TWO: WEDDING VOWS AND FAMILY SECRETS

11 *invented in the wake of the French Revolution*: Dror Wahrman, *The Making of the Modern Self: Identity and Culture in Eighteenth-Century England* (New Haven, CT: Yale University Press, 2004).

12 *embraced fashion, which also became democratic*: Madeleine Delpierre, *Dress in France in the Eighteenth Century*, trans. Caroline Beamish (New Haven, CT: Yale University Press, 1997), pp. 150–151. Also Caroline Weber, *Queen of Fashion: What Marie Antoinette Wore to the Revolution* (New York: Henry Holt & Co., 2006).

12 *wearing blood-red ribbons around their necks*: Mary Sophia Hely-Hutchinson, *Fashion in Paris: The Various Phases of Feminine Taste and Aesthetics from the Revolution to the End of the 19th Century* (London: W. Heinemann, 1901); Aileen Ribiero, *Fashion in the French Revolution* (New York: Holmes & Meier, 1988).

12 *"coiffure of white tulle and celestial blue ribbons"*: Manuscript, *Memoirs of Madame Maldan*, quoted in Crestin-Billet, p. 15.

13 *bureaucrat conceded was a poetic "ardent" blond*: Etienne, p. 22.

13 *white dresses were more than just a popular—and populist—fashion*: See

Ribiero; on the national dress code and the French Revolution, see James H. Johnson, "Versailles, Meet Les Halles: Masks, Carnival, and the French Revolution," *Representations* 73 (Winter 2001): 89–116.

14   *Madame Tallien*: Thérésa, *née* Cabarrús (1773–1835), Parisian socialite during the Revolution and political opponent of Maximilien Robespierre (1758–1794), the man credited with leading the deadly purges during the Terror (1794); Madame Tallien later married into the noble Riquet family of Chimay (Belgium), becoming the Princess de Caraman-Chimay in 1805. Louis de Chevigné encountered her son during exile in Chimay during the Franco-Prussian War (p. 231). See Arsène Houssaye, *Notre-Dame de Thermidor: Histoire de Madame Tallien* (Paris: H. Plon, 1866).

14   *the Catholic rites were criminal*: The state authority of the Catholic Church in France is widely considered by historians as one of the causes of the Revolution, and by 1793 practice of the religion was formally banned, soon to be replaced, first, by the Cult of Reason and, later, by the Cult of the Supreme Being. Antireligious sentiment was at its height during 1794, although clergy were particular targets of revolutionary violence throughout the period. These strictures were relaxed during 1795, after the execution of Robespierre, but Catholicism remained formally outlawed and legally punishable until 1801. See Claude Geffré and Jean-Pierre Jossua, *1789: The French Revolution and the Church* (Edinburgh: T. and T. Clark, 1989); and Nigel Aston, *The End of an Élite: The French Bishops and the Coming of the Revolution, 1786–1790* (Clarendon: Oxford University Press, 1992).

14   *in a damp cellar*: Chimay, p. 3; Gmeline, p. 15.

15   *bridal bouquet of roses and orange blossoms*: Pierre-Louis Menon and Roger Lecotté, *Au village de France, les traditions, les travaux, les fêtes: La vie traditionnelle des paysans* (Entrépilly: Christian de Bartillat, 1993), pp. 43, 101, 138.

15   *married Citizen Ponsardin on June 10, 1798*: Diane de Maynard, *La descendance de Madame Clicquot-Ponsardin, préface de la Vicomtesse de Luppé* (Mayenne: Joseph Floch, 1975), n.p.

16   *Barbe-Nicole's great-grandfather had invented the industry*: Robert

Tomes, *The Champagne Country* (New York: Hurd & Houghton, 1867), pp. 94–95: "The Viscount of Brimont [Jean-François Irénee Ruinart de Brimont] is known to champagne drinkers by his family name of Ruinart. He is a descendant—a collateral one, it is supposed—of one Dom [Thierry] Ruinart [1657–1709], who was of the convivial and holy brotherhood of the monastery of Hautvillers . . . the wine manufactory of which he is proprietor is one of the most ancient in Champagne. . . . His wine was in former times in considerable vogue, and his bottles may now occasionally be seen."

The Ruinart champagne company was originally established by Nicolas Ruinart (1697–1769) immediately after the royal decree of May 25, 1728, which granted the merchants of Reims the exclusive right to transport the local sparkling wines in bottles. After his death in 1769, Marie-Barbe-Nicole Ruinart's brother Claude ran the family wine trade. He was married to the daughter of another champagne house, Hélène Héloïse Françoise Tronsson, of Champagne Tronsson. After the death of Claude, his son Irénee (1770–1850) inherited the business; also the mayor of Reims for a period and a local recipient of the French Legion of Honor, Irénee was a close associate of Nicolas Ponsardin. According to company promotional materials, Champagne Ruinart was producing on the order of forty thousand bottles of champagne a year by 1769, making it the major champagne house of the late eighteenth century, along with Champagne Moët; by the early nineteenth century, it was a contracting business. Marie-Barbe-Nicole Le Tertre, *née* Ruinart was born c. 1733.

For scholarly accounts of the Ruinart family and the business climate of eighteenth-century wine brokers in the Champagne, see Patrick de Gmeline, *Ruinart, la plus ancienne maison de champagne, de 1729 à nos jours* (Paris: Stock, 1994); Charles Henri Jadart, *Dom Thierry Ruinart . . . Notice suivie de documents inédits sur sa famille, sa vie, ses œuvres, ses relations avec D. Mabillon* (Paris: n.p., 1886).

16   *gray cobblestone street known as rue de la Vache*: Etienne identifies this as present-day rue de la Nanteuil; p. 10, n. 9.

17   *he played the violin beautifully*: Detail from Crestin-Billet, p. 36.

17   *François's spelling, however, was dismal*: Bertrand de Vogüé,

L'Éducation d'un jeune bourgeois de Reims sous la Révolution (n.p.: Marsh, 1942); also Etienne, pp. 10–17.

18   *begged his son to fight melancholy*: Etienne, pp. 11–19.

19   *an appointment to the medical corps*: Etienne, pp. 11–14.

19   *"retired from active service"*: Charles Tovey, *Champagne: Its History, Properties, and Manufactures* (London: James Camden Hotten, 1870), p. 50; also in Fiévet, *Madame Veuve Clicquot*, who writes, with questionable accuracy, "an officer retired from active service on account of his injuries," p. 55.

20   *system of the* échelle des crus: Tom Stevenson, *Champagne and Sparkling Wine Guide* (San Francisco: Wine Appreciation Guild, 2002), p. 204; see also the official website of the Syndicat Professionnel des Courtiers en Vins de Champagne for details on the early-twentieth-century history of regulation and ratings in the wine industry: www. spcvc.com/historique.php?go=3&art=2.

20   *Robert Joseph explains that*: Robert Joseph, *French Wine Revised and Updated* (London: Dorling Kindersley, 2005).

20–21 *"the nature of the* terroir *contributes greatly"*: Denis Diderot, *Encyclopédie; ou Dictionnaire raisonné des sciences, des arts et des métiers* (Neufchastel [*sic*]: Samuel Faulche, 1765), vol. 17, p. 292.

21   *properties in the heart of the French wine country*: Champagne Veuve Clicquot Ponsardin, tasting-room promotional materials.

21   *Traveling in an open carriage*: Detail in various sources, including Gmeline, p. 16; Chimay, p. 3.

21   *in the Champagne the roses come tumbling out of the sides of the vineyards*: David G. James, "Opportunities for Reducing Pesticide Use in Management of Leafhoppers, Cutworms, and Thrips," conference proceedings of the Washington State Grape Society (2002), available at www.grapesociety.org. James writes: "Roses have been cultivated in and around vineyards in Europe and Australia for many years and for many reasons . . . as an indicator for powdery mildew," p. 3.

22   *the Cattier family*: Interview, January 19, 2007, Philippe Bienvenue; also Champagne Cattier promotional materials.

23   *small commission of around 10 percent*: Brennan, p. 269.

CHAPTER THREE: CHAMPAGNE DREAMS

25   *Clicquot-Muiron were shipping about 15,000 bottles*: Brennan, p. 269.

25   *champagne is ranked from driest to sweetest*: Stevenson, p. 200; see also Syndicat Professionnel des Courtiers en Vins de Champagne, available at www.spcvc.com/memento.php?go=6.

25   *The Russians liked it sweeter still*: Tomes, p. 68; also Henry Vizetelly, *Facts About Champagne and Other Sparkling Wines, Collected During Numerous Visits to the Champagne and Other Viticultural Districts of France and the Principal Remaining Wine-Producing Countries of Europe* (London: Ward, Lock, & Co., 1879), pp. 192, 198, 214.

26   *Château d'Yquem*: Promotional fact sheets, 2001 vintage, available at www.yquem.fr; promotional fact sheets, Grgich Hills, available at www.grgich.com.

26   *"a faint redish colour like Champane wine"*: *OED*, "champagne"; according to the same entry, in 1903 "champagne" was "a beautiful shade of pale straw, with a suggestion of pink about it."

26   *"Oiel du Pedrix"*: Anonymous [S. J.], *The Vineyard, Being a Treatise Shewing the Nature and Method of Planting, Manuring, Cultivating, and Dressing Vines* (London: W. Mears, 1727), p. 46.

26   *brandy often tinted the wine a light golden brown*: Phillips, p. 243.

27   *"Gray wine is made with black grapes"*: Charles Joseph Ligne, Prince de, *Mémoires et mélanges historiques et littéraires* (Paris: A. Dupont, 1827–1829).

27   *Under current French law, champagne is still made*: Liger-Belair, p. 19. Complete guidelines for winemakers in the Champagne AOC are provided by the governing professional bodies, including the Comité Interprofessionnel du Vin de Champagne, available at www.champagne.fr, and the Institut National de l'Origine et de la Qualité, available at www.inao.gouv.fr. For a scholarly account of the history of champagne regulation, see Kolleen Guy, *When Champagne Became French: Wine and the Making of National Identity* (Baltimore: Johns Hopkins University Press, 2003).

27   *nobody put labels on their bottles*: André Simon, *History of the Champagne Trade in England* (London: Wyman & Sons, 1905): "During the

second half of the eighteenth century . . . there were no labels of any shape or form and the consumer never inquired about the name of the man who had made the wine," p. 59.

27   *half the pressure champagne makers use today*: Liger-Belair, p. 15; champagne today is generally bottled at up to 6 atmospheres (14.7 pounds per square inch) of pressure. Because the internal pressure is reduced when the temperature is lowered, bubbles last longer in chilled champagne.

28   *appearance of vines in the area around Reims to the fourth century AD*: Roger Dion, *Histoire de la vigne et du vin en France* (Paris: Flammarion, 1959).

28   *finding a way to get rid of the bubbles*: Various sources, including Liger-Belair, p. 9; see also René Gandilhon, *Naissance du Champagne: Dom Pierre Pérignon* (Paris: Hachette, 1968); François Bonal, *Dom Pérignon: Vérité et légende* (Langres: D. Guéniot, 1995).

29   *extends across the English Channel to Great Britain*: On recent growth in the British sparkling wine industry, see Mark Phillips, "Global Warming Spawns Wine in U.K.," CBS Evening News, September 25, 2006, available at www.cbsnews.com/stories/2006/09/25/eveningnews/main2037991.shtml; and Valerie Elliott, "English Wine Sparkles as Global Climate Warms Up," *The Times*, September 11, 2006, available at www.timesonline.co.uk/tol/news/uk/article635009.ece. Historical evidence suggests that Great Britain once had a flourishing wine trade; see D. Williams, "A Consideration of the Sub-Fossil Remains of 'Vitis vinifera' L. as Evidence of Viticulture in Roman Britain," *Britannia* 8 (1977): 327–334; and William Hughes, *The Compleat Vineyards, or, A Most Excellent Way for the Planting of Wines Not Onely* [sic] *According to the German and French Way, but Also Long Experimented in England* (London: W. Crooke, 1665).

29   *wine known as* piquette: Classified in the "Working Paper," European Commission Directorate General for Agriculture and Rural Development: Wine, Common Market Organisation, 2006, which bans its export; see http://ec.europa.eu/agriculture/markets/wine/studies/rep_cmo2006_en.pdf, p. 21.

30   *the devil's wine*: Kladstrup, p. 46.

31   *Hautvillers didn't even start bottling their wines*: Brennan, p. 251.

32   *wealthy British consumers*: An argument first put forward by Tom Stevenson, *World Encyclopedia of Champagne and Sparkling Wine* (San Francisco: Wine Appreciation Guild, 1999).

32   *Great Britain was producing far stronger and less expensive glass*: See Ward Lloyd, *A Wine Lover's Glasses: The A. C. Hubbard Jr. Collection of Antique English Drinking Glasses and Bottles* (Yeovil, UK: Richard Dennis, 2000); Roger Dumbrell, *Understanding Antique Wine Bottles* (San Francisco: Antique Collector's Club, 1983).

32   *Charles de Saint-Évremond*: Born Charles de Marguetel de Saint-Denis, Seigneur de Saint-Évremond (1610–1703); an edition of his writings on gourmet pleasures has been edited by Claude Taittinger, *Saint-Évremond, ou, Le bon usage des plaisirs* (Paris: Perrin, 1990). On Saint-Évremond's time in Great Britain, see Walter Daniels, *Saint-Évremond en Angleterre* (Versailles: L. Luce, 1907).

33   *Merrett's lecture on winemaking*: Christopher Merrett, *Some Observations Concerning the Ordering of Wines* (London: William Whitwood, 1692).

33   *John Evelyn's* Pomona: John Evelyn, *Sylva, or A Discourse of Forest-Trees, and the Propagation of Timber in His Majesties Dominions. By J. E. Esq. As it was deliver'd in the Royal Society the XVth of October, MDCLXII . . . To which is annexed Pomona; or, an appendix concerning fruit-trees in relation to cider* (London: Joseph Martyn & James Allestry, 1664).

33   *a full decade before the wine was first produced in France*: Liger-Belair, p. 10; Brennan, p. 249; Delpal, p. 127.

34   *owned lucrative property in the Champagne*: Kladstrup, p. 50; see also Christine Pevitt, *Madame de Pompadour: Mistress of France* (New York: Grove Press, 2002).

34   *50 percent of it was sold directly to the palace at Versailles*: Brennan, p. 255.

CHAPTER FOUR: ANONYMITY IN THEIR BLOOD

36   *The country had been at war since the early days*: The history of the Napoleonic Wars (often chronicled as a continuation of the wars that followed from the French Revolution) can be understood in a general way by talking of a series of coalitions. But the truth of the matter is

that throughout the period, dozens of countries or principalities were involved, and they were often engaged in maddeningly complex multilateral conflicts.

The war of the First Coalition, a French victory principally over Austria and the Italian states, formally ended in 1797 and extended the boundaries of France as far as the Rhine River. This was economically important for the Champagne region in particular. Even after the treaty in 1797, France remained at war with Great Britain.

The Second Coalition focuses on the years from 1798 until about 1805 and pitted France against Great Britain, Austria, Russia, the Ottoman Empire, and several of the Italian states. There was a peace with Austria and most of the coalition members in February 1801, and a peace with Great Britain was set out in the Treaty of Amiens, brokered in March 1802. Until May 1803—for fourteen months—there was a brief peace in France.

In 1804, Napoléon crowned himself the emperor of France, and by 1805 a Third Coalition of primarily Russia, Great Britain, and Austria had developed. This period of the conflict was focused largely on Napoléon's plans to conquer Great Britain, which were ended with the defeat at Trafalgar in the autumn. Napoléon also famously defeated the Austrians at Austerlitz at the end of the year.

The Fourth Coalition was France primarily against Prussia, Russia, Great Britain, and some of the German states and ended with Napoléon's conquest over Prussia in 1806 and over Russia in 1807. In 1806, France introduced the Continental System—a series of trade restrictions aimed at isolating Great Britain from world trade and bringing about an economic conquest. By at least 1810, many people in France were either buying or selling contraband goods in defiance of the ban, which lasted until 1812.

From 1809 until 1812, the Fifth Coalition largely pitted Great Britain and Austria against France. Importantly for Barbe-Nicole's champagne dreams, the Russian market was theoretically (if not practically) open to French traders from 1807 to 1812. However, it was Russia's refusal to blockade British goods that led, in part, to Napoléon's disastrous invasion of the country in 1812.

After Napoléon's wintertime retreat from Russia, the Sixth Coalition formed to take advantage of his weakness, with Prussia, Austria, and the German states joining Russia and Great Britain. In the summer of 1813, there was a brief period of peace from early June to mid-August, and by the spring of 1814 Napoléon had been defeated in France. The French king was restored, and Napoléon was shipped off to exile. Then, with his characteristic pluck, Napoléon famously returned to France in 1815 for the so-called Hundred Days, in a last-ditch effort to save his empire. He was finally defeated at Waterloo by the Seventh Coalition: Russia, Prussia, Austria, Great Britain, and Germany. For a detailed historical overview, see Gunther Rothenberg, *The Napoleonic Wars* (New York: Collins, 2006).

37   *one-in-twenty chance of dying as a result of the delivery*: On infant and maternal mortality in eighteenth-century France, see Yves Blayo, "La mortalité en France de 1740 à 1829," *Population* (November 1975): 124–142; Nancy Senior, "Aspects of Infant Feeding in Eighteenth-Century France," *Eighteenth-Century Studies* 16, no. 4 (Summer 1983): 367–388; Nina Rattner Gelbart, *The King's Midwife: A History and Mystery of Madame du Coudray* (Berkeley: University of California Press, 1998); and Jenny Carter and Therese Duriez, *With Child: Birth Through the Ages* (Edinburgh: Mainstream Publishing, 1986). On British mortality rates, but nevertheless useful, is Jona Schelleken, "Economic Change and Infant Mortality in England, 1580–1837," *Journal of Interdisciplinary History* 32, no. 1 (Summer 2001): 1–11.

38   *widow named Thérèse*: Thérèse Pinchart (1775–1859) married Jean-Louis Doé de Maindreville (d. 1798), a parliamentary lawyer, in 1795. Their son, Pierre (1796–1870), was born the following year, and she was widowed in 1798.

38   *Clémentine and Thérèse quickly established themselves*: Crestin-Billet, p. 15.

38   *It is probably not a coincidence that the public still thought of them both as whores*: Susan P. Conner, "Public Virtue and Public Women: Prostitution in Revolutionary Paris, 1793–1794," *Eighteenth-Century Studies* 28, no. 2 (Winter 1994): 221–240, writes that "in the name of 'virtue' they had executed Marie-Antoinette, the quintessential whore of the eighteenth cen-

tury," p. 222. The infidelities of Joséphine Bonaparte, meanwhile, were legend; on the political use made of her indiscretions by her enemies, see, for example, Evangeline Bruce, *Napoleon and Josephine: An Improbable Marriage* (New York: Scribner, 1995).

38 *"Anonymity runs in their blood"*: Virginia Woolf, *A Room of One's Own* (New York: Harcourt Brace, 1981), p. 50.

38 *Lady Bessborough*: Quoted in Woolf, p. 55; see also Janet Gleeson, *Privilege and Scandal: The Remarkable Life of Harriet Spencer, Sister of Georgiana* (New York: Crown, 2007).

39 *"A prejudice against women acting in the marketplace"*: Bonnie G. Smith, *Ladies of the Leisure Class: The Bourgeoisies of Northern France in the Nineteenth Century* (Princeton, NJ: Princeton University Press, 1981), p. 47; *Code Napoléon; or, The French Civil Code. Literally Translated from the Original and Official Edition, Published at Paris, in 1804*, trans. George Spence (London: William Benning, 1827).

40 *Today, wine tasting is a multimillion-dollar tourist industry*: According to the Sonoma County Tourism Board, wine tourism generates over $1 billion in revenue in Sonoma County, California, alone; statistics available at www.sonomacounty.com.

40 *expect to find their wines labeled*: Tomes, p. 173.

41 *"opportunities for women to participate in rebuilding the industry"*: Ann B. Matasar, *Women of Wine: The Rise of Women in the Global Wine Industry* (Berkeley: University of California Press, 2006), p. 75.

42 *Dame Geoffrey . . . Widow Germon*: Brennan, pp. 261–262.

42 *Widow Robert and the Widow Blanc*: Brennan, p. 261; Claire Desbois-Thibault, *L'extraordinaire aventure du Champagne Moët et Chandon, une affaire de famille* (Paris: Presses Universitaires de France, 2003), p. 31; Etienne, p. 59.

43 *Historian Béatrice Craig*: Béatrice Craig, "Where Have All the Businesswomen Gone?: Images and Reality in the Life of Nineteenth-Century Middle-Class Women in Northern France," in *Women, Business and Finance in Nineteenth-Century Europe: Rethinking Separate Spheres*, eds. Robert Beachy, Béatrice Craig, and Alastair Owens (Oxford: Berg Publishers, 2006), p. 54.

44 *salesman from Mannheim, Germany*: Alain de Vogüé, *Une maison*

de vins de champagne au temps du blocus continental, 1806–1812, thesis for the Diplôme d'Études Supérieures d'Histoire, June 1948, p. 3.

44   *grand plan for selling wines in Great Britain*: Ibid.

44   *luxuries like French wine and silk had been contraband*: Gavin Daly, "Napoleon and the 'City of Smugglers,' 1810–1814," *Historical Journal* 50, no. 2 (June 2007): 333–352; for a more complete account of Anglo-French trade relations during the Napoleonic period, see François Crouzet, *L'économie britannique et le blocus continental* (Paris: Economica, 1987).

45   *mildly effervescent champagne known as* crémant: Etienne, p. 96.

45   *more than half the weekly salary of many of the people*: Brennan, p. 261.

46   *If his portraits are any indication, Jean-Rémy*: Promotional display materials, Champagne Moët et Chandon, Reims; portraits reproduced in Victor Fiévet, *Jean-Rémy Moët et ses successeurs* (Paris: E. Dentu, 1864).

46   *since the heyday of the 1730s*: Brennan, p. 198.

46   *a deal for the sale of two or three thousand bottles of nearly flat champagne*: Etienne, p. 96.

47   *"The day very hot"*: Dorothy Wordsworth, *The Grasmere Journals,* ed. Pamela Woof (Oxford: Oxford University Press, 1991), p. 125.

47   *"In the memory of man"*: Quoted in Etienne, p. 36; letter of August 20, 1802.

48   *Allart de Maisonneuve woke up to find*: Brennan, p. 252.

48   *"foundation of an entirely different commercial system"*: Fiévet, *Madame Veuve Clicquot,* p. 56.

CHAPTER FIVE: CRAFTING THE CUVÉE

49   *Jean-Antoine Chaptal's treatise*: Jean-Antoine-Claude Chaptal, Comte de Chanteloup, *L'art de faire le vin* (Paris: Madame Huzard, 1819).

49   *"a decisive turning point in the history of wine technology"*: Jerry B. Gough, "Winecraft and Chemistry in Eighteenth-Century France: Chaptal and the Invention of Chaptalization," *Technology and Culture* 39, no. 1 (January 1998): 74–104, 102.

49   *Napoléon ordered departmental prefects throughout France*: Gough, p. 102.

50   *worth three times what it sold for by the barrel*: Brennan, p. 250.

50   *springtime moon had the power to raise a tide of bubbles*: Louis Saint-Pierre, *The Art of Planting and Cultivating the Vine; and Also of Making, Fining, and Preserving Wines, &c.* (London: n.p., 1722), p. 230.

50   *ancient festival of St. Vincent*: Émile Moreau, *Le culte de Saint Vincent en Champagne* (Épernay: Éditions le Vigneron de la Champagne, 1936).

51   *guests consumed a thousand bottles in a night*: Desbois-Thibault, p. 35.

51   *his own boyhood in the region*: Napoléon spent five years at the military academy in Briennes-le-Château (Aube); "Napoleon I," *Encyclopædia Britannica Online*, available at http://www.search.eb.com.prxy5. ursus.maine.edu/eb/article-9108752; see also Alexandre Assier, *Napoléon Ier à l'École Royale Militaire de Brienne d'après des documents authentiques et inédits, 1779–1784* (Paris: n.p., 1874). Jean-Rémy Moët was educated at the same academy, and there is a charming tradition that tells how the two young men first became friends as students. Unfortunately, the dates of their attendance do not correspond. However, it seems likely that their shared experiences at Brienne provided a foundation for the warm personal relationship that developed in later years. On Moët's education, see Desbois-Thibault, p. 26, n. 1.

51   *books such as Jean Godinot's*: Jean Godinot, *Manière de cultiver et de faire le vin en Champagne* (1722), ed. François Bonal (Langres: Dominique Guéniot, 1990); Nicolas Bidet, *Traité sur la culture des vignes, sur la façon du vin, et sur la manière de le gouverner: Ouvrage orné de figures, & en particulier de celle d'un pressoir d'une nouvelle invention* (Paris: Chez Savoye, 1752).

52   *According to local custom, it lasted for twelve days*: The so-called *bans de vendange* had their origins in medieval feudalism; today, the Comité Interprofessionnel du Vin de Champagne, a trade organization comprising growers and champagne producers, regulates all aspects of the champagne harvest, in collaboration with the French government; details available at www.champagne.fr.

52   *favorite haunt at harvest-time was in the village of Bouzy*: Etienne, p. 32.

53   première taille, *or the first cutting*: Anonymous [S. J.], *The Vineyard*, pp. 49–52.

54   *some unlucky people find that it gives them a pounding headache*: Medical scientists distinguish between a typically mild reaction to red wine known as "red wine headache," or RWH, which is thought to result

either from a histamine or prostaglandins response or from a reaction to tannins, and a sometimes much more serious and potentially fatal sulfite allergy. See, for example, A. T. Bakalinsky, "Sulfites, Wine and Health," in *Wine in Context: Nutrition, Physiology, Policy: Proceedings of the Symposium on Wine and Health*, eds. Andrew L. Waterhouse and R. M. Rantz (Davis, Calif.: American Society for Enology and Viticulture, 1996); C. S. Stockley, "Histamine: The Culprit for Headaches?" *Australian and New Zealand Wine Industry Journal* 11 (1996): 42–44.

54   *known as "powder number three"*: Godinot, p. 65.

55   *the skill in French cooking of clarifying a consommé*: *The Professional Chef: The Culinary Institute of America* (New York: John Wiley & Son, 2002), pp. 300–303.

55   *a good eye to track the sediment and an excellent thumb*: André Jullien, *Manuel du sommelier, ou Instruction practique sur la manière de soigner les vins* (Paris: Encyclopédie de Roret, 1836), p. 189.

56   *chemical process called "autolysis"*: Carlo Zambonelli et al., "Effects of Lactic Acid Bacteria Autolysis on Sensorial Characteristics of Fermented Foods," *Food Technology/Biotechnology* 40, no. 4 (2002): 347–351.

56   *fine champagne its characteristic rich, nutty flavors*: Stevenson, p. 9.

56   *its northern location prevents the grapes from developing too many natural sugars*: Liger-Belair, p. 137.

57   *without being overshadowed by foliage*: Hervé This, *Molecular Gastronomy: Exploring the Science of Flavor*, trans. M. B. Debevoise (New York: Columbia University Press, 2006), p. 232.

57   *ordering bottles could be maddening*: See *Champenoises: Ecomusée de la région de Fourmies Trélon* (Trélon: Atelier-Musée du Verre de Trélon, 2000), courtesy of the resource library, Champagne Moët et Chandon, which describes Barbe-Nicole's problems with ordering bottles in consistent size and quality. Champagne production required specialized bottles, in form, color, resistance to pressure and acidity, and *embouchure* (bottle opening), and poor glassware was a significant obstacle to the development of the industry. By the 1820s, Barbe-Nicole was precise in the orders that she placed to her manufacturers, but the glassmakers "had serious technical difficulties and reticence about fabricating this model," because she wanted functional, cylindrical, and aesthetically

pleasing bottles "before their time" (p. 80). She disliked, in particular, the appearance of pear-shaped bottles, writing: "This form is without elegance" (p. 152; letter of March 1856). By the 1830s, Barbe-Nicole was also beginning to regard bottle shape as a marketing device, and she insisted that her suppliers not sell bottles made to her "form" to her competitors (p. 151; letter of October 1831, to Haumont). As a result of her persistence and buying power (she purchased approximately sixty-five million bottles over sixty-five years in business), the glassmaking industry in wine developed rapidly during the mid-nineteenth century, and the company archives, with over seven hundred letters on the topic, reveal a great deal about her "role in the elaboration of the champagne bottle" as we know it today (p. 148).

58   *Until then, wine bottles were blown by hand*: Dumbrell, p. 16

58   *Perhaps she was what wine experts today sometimes call a "supertaster"*: Jamie Goode, *The Science of Wine: From Vine to Glass* (Los Angeles: University of California Press, 2005), p. 170.

58   *Sulfur gives a cool summer's glass of* sauvignon blanc: This, p. 236.

59   *white wines are aged "on the lees"*: Ibid., p. 250.

CHAPTER SIX: THE CHAMPAGNE WIDOW

60   *Sales in France were now a mere 7 percent of their sales*: Etienne, p. 269.

60   *from Prussia and Austria or not at all*: During the period, control of central and eastern Europe was divided largely between two powers, the Austrian or Hapsburg Empire and the independent kingdom of Prussia. Although territorial boundaries shifted, especially during the Napoleonic period, Prussia generally included parts of the modern states of Germany and Poland, territories along the Baltic, and several former Soviet states. The Austrian Empire included much of modern Austria, Hungary, Romania, and numerous Adriatic states, including the northeast territories in modern Italy. The Ottoman Empire, although in decline during the early nineteenth century, controlled the large extent of territories to the south, including modern Turkey, some of the contested Adriatic states, most of the areas around the Black Sea, and significant parts of the Near East, Middle East, and northern Africa. For a more complete account of early-nineteenth-century political geogra-

phy, see Christopher Clark, *Iron Kingdom: The Rise and Downfall of Prussia, 1600–1947* (New York: Penguin, 2007); and Andrew Wheatcroft, *The Hapsburgs* (New York: Penguin, 1997).

61   *"The excess of luxury [here] means that the broker"*: Quoted in Etienne, p. 262.

61   *"The commerce in this place is excessively rotten"*: Alain de Vogüé, *Une maison de vins*, p. 5.

61   *"Foreign companies are seen as nanny goats"*: Quoted in Etienne, p. 263.

62   *Russia . . . would account for an astonishing third of their sales*: Ibid., pp. 269, 95.

63   *black crust of infection, and everywhere, he ached*: William Buchan, *Domestic Medicine, or, A Treatise on the Prevention and Cure of Diseases, by Regimen and Simple Medicines: With an Appendix, Containing a Dispensatory for the Use of Private Practioners* (Philadelphia: Richard Folwell, 1797), ch. 10.

63   *she could only feel relief to hear that François was dead*: Fiévet, *Madame Veuve Clicquot*, p. 59.

64   Question Agitated in the School of the Faculty of Medicine at Reims: Jean-Claude Navier, *Question Agitated in the School of the Faculty of Medicine at Reims . . . on the Use of Sparkling Champagne Against Putrid Fevers and Other Maladies of the Same Nature* (Reims: Cazin, 1778).

64   *"It contains," Dr. Navier wrote*: Ibid., p. x.

64   *Dr. Navier's brother-in-law was none other than Jean-Rémy Moët*: Jacqueline Roubinet and Gilbert and Marie-Thérèse Nolleau, *Jean-Rémy Moët: A Master of Champagne and a Talented Politician*, trans. Carolyn Hart (Paris: Stock, 1996), p. 38.

64   *experiments with wine cures*: See, for example, Jacques Moreau, *De la connoissance* [sic] *des fièvres continues, pourprées et pestilentes* (Paris: Laurent D'Houry, 1689); and William Guthrie, *Remarks upon Claret, Burgundy, and Champagne, Their Dietetic and Restorative Uses, Etc.* (London: Simpkin, Marshall & Co., 1889).

64   *"Champagne, if pure, is one of the safest wines that can be drunk"*: Charles Tovey, *Champagne: Its History, Properties, and Manufactures* (London: James Camden Hotten, 1870), p. 105; reiterated in Charles Tovey, *Wine Revelations* (London: Whitaker, 1880), p. 38.

65   *"Nothing . . . can ever assuage the deep sorrow I feel"*: Quoted in Crestin-Billet, p. 69.

65   *the slain revolutionary Jean-Paul Marat*: Jacques-Louis David, "The Death of Marat" (*La mort de Marat*), ca. 1794, oil on canvas, Reims, Musée des Beaux-Arts de la Ville de Reims, gift of Paul David, 1879 (879.8); Marat was murdered by Charlotte Corday during the Revolution.

65   *"The malignant fever is generally preceded by a remarkable weakness"*: Buchan, ch. 10.

66   *"Do not abandon yourself to a sort of melancholy gloom"*: Quoted in Etienne, p. 12.

66   *"While big with this magnificent project"*: Tomes, p. 66.

67   *"profound depression"*: Alain de Vogüé, *Une maison de vins*, p. vi.

68   *"the* bourgeoisie *of yesteryear who had tended the [company] books had . . . metamorphosed"*: Smith, p. 46.

CHAPTER SEVEN: PARTNER AND APPRENTICE

71   *tune of nearly half a million dollars*: Etienne, pp. 179–181; using a one-to-twenty ratio.

72   *Under the laws of the Napoleonic Code*: According to statute, a "wife [could not] plead in her own name, without the authority of her husband, even though she should be a public trader," *Code Napoléon*, ch. 6, sect. 4.

72   *She and Alexandre had each invested 80,000 francs*: Etienne, pp. 178–181. Currency in nineteenth-century France was a complex system; for the sake of clarity, all references are to francs, although many continued to refer to values in "livres" or even "napoleons." The livre— abolished in 1795 by the revolutionary government—had near parity with the franc during the period.

72   *thirty years later an unskilled laborer*: Contemporary figures from L. and D. Noack, "Cost of Living in Daumier's Times," available at www.daumier.org/index.php?id=176; see also Gilles Postel-Vinay and Jean-Marc Robin, "Eating, Working, and Saving in an Unstable World: Consumers in Nineteenth-Century France," *Economic History Review* 45, no. 3 (August 1992): 494–513; British comparative data is

included in Liza Picard, *Dr. Johnson's London* (New York: St. Martin's Press, 2000).

73   *Philippe brought to the table another 30,000 francs*: Etienne, p. 180.

73   *"Renouncing the commerce in textiles"*: Alain de Vogüé, *Une maison de vins*, p. 5

73   *approximately 75 percent of the wines sold by this new company*: Etienne, pp. 39–41.

74   *"Sea commerce is totally ruined"*: Alain de Vogüé, *Une maison de vins*, p. 8.

75   *ideally be stored in cool darkness at around 55°F*: This, p. 254.

75   *5 percent of the wine sold to customers is "corked"*: Goode, p. 145.

75   *and they would sacrifice taste in order to achieve it*: Etienne, p. 74.

75   *Likely, the culprit was problems that had begun during the cask stage*: See C. R. Davis et al., "Practical Implications of Malolactic Fermentation: A Review," *American Journal of Enology and Viticulture* 36, no. 4 (1985): 290–301; and Émile Peynaud, *Knowing and Making Wine*, trans. Alan F. G. Spenser (Chichester, UK: Wiley Interscience, 1984).

77   *"I prayed to the Good Lord"*: Quoted in Etienne, p. 116.

77   *"I pray to the Good Lord day and night to send some corsair to take them"*: Alain de Vogüé, *Une maison de vins*, p. 8.

77   *"This country has lacked even money for the worst vintage this past year"*: Ibid., p. 10.

77   *"What a blessing for us"*: Ibid., p. 16.

78   *Avoid "talking politics," he pleaded*: Ibid., p. 20.

78   *"In the name of God, don't ever talk of politics"*: Ibid., p. 28.

79   *The empress had given birth to a daughter in the autumn:* Reputed to be the son of her lover, Adam Czartoryski, a Polish prince, the child was born Maria Alexandrovna and lived just fourteen months (1799–1800); Henri Troyat, *Alexander of Russia: Napoleon's Conqueror* (New York: Grove Press, 2003), pp. 43–46.

80   *Today, the region is limited to 323 classified villages*: According to the Office of Champagne's Cultivation Regulations (the United States representative of the Comité Interprofessionnel du Vin de Champagne, or CVIC), grapes grown within the "champagne" appellation are limited to strictly controlled vineyards, and growers must agree to abide

by restrictions governing everything from the distance between vines to the extent and timing of vine pruning, the maximum yield per hectare, and the dates of harvest; details available at www.champagne.us/index. cfm?pageName=appellation_cultivationregs.

81   *Even the descriptive term* champenoise, *or "champagne style"*: The use of the label *méthode champenoise* on wines produced outside the champagne AOC was outlawed in the European Union in 1994 (*SMW Winzersekt GmbH v. Land Rheinland-Pfalz Ase C-306/93 [1994], European Court Reports 1994*, p. I-05555). The legal status of the term in the United States is the subject of complex litigation, but the use of the term is increasingly controversial. The history of American "champagne" is documented in William Heintz et al., *A History of Champagne in California and the United States: With Particular Emphasis on How the Word "Champagne" Has Been Used by Journalists and Writers and the Understanding of Its Definition by the American Wine Consumer*, unpublished archival collection, 1984, Saint Helena Public Library, Napa, California.

81   *"a large part of Europe [was] ruined by the famine"*: Alain de Vogüé, *Une maison de vins*, pp. 58–60.

82   *"there are rare advantages that give us a rising name brand"*: Ibid., p. 65.

82   *"Everywhere . . . business is absolutely dead"*: Ibid., p. 76.

82   *"an order to leave the city and the states of Austria"*: Ibid., p. 72.

82   *In 1809, she managed to sell only forty thousand bottles of wine*: Etienne, p. 269.

83   *the only news he could send: "Business totally dead"*: Alain de Vogüé, *Une maison de vins*, p. 96.

CHAPTER EIGHT: ALONE AT THE BRINK OF RUIN

84   *founded in 1734 by Alexandre's grandfather under the name Forest-Fourneaux*: Promotional materials, Champagne Taittinger, available at www.taittinger.com; see also Delpal, p. 58.

85   *Nicolas's reward for his hospitality*: George Lallemand, *Le Baron Ponsardin* (Reims: Chamber of Commerce/Société des Amis de Vieux Reims, 1967).

85   *Austrian archduchess Marie Louise—niece to the ill-fated Marie Antoinette*: Marie Louise of Austria (1791–1847); see Edith Cuthell, *An Imperial*

Victim: Marie Louise, Archduchess of Austria, Empress of the French, Duchess of Parma (London: Brentanto's, 1912).

85   *her father, always a royalist at heart*: Fiévet, *Madame Veuve Clicquot*, p. 24.

86   *"marriage of the Archduchess Louise is fixed for the 25 of March*: Champagne Veuve Clicquot Ponsardin, Company Archives, 1A E 086, *Copie de lettres du 1er Julliet au 9 Novembre 1812*, p. 243; letter of March 3, 1810.

86.   *she and Louis referred to him in their letters simply as "the devil"*: Interview, January 8, 2007, Fabienne Huttaux, Historical Resources Manager, Champagne Veuve Clicquot Ponsardin, Reims.

86   *the emperor's personal appreciation of "the beauty and richness of their cellars"*: Promotional materials, Champagne Jacquesson, available at www.champagnejacquesson.com.

87   *Her account book showed*: Etienne, p. 184.

87   *Now he was engaged to Miss Rheinwald*: Crestin-Billet, p. 89.

88   *burned the symbol of the anchor into the corks*: Delpal, p. 173.

88   *brilliant greens flecked with gold or silver*: Desbois-Thibault, p. 57.

89   *it had always been used because it was the traditional symbol of hope*: Champagne Veuve Clicquot Ponsardin, tasting-room promotional materials.

89   *selling more local red wines by the barrel*: Etienne, p. 44.

89   *high-end vintages from other, more fashionable parts of France*: Etienne, pp. 47–49.

90   *daughter, Clémentine, away to a convent boarding school in Paris*: Chimay, p. 31.

90   *challenges of raising a child while running a business*: "Women integrated their sense of parenthood with the general business orientation of their lives . . . evidence does not appear . . . to suggest that the businesswoman spent much time beyond the market world"; Smith, p. 45.

90   *Her letters show that she was a devoted and pragmatic mother*: See, for example, Chimay, pp. 31–42.

91   *"I pray that you will keep it on your person"*: Champagne Veuve Clicquot Ponsardin, Company Archives, 1A E 086, *Copie de lettres du 1er Juillet 1809 au 9 Novembre 1812*, p. 429; letter of October 19, 1810.

92   *"This is a terrible thing that gets up and goes to bed with me"*: Chimay, p. 18.

92   *"never use the present round saucer animalcula-catching champagne glasses"*: Anonymous, *London at Table: or, How, When, and Where to Dine and Order a Dinner, and Where to Avoid Dining, with Practical Hints to Cooks* (London: Chapman & Hall, 1851), vol. 2, p. 45.

92–93   *Owing to basic mechanics, the bubbles are smaller and prettier in narrow glasses*: This, p. 257.

93   *country estate outside Oger*: Chimay, p. 17.

94   *"maritime harpies" and the "assassins of prosperity"*: Quotations here and following from Bertrand de Vogüé, *Madame Clicquot à la conquête pacifique de la Russie* (Reims: Imprimerie du Nord-Est, 1947), p. 8.

94   *"2,000 bottles have been easily sold because of the season"*: Alain de Vogüé, *Une maison de vins*, p. 112.

94   *That spring, she had orders for fewer than thirty-three thousand bottles*: Etienne, p. 269.

95   *Lower the prices if need be, she wrote to Louis in Holland*: Crestin-Billet, p. 77.

95   *"There had never been . . . a grape so ripe, so sugary, and one harvested under such favorable circumstances of weather"*: Tomes, p. 129.

95   *"the great comet was attracting all eyes"*: Harriet Martineau, *Autobiography* (Boston: James R. Osgood, 1877).

95   *"how many superstitious terrors it gave rise to"*: Anonymous, "The Comet," *Robert Merry's Museum* (November 1858), pp. 137–139, p. 137.

97   *Louis spent the spring of 1812 hunting orders*: Alain de Vogüé, *Une maison de vins*, p. 118.

97   *pushing the development of new sugar sources for winemakers*: With the continental blockades during the Napoleonic Wars, popular British colonial commodities, including sugar and cotton, were scarce and costly. Because of the need for sugar in the production of wine—and in the production of champagne in particular—"the French wine trade suffered," and in order to protect his favorite industry, Napoléon saw to it that "investigations were carried out in France to find substitutes for British colonial produce," including the large-scale extraction of sugar from the locally grown beetroot; William G. Freeman, *New Phytologist* 6,

no. 1 (January 1907): 18–23, 20. See also Phillips, pp. 186–195. According to Robert Tomes, the winemakers still preferred cane sugar, and he reported that beet sugar is "said to poison wine" and give it a "nauseous flavor"; Tomes, p. 145.

97   *"an infernal genie who has tormented and ruined the world for five or six years"*: Bertrand de Vogüé, *Conquête pacifique de la Russie*, p. 8.

98   *"The Good Lord is a joker: eat and you will die, do not eat and you will die, and so patience and perseverance"*: Alain de Vogüé, *Une maison de vins*, p. 125.

98   *"All the houses of the nobility," wrote a British witness*: Quoted in George Rudé, *Revolutionary Europe: 1783–1815* (Glasgow: Fontana Press/HarperCollins, 1985), p. 273.

98   *"If circumstances were less sad," he told Jean-Rémy*: Victor Fiévet, *Histoire de la ville d'Épernay* (Épernay: V. Fiévet, 1868), p. 151.

98   *More than half a million men had been sent to fight in Russia*: For an account of the Russian campaign, see, for example, Henry Houssaye, *Napoleon and the Campaign of 1814* (Uckfield, UK: Naval and Miltary Press, 2006).

CHAPTER NINE: WAR AND THE WIDOW'S TRIUMPH

100   *Sales of her wine had been down again that year . . . a staggering 80 percent*: Alain de Vogüé, *Une maison de vins*, pp. 64, 123.

102   *he would lose over half a million bottles of champagne*: Kladstrup, p. 67.

102   *Mademoiselle Gard—to the family, simply Jennie*: Chimay, p. 38.

102   *"I have been occupied for many days with walling up my cellars"*: Bertrand de Vogüé, *Conquête pacifique de la Russie*, p. 26.

102   *Her brother's textile factory at Saint-Brice was destroyed*: Fiévet, *Madame Veuve Clicquot*, p. 33.

103   *Serge Alexandrovich Wolkonsky, insisted that there would be no looting*: Kladstrup, p. 83; Chimay, p. 24.

103   *"as for your insolent threat of sending troops to Rheims"*: Chimay, p. 24.

103   *"Tomorrow they will pay!"*: Ibid.

103   *"All these officers who ruin me today"*: Desbois-Thibault, p. 35.

103   *General Corbineau recaptured Reims*: Louis Antoine Fauvelet,

Memoirs of Napoleon Bonaparte (London: Richard Bentley, 1836); also Houssaye.

104 *"about a dozen prisoners were made, who had been laid under the table"*: Tomes, p. 67.

104 *"Madame Clicquot . . . gave Napoléon's officers Champagne and glasses"*: Details from "The Noble Art of Sabrage," available at www .champagnesabering.com.

105 *Hedging his bet, he wrote Napoléon a letter*: According to Fiévet, *Madame Veuve Clicquot*, the letter read: "Sire, at this instant, the city and those who protect it are in your power," p. 39.

105 *Barbe-Nicole who greeted the emperor at the door of the Hôtel Ponsardin*: Fiévet, *Madame Veuve Clicquot*: "The Widow Clicquot, it was said, welcomed the emperor to the Hôtel Ponsardin herself, deserted by her father, mayor of the village," p. 19.

105 *As was the custom, she herself filled the emperor's pillows with the softest new down*: Crestin-Billet, p. 24.

106 *"If fate intervenes and dashes my hopes, I want at least to be able to reward you for your loyal service and steadfast courage"*: Roubinet and Nolleau, p. 63.

107 *"Russian officers . . . lifted the champagne glass to their lips"*: Tomes, p. 67.

107 *Lord Byron wrote to his friend Thomas Moore*: Thomas Moore, *Life of Lord Byron, with His Letters and Journals*, 6 vols (London: John Murray, 1854), vol. 3, letter 174; letter of April 9, 1814.

107 *"At last the time has come"*: Chimay, p. 24.

107 *Within decades of Napoléon's defeat, it would multiply more than tenfold*: Brennan, p. 272.

108 *Still, when the Russian czar Alexander ordered provisions*: Roubinet and Nolleau, p. 43.

108 *"Thanks are due to Heaven . . . I do not have any losses to regret"*: Bertrand de Vogüé, *Conquête pacifique de la Russie*, p. 9.

109 *Monsieur Rondeaux, a shipping merchant in Rouen*: Ibid., p. 11.

109–110 *"our wines must be properly cared for"*: Chimay, p. 26.

110 *Jean-Rémy was already writing to Count Tolstoy*: Michel Refait, *Moët*

& Chandon: De Claude Moët à Bernard Arnault (Paris: Dominique Gueniot, 1998), p. 41.

110 *she had also slyly included a present for Louis*: Bertrand de Vogüé, *Conquête pacifique de la Russie*, p. 12.

111 *"as strong as the wines of Hungary, as yellow as gold, and as sweet as nectar"*: Ibid., p. 15.

111 *"Our ship is the first, in many years, to travel to the North"*: Ibid., p. 12.

CHAPTER TEN: A COMET OVER RUSSIA: THE VINTAGE OF 1811

113 *"I am bored of seeing them leave us in peace taking the money"*: Bertrand de Vogüé, *Conquête pacifique de la Russie*, p. 18.

114 *"Great God! What a price! How novel!"*: Ibid., p. 17.

114 *"I am adored here . . . because my wines are adorable"*: Quotations in this paragraph from ibid., p. 14.

115 *"I have already in my portfolio [orders for] a new assault on your caves"*: Ibid., p. 18.

117 *"If my business continues as it has gone since the invasion"*: Ibid., p. 20.

118 *"your judicious manner of operating, your excellent wine"*: Ibid., p. 19.

119 *In the company archives in Reims . . . she writes about the shape of the bottles*: Interview, January 8, 2007, Fabienne Huttaux, Historical Resources Manager, Champagne Veuve Clicquot Ponsardin.

119 *"The world market which was slowly coming into existence"*: Peter Kriedte, *Peasants, Landlords, and Merchant Capitalists: Europe and the World Economy, 1500–1800* (Leamington Spa, UK: Berg, 1983), p. 13, quoted in "Proto-Industrialization in France," Gwynne Lewis, *Economic History Review* (New Series) 47, no. 1 (February 1994): 150–164, 155.

120 *"business historians, agree that those women would have disappeared"*: Craig, p. 52.

CHAPTER ELEVEN: THE INDUSTRIALIST'S DAUGHTER

121 *In France, a handful of women run wine estates*: Matasar, p. 2.

121 *Today, in all of Europe, there is not a single woman who does both*: In-

terview, October 2007, Eileen Crane, President, Champagne Domaine Carneros, Napa, California.

122 *An "industry in retreat" opened doors for new entrepreneurs*: Ibid.

122 *Built in the 1750s on the site of the ancient estate of the monks of Saint-Pierre aux Monts de Châlons*: Promotional materials, Champagne Taittinger, available at www.taittinger.com.

123 *"Any big glass is good for champagne"*: Hugh Johnston, *Wine* (New York: Simon & Schuster, 1979), p. 71.

123 *miniature versions of the V-shaped stemware*: Ibid., p. 63.

124 *Barbe-Nicole today is credited with three achievements*: Matasar, p. 27.

124 *her name was celebrated in some of the greatest nineteenth-century works*: Detail from Natalie MacLean, "The Merry Widows of Mousse," *International Sommelier Guild,* 3:63AJ (December 2003): 1–2, 1.

On the literary representations of the Widow Clicquot, see in particular Anton Chekhov's "Champagne, A Wayfarer's Story" and Alexander Pushkin's *Eugene Onegin*, where he famously writes: "Of Veuve Clicquot or of Moët / the bless'd wine / . . . / Its magic stream / no dearth of foolishness engendered / but also what a lot of jokes, and verse, / and arguments, and merry dreams!!" (st. xlv, ll. 1–14); *Eugene Onegin*, trans. Vladmir Nabokov (Princeton, NJ: Princeton University Press, 1991), p. 196. The champagne of the Widow Clicquot also appears in various works of twentieth-century literature, including, memorably, Ernest Hemingway's *The Sun Also Rises* (ch. 7).

124 *"It is cruel," Louis wrote, "to have to refuse orders"*: Bernard de Vogüé, *Conquête pacifique de la Russie*, p. 18.

125 *By winter, grain was impossible to come by in the markets*: Fiévet, *Madame Veuve Clicquot*: "In 1816 after the war, there were no cereals at the public markets. . . . Many of the peasants turned in their misery to vagrancy and robbery," pp. 41–42.

125 *"The old way, which involved knocking the bottles upside down to settle the sediment, used drugs and clarifiers"*: Tomes, p. 150.

126 *"You only have fifty thousand bottles ready"*: Fiévet, *Madame Veuve Clicquot*, p. 65.

126 *"Great advance," they whispered*: Quotations in this paragraph from

Fiévet, *Madame Veuve Clicquot*, p. 66. A point reiterated by Kolleen M. Guy, "Drowning Her Sorrows: Widowhood and Entrepreneurship in the Champagne Industry," *Business and Economic History* 26, no. 2 (Winter 1997): 505–512: "In the early nineteenth century, it was believed that this kind of manipulation of the wine would not serve to speed up the process of removing the sediment and that it would only trouble the already volatile wines. Clicquot's early experiments were met with ridicule and sarcasm by male contemporaries," p. 508. See also Tomes, who records details of Barbe-Nicole "slipping quietly into the cellar day after day, while all the workmen were at dinner," p. 154.

127 *preliminary cellar experiments with siphons, "rigid tubes fitted with a tap"*: Jullien, p. 139.

127 *What she and Antoine Müller discovered changed the way champagne is finished to this day*: Fiévet, *Madame Veuve Clicquot*: "The spirit and tenacity of a woman triumphed over these stubborn cellar workers, stuck in their routine. All the Champagne today has adopted the method of Madame Veuve Clicquot," p. 68.

Henry Vizetelly, in his *History of Champagne, with Notes on the Other Sparkling Wines of France* (New York: Scribner & Welford, 1882), gives Müller credit for suggesting the idea to Barbe-Nicole: "Already in 1806 . . . the bottles were placed on tables, like to-day, with their heads downward; each bottle being taken out of its hole, raised, in the air, and shaken with the hand, so as to cause the cream of tartar and the deposit it contained to fall upon the cork. . . . This lasted till 1818, when a man named Müller . . . suggested to her that the bottles should be left in the table whilst being shaken, and that the holes should be cut obliquely. . . . The trial was made, and every day, with a view of keeping this new process a secret, Müller and Madame Clicquot shut themselves up in the cellars, and shook the bottles unperceived," pp. 161–162, n. 1.

Accounts of this sort led Matasar to observe: "There is disagreement regarding the degree of the Veuve Clicquot's personal involvement in developing this process. Her detractors, including her winemaking contemporaries who dismissed her experimentation on the basis of her gender, give all the credit to Müller. Some, however, view her as the sole inventive genius. She surely instigated the research, encouraged and participated in developing the process, and can lay claim to it as the firm's owner," pp. 27–28.

Vizetelly suggests 1818 as the date when *remuage* was invented, although some recent sources propose 1816, including Crestin-Billet and Etienne.

127 *wine aficionado Henry Vizetelly describes* remuage: Quotations here and in the following paragraph from Vizetelly, pp. 160–161.

128 *"from which tragic instrument"*: Tomes, p. 159.

128 *a move by the large commercial producers to mechanized rotation in crates known as* giropalettes: Interview, Champagne Cattier, January 19, 2007; see also Bruce Zoecklein, "A Review of *Méthode Champenoise* Production," Virginia State University/Virginia Tech, Cooperative Extension Publication, Publication Number 463-017, December 2002, available at www.ext.vt.edu/pubs/viticulture/463-017/463-017.html.

128 *expert cellar worker, it is said, can turn as many as fifty thousand bottles in a day*: Vizetelly, p. 161.

128 *"We must wrack our brains to obtain as good a result"*: Quoted in Desbois-Thibault, p. 47.

128 *"The adventure of Madame Clicquot," wrote Jean-Rémy, "is infamous"*: Ibid., p. 50.

128 *"sufficiently eloquent to show the rivalry that existed"*: Ibid., p. 49.

128 *The climate of espionage aside, Jean-Rémy would not discover her secret*: There is some disagreement regarding how long Barbe-Nicole was able to keep *remuage* a company secret. Roderick Phillips claims it was a matter of only a few years and that the technique was widely used in the region by the 1820s; see Phillips, p. 243. However, all the evidence suggests that Jean-Rémy Moët—despite his enthusiasm for technological innovation in the champagne industry—didn't begin using the technique until 1832, surely a curious situation if *remuage* was already widely used throughout the Champagne. On Moët's use of *remuage*, see Desbois-Thibault, p. 49.

129 *"It is only within the last fifty years that the trade in champagne has become important"*: Tomes, p. 74.

129 *Barbe-Nicole was scraping by on sales of under 20,000*: Etienne, p. 277. In 1812, Moët sold approximately thirty-five thousand bottles; see Desbois-Thibault, p. 36.

129 *exporting upward of 175,000 bottles a year*: Desbois-Thibault, p. 36; Crestin-Billet, p. 88.

CHAPTER TWELVE: THE WINE ARISTOCRATS

130 *Two eligible bachelors were vying for the attentions of her daughter*: Chimay, pp. 31–33.

130 *Marie's husband, Florent Simon*: Florent Simon Andrieux (1761–1835) and Marie *née* Lasnier (1768–1842). The visits of Barbe-Nicole, Édouard, and her family to the Andrieux salon were recorded by Marie's grandson Arthur Barbat de Bignicourt (1824–1888) in his *Un salon à Reims en 1832* (Reims: n.p., 1879).

In 1820, the two families became even more closely connected when the stepson of Barbe-Nicole's sister, Clémentine Barrachin, a young man named Augustin (1797–1883), married one of the Andrieux daughters, Elisabeth (1799–1846). Augustin was the child of Jean-Nicolas Barrachin's first wife, Charlotte Augustine, *née* Raux.

Florent Simon was mayor of Reims from 1828 to 1835, after the retirement of Nicolas Ponsardin from that office. Throughout the early nineteenth century, champagne dealers were well represented in city politics, with other notables including Barbe-Nicole's distant relation Irénee Ruinart de Brimont (Champagne Ruinart, 1820–1827) and, later, Édouard Werlé (Champagne Veuve Clicquot Ponsardin, 1852–1868). Details available at www.reims.unblog.fr/tag/generale.

131 *"Don't cry, Mentine," her mother had told her only recently*: Gmeline, p. 20; Chimay, p. 31.

131 *she had proposed the generous dowry of 100,000 francs*: Chimay, pp. 31–33.

131 *"like cabbages in the market"*: Crestin-Billet, p. 24.

131 *"All this marriage talk," she wrote to Mademoiselle Gard*: Chimay, p. 31.

132 *King Louis XVIII had reconfirmed his title*: Fiévet, *Madame Veuve Clicquot*, p. 47.

132 *Barbe-Nicole "was infatuated"*: Chimay, p. 42.

132 *"easy living for the time being, and opulence in the future"*: Ibid., p. 35.

132–133 *"assisting at the balls of Marie Antoinette"*: Tomes, p. 95;
Fiévet, *Madame Veuve Clicquot*, p. 115.

133 *"a mandate of arrest to direct the taking of 'Citizen Such-a-one'"*:
Anonymous, *A Residence in France During the Years 1792, 1793, 1794, and
1795*, n.p.

133 *her sister, the Countess de Marmande*: Various details on Louis de
Chevigné's family and childhood from Gmeline, pp. 21–25.

134–135 *"obtaining noble titles was a shrewd marketing strategy"*: Kolleen
Guy, "'Oiling the Wheels of Social Life': Myths and Marketing in
Champagne during the Belle Epoque," *French Historical Studies* 22, no. 2
(Spring 1999): 211–239, 218.

135 *"a mother with an only daughter"*: Chimay, p. 35.

135 *"the less she will be able to refuse"*: Chimay, p. 35.

135 *Clémentine, perhaps tired of this parade of suitors, for once insisted*: Éric
Poindron, "Promenade et *Conte rémois*, en guise d'introduction, ou,
tentative de nouvelle essai à la manière modeste des *Contes* de Louis de
C[hevigné]," available at http://blog.france3.fr/cabinet-de-curiosites/
tb.php?id=59083.

135 *"I won't make myself destitute"*: Chimay, pp. 32, 38.

135 *plus free accommodation with her in the family home*: On conventional family arrangements in nineteenth-century France, see David
I. Kertzer and Marzio Barbagli, *Family Life in Early Modern Times,
1500–1789* (New Haven, CT: Yale University Press, 2001); and Frederic
Le Play, *La reforme sociale* (1872), reprinted in Catherine Bodard Silver,
ed., *On Family, Work and Social Change* (Chicago: University of Chicago
Press, 1982).

135 *"awaiting the rest of the inheritance—which shouldn't take long"*:
Chimay, p. 35.

135 *the wedding was planned in Reims on the tenth of September*: A fac-
simile of the wedding invitation is reproduced in Diane de Maynard,
La descendance de Madame Clicquot-Ponsardin, preface de la Vicomtesse de Luppé
(Mayenne: Joseph Floch, 1975).

136 *"Arrange as you like with Monsieur de Chevigné about the trousseau"*:
Chimay, p. 36.

136 *"Clémentine is no longer shy with her husband, she* tutoies *him"*: Gmeline, p. 23; Chimay, p. 37.

137 *locker-room references from his friend Richard Castel*: Chimay, pp. 40–41.

137 *"The Comte de Chevigné, who had not yet written his [erotic] fables"*: Barbat de Bignicourt, *Un salon à Reims en 1832* (1879), quoted in Eugène Dupont, *La vie rémoise*, ed. Jean-Yves Sureau, available at www .lavieremoise.free.fr.

137 *In London, the Duchess of Devonshire*: See Amanda Forman, *Georgiana: Duchess of Devonshire* (New York: Random House, 1999).

137 *the lowly sandwich was a sign of the times*: According to a contemporary travel account, the sandwich was invented at the gambling table by John Montagu, the fourth Earl of Sandwich (1718–1792); see Pierre Jean Grosley, *A Tour to London, or, New Observations on England and Its Inhabitants* (London: Lockyer Davis, 1772).

137 *"a protest against bourgeois and capitalist modernity"*: E. J. Carter, "Breaking the Bank: Gambling Casinos, Finance Capitalism, and German Unification," *Central European History* 39 (2006): 185–213, 186.

139 *Philippe Clicquot . . . died in the final months of 1819*: His death is recorded on October 23, 1819; see Lallemand, *Le Baron Ponsardin*.

139 *her father, Nicolas, passed away at seventy-three years old*: Fiévet, *Madame Veuve Clicquot*, records the date as October 25, 1820; p. 50.

139 *"pliable and pragmatic in his beliefs"*: Ibid., p. 51.

139 *"skillful in his acquaintances"*: Ibid., p. 50.

140 *He slipped off an icy bridge*: Crestin-Billet, p. 89.

140 *she intended to retire—and to give George the entire business as a gift*: Ibid., p. 91.

140 *At the beginning of the century . . . there were ten champagne houses*: Details from website of the Union des Maisons de Champagne, available at www.maisons-champagne.com.

140–141 *"There is no country where you can make a fortune so easily"*: See "L'insertion de la maison Pommery dans le négoce du champagne," available at www.patrimonieindustriel-apic.com, p. 8.

141 *German named Matthieu-Édouard Werler*: Crestin-Billet, pp. 91–94.

141   *"Werler . . . came a poor boy to Rheims from the Duchy of Nassau"*:
Tomes, p. 87.

CHAPTER THIRTEEN: FLIRTING WITH DISASTER

144.   *In one room, the ceiling was decorated with sculpted figures*: Paul Vitry,
L'Hôtel le Vergeur, notice historique (Reims: Société des Amis du Vieux
Reims/Henri Matot, 1932), p. 11. According to town records, a gentle-
man by the name of Vanin-Clicquot, a manufacturer in Reims and
probably a family relation, purchased the building on 27, brumaire an
II. He updated and renovated the mansion and sold it in 1822 to Barbe-
Nicole. The building was subsequently sold in 1895 by the Werlé family,
who had come into possession of the building after Barbe-Nicole's death.

144.   *More solid companies are destroyed by overreaching expansion than almost
anything else*: See, for example, Carlos Grande, "Stretching the Brand:
The Risk of Extension," *Financial Times*, June 4, 2007, available at www.
ft.com; and Dennis Berman, "Growing Danger: Relentless Prosperity Is
Forcing a Choice on Many Small Companies: Expand or Die," *Business
Week*, October 8, 1999, available at www.businessweek.com.

144–145   *"bankers played a secondary role . . . in the production cycle"*:
Desbois-Thibault, p. 80.

145   *typically required to loan his personal savings*: George V. Taylor,
"Notes on Commercial Travelers in Eighteenth-Century France," *Business History Review* 38, no. 3 (Autumn 1964): 346–353, 348.

145.   *Jean-Rémy Moët started self-financing his production costs as early as
1819*: Desbois-Thibault, pp. 80–81.

145   *what the poet William Blake called "dark satanic mills"*: From "And
did those feet in ancient times," *Milton* (1804), preface. At this point in
British industrial history, the mills in and around London would have
been primarily water-powered textile mills and not the steam-powered
mills that were later so common; see Sir Edward Baines, *History of the
cotton manufacture in Great Britain, with a notice of its early history on the East,
and in all the quarters of the globe: A description of the great mechanical inventions,
which have caused its unexampled extension in Britain: And a view of the present state of the manufacture, and the conditions of the classes engaged in its several
departments* (London: H. & R. Fisher, P. Jackson, 1835).

145 *Louis-Philippe, the Duke of Orléans*: Fiévet, *Madame Veuve Clicquot*: "At the moment of the coronation of Charles X, Madame Clicquot had the honor of lodging during his visit . . . the duke of Orléans, after Louis-Philippe," p. 23. Charles-Philippe, Comte d'Artois, the younger brother of Louis XVI and brother-in-law to Marie Antoinette, became king in 1824, at the age of sixty-seven, after the death of Louis XVII. He was deposed during the revolution of 1830, and Louis-Philippe became king by popular acclaim.

146 *Barbe-Nicole was almost $14 million*: 700,000 French francs; statistics from Crestin-Billet, p. 91.

146 *When a tearful and frightened young lad was sent to deliver a defective load of glass bottles*: Interview, January 8, 2007, Fabienne Huttaux, Historical Resources Manager, Champagne Veuve Clicquot Ponsardin.

147 *poor Thérèse had lost her husband*: Adrien lived from 1802 to 1826; her son, Pierre, from her first marriage, survived until 1870.

147 *Édouard's wedding to a young woman named Louise-Émilie Boisseau*: Crestin-Billet, p. 43.

147 *engaged to marry the daughter of an important state official back in Germany*: Vizetelly writes: "Establishment of G. C. Kessler and Co. at Esslingen—formerly one of the most important of the free imperial cities, and picturesquely situated on the Neckar—was founded as far back as 1826, and claims to be the oldest sparkling wine factory in Germany," p. 192. Details here from G. C. Kessler promotional materials, available at www.kessler-sektkellerei.de.

148 *Barbe-Nicole was running a large operation*: Vizetelly records that her competitors at Moët et Chandon, for example, had 1,500 employees by 1879; p. 113.

148 *"the superiority of her brand"*: Fiévet, *Madame Veuve Clicquot*, p. 63.

148 *Barbe-Nicole knew what historian Kolleen Guy has recently discovered*: Guy, "Oiling the Wheels of Social Life," p. 216, n. 20; quoting U.S. Department of State, dispatches from U.S. consul at Rheims, January 15, 1869.

149 *began to wonder if it might not be a good idea to protect her good name*: Delpal, p. 173.

149 *she went through the trouble of registering her trademark*: Crestin-Billet, p. 134.

149 *André Jullien had been working in Jean-Rémy's cellars*: Desbois-Thibault, p. 141; Fiévet, *Histoire de la ville de Épernay*, p. 82, discusses mechanization of industry by the late 1830s in greater detail. See also François Bonal, *Champagne Mumm: Un champagne dans l'histoire* (Paris: Arthaud, 1987).

149 *Cyrus Redding's monumental* History and Description of Modern Wines: Cyrus Redding, *A History and Description of Modern Wines* (London: Whittaker, Treacher, & Arnot, 1833), p. 56.

150 *massive crop failures across France*: David H. Pinkney, "A New Look at the French Revolution of 1830," *Review of Politics* 23, no. 4 (October 1961): 490–506, 492.

150 *with the large and well-established firm of Poupart de Neuflize*: Fritz Redlich, "Jacques Laffitte and the Beginnings of Investment Banking in France," *Bulletin of the Business Historical Society* 22, nos. 4–6 (December 1948): pp. 137–161; and Richard J. Barker, "The Conseil General des Manufactures under Napoléon (1810–1814)," *French Historical Studies* 6, no. 2 (Autumn 1969): pp. 185–213, 196, n. 36.

151 *losses of almost $5.5 million*: 270,000 francs; Crestin-Billet, p. 93.

152 *an astonishing 280,000 bottles of champagne*: Ibid., pp. 88, 94; Desbois-Thibault, p. 333.

152 *Soon, it was not a middle-class protest at all*: Edgar Leon Newman, "The Blouse and the Frock Coat: The Alliance of the Common People of Paris with the Liberal Leadership and the Middle Class during the Last Years of the Bourbon Restoration," *Journal of Modern History* 46, no. 1 (March 1974): 26–59, 31.

152 *more than half the population was living in squalid poverty*: Statistics here and following from Pinkney, p. 494.

152 *"his jacket with its [royal] fleur-de-lis buttons"*: François-René de Chateaubriand, *Mémoires d'outre-tombe* [Memoirs from Beyond the Tomb] (1849–1850), trans. A. S. Kline, sect. 31, pt. 8, available at www.tkline. pgcc.net/PITBR/Chateaubriand/Chathome.htm.

153   *the town hall had been sacked*: Fiévet, *Histoire de la ville d'Épernay,* pp. 318–320.

153   *dislike of the Bourbon kings—and their supporters—was especially intense*: Pamela Pilbeam, "The 'Three Glorious Days': The Revolution of 1830 in Provincial France," *Historical Journal* 26, no. 4 (December 1983): pp. 831–844, 837.

154   *waving the tricolor flag of an earlier, more radical, generation*: The National Guard was revived with particular intensity in the nearby Haut-Marne and was associated specifically with the revival of the *tricolore* and with the democratic election of officers to serve as local civic and military leaders; see Pilbeam, p. 836.

154   *"My feelings are divided . . . but I regret more than anything the family ties"*: Quoted in Poindron, n.p.

154   *"The reign of Louis-Philippe was a business régime"*: Anonymous, "Entertaining the Son of the 'Bourgeois King,'" *Bulletin of the Business Historical Society* 3, no. 4 (June 1929): 15–17, 15.

154   *the vast majority of them a new economic boom time*: Pilbeam, p. 832.

CHAPTER FOURTEEN: THE CHAMPAGNE EMPIRE

155   *made his first visit to the Champagne wine country*: Fiévet, *Histoire de la ville d'Épernay,* pp. 334–335.

157   *what historians call "the managerial revolution"*: Alfred D. Chandler Jr., "The Emergence of Managerial Capitalism," *Business History Review* 58, no. 4 (Winter 1984): 473–503, 473.

157   *"personally managed enterprises . . . had become specialized"*: Ibid., p. 383.

157   *the Widow Clicquot might easily have shared the same fate as those of the Widow Binet*: For historical details on the Widow Binet, see Union des Maisons de Champagne, available at www.maison-champagne.com.

157   *Already, the first railroad tracks were being laid in France*: Fiévet, *Histoire de la ville d'Épernay,* p. 108.

158   *He was also a gentle man possessed of an artistic sensibility*: Tomes, p. 95; Gmeline, pp. 30, 170.

160   *the average woman in France lived fewer than forty-five years*: "Data on Healthy Life Years in the European Union," avail-

able at http://ec.europa.eu/health/ph_information/indicators/
lifeyears_data_en.htm.

160   *"a dwarfish, withered old woman of eighty-nine years"*: Tomes, p. 68.

160   *"He is also a German, and a nephew, it is believed, of [Édouard]
Werler"*: Ibid., p. 89.

161   *"I have my grandchildren and great-grandchildren around me"*: Quoted
in Crestin-Billet, p. 94.

161   *"I am making preparations . . . for my removal to the country"*: Details
here and following from Fiévet, *Madame Veuve Clicquot*, p. 94.

162   *an amusing story of its construction*: Tomes, pp. 96–97.

162   *"It was a grand château"*: Maynard, preface, n.p.

162   *"adorned with modern tapestries and richly sculptured panels"*: Quotes
here and following from Chimay, pp. 50–51.

164–165   *"none of the wit and grace, but all the grossness, of those authors"*:
Tomes, p. 97.

165   *if Louis had not found himself needing cash again*: Gmeline, p. 25.

CHAPTER FIFTEEN: LA GRANDE DAME

166   *what the doctors then called a cerebral congestion*: Gmeline, p. 2;
Gustavo C. Roman, "Cerebral Congestion, a Vanished Disease," *Archives
of Neurology* 44, no. 4 (April 1987), abstract summary: "It accounted not
only for cerebral hemorrhage, but also for lacunae (Dechambre, 1838),
etat crible [*sic*; cribriform state] (Durand-Fardel, 1842), depression, manic
outbursts, headaches, coma, and seizures. According to Hammond
(1871, 1878), cerebral congestion was 'more common . . . than any other
affliction of the nervous system.'" See also Gustavo C. Roman, "On the
History of Lacunes, *État Criblé*, and the White Matter Lesions of Vascular Dementia," *Cerebrovascular Diseases* 13, no. 2 (2002): 1–6. Some have
suggested this cerebral congestion was used to describe malaria, although cholera is more likely. By the 1820s, quinine had been extracted
as a relatively reliable treatment for malaria, and it was commonly
recognizable as ague. The symptoms are similar to cholera, which was
still pandemic in Europe during the first part of the 1850s. However,
cerebral congestion may have been a result of any other number of diseases. On possible diagnoses, see "Old Diseases and Their Symptoms,"

available at http://web.ukonline.co.uk/thursday.handleigh/history/ health/old-diseases.htm.

167 *"I was already six when my brother Paul fell ill"*: Gmeline, pp. 1–2.

167 *Within days, everyone knew Anne, too, had contracted the illness*: Ibid., p. 31.

167 *continued outbreak of cholera in 1854*: Ibid., p. 2.

167 *"sad parents and aged grandparents"*: Ibid., p. 3.

168 *The two men, especially, did not get along*: Ibid., p. 35.

168 *"My dear mother had such a weak character"*: Ibid., p. 30.

168 *"life was not always easy"*: Ibid., p. 7.

168 *"animosity reigned"*: Ibid.

168 *Victor Fiévet's* Madame Veuve Clicquot: Published at the specific request of Louis de Chevigné, who contacted the author after reading his earlier biography of Jean-Rémy Moët.

169 *Alphonse Marie Louise de Lamartine*: French novelist and politician (1790–1869), author of *Histoire des Girondins* (Paris: Furne et Cie., 1847).

169 *For a short while, there was a second republic in France*: Following the abdication of King Louis-Philippe and the end of his so-called July Monarchy in 1848. By 1852, Louis-Napoléon had assumed the title of Emperor Napoléon III, which he retained until the intensification of the Franco-Prussian War in 1870.

169 *"Working women had emerged as a locus of tension and debate"*: Judith A. DeGroat, "The Public Nature of Women's Work: Definitions and Debates During the Revolution of 1848," *French Historical Studies* 20, no. 1 (Winter 1997): 31–47, 32.

169 *"Woman . . . was not made to manufacture our products"*: *L'Atelier*, January 4, 1841; quoted in DeGroat, p. 34.

170 *sounds of low voices in the distance and the creaking wheels of donkey carts*: Vizetelly, p. 119.

170 *the Clicquot-Werlé crushing rooms now had eight presses*: Ibid., p. 39.

170 *vats large enough to supply the international market*: Tomes, p. 68.

171 *known as "Consular Seal" champagne*: Advertised in *Harper's Weekly*, July 25, 1868; Tomes, p. 62.

171 *"RHEIMS printed conspicuously on the labels of a bottle of* Clicquot*"*: Ibid., p. 59.

172   *"accumulated a fortune of four or five millions of dollars"*: Ibid.,
p. 87; $1.00 in 1850 was worth $21.11 in 2003; statistical details available at http://listlva.lib.va.us/cgibin/wa.exe?A2=ind0410&L=VA-
ROOTS&P=3010.

172   *80,000 francs . . . to establish a home for poor children*: Fiévet, *Madame
Veuve Clicquot*, p. 103.

172   *"Madame Clicquot . . . is queen of Reims"*: Prosper Mérimée, *Oeuvres
complètes de Prosper Mérimée*, ed. Pierre Trahard and Edouard Champion
(Paris: H. Champion, 1927); letter of July 26, 1853. This is an amount
on the order of $700,000.

172   *"Don't ever accuse me of being jealous!"*: Fiévet, *Madame Veuve Clicquot*, pp. 73–74.

172   *Édouard was appointed mayor of Reims*: Details available at www.
reims-web.com/reims/champagne-reims-veuve-clicquot.html.

172   *"an ardent imperialist"*: Tomes, p. 88.

173   *"will do anything for his favorite wine-merchant but drink his champagne"*: Ibid.

173   *"the shrewdest manipulator of the sparkling products of Aÿ and Bouzy of
her day"*: Vizetelly, p. 21.

173   *"made to suit the Russian taste, which likes a sweet and strong champagne"*: Tomes, p. 68.

174   *her husband, Alexandre, another of Reims's dabbling wool merchants*: Details here and following from "L'insertion de la maison Pommery dans
le négoce du champagne," available at www.patrimonieindustriel-apic.
com.

175   *"was just as equipped to run a government as a business"*: François
Bonal, *Le livre d'or du champagne* (Laussane: Édition du Grand Pont, 1984),
p. 66.

175   *Veuve Pommery and Company into an immensely profitable and important
business*: Raphaël Bonnedame, *Notice sur la maison Veuve Pommery, Fils &
Cie.* (Épernay: n.p., 1892), quoted at www.patrimoineindustrielapic.com/
documentation/maitrise%20piotrowski/partie%201%20chap%201.htm.

175   *champagne in the style we still enjoy today as brut*: "In 1860, she
[Madame Pommery] understood that sweet champagne, doux or demi-
sec, will always remain a wine without a big future. She saw that bring-

ing these wines to the market as *brut* wines, under the names *sec* or *extra sec* would lead to bigger growth in the Champagne. And after investigating, she finally decided to market wines *brut nature* to accompany any meal . . . the *brut nature*, with no added sugar, was commercially released in 1874"; Glatre, p. 95. Vizetelly adds: "To the extra-dry champagnes a modicum dose is added, while the so-called '*brut*' wines receive no more than from one to three per cent. of liqueur"; Vizetelly, p. 60.

175   *in the style of the noble British estates*: Helen Gillespie-Peck suggests a design based on Inveraray Castle and Mellerstain House; see Peck, *WineWoman@Bergerac.France* (Ely, UK: Melrose Books, 2005), p. 119. The domaine was built during the 1860s and 1870s.

176   *cellars were adorned with great works of art in carved stone*: Louise Pommery commissioned sculptor Henri Navlet to decorate some of her more than ten miles of cellars with bas-reliefs on the theme of wine and Bacchus; promotional materials, Champagne Pommery.

176   *her ancestors still run Champagne Henriot*: Promotional materials, Champagne Henriot, available at www.champagne-henriot.com/histoire.php.

176   *"the largest and wealthiest of all" the local companies*: Tomes, p. 69. On Madame Jacques Olry, see www.maisons-champagne.com/bonal/pages/04/04-01_1.htm.

177   *"the high-class English buyer [who] demands a dry champagne"*: Vizetelly, p. 60.

177   *"color of the egg yolks of the famous corn-fed hens of Bresse"*: Matasar, p. 29; see also Marion Winik, "The Women of Champagne," *American Way*, March 1, 1997, p. 113. Although commonly considered a bright orange, the color is registered as "Clicquot Yellow."

CHAPTER SIXTEEN: THE QUEEN OF REIMS

179   *"Strangers and visitors were welcomed with an open hospitality"*: Fiévet, *Madame Veuve Clicquot*, pp. 90–91.

180   *"the Château de Boursault was a must see on their list"*: Fiévet, *Madame Veuve Clicquot*, pp. 16, 98.

180   *"every prince, czar, archduke, Roman cardinal, nabob, or lord mayor"*: Quoted in Gmeline, p. 36.

180   *"delicate features and full of energy"*: Fiévet, *Madame Veuve Clicquot*, pp. 88–91.

180   *Half the dukes of France and the king of Serbia were vying for her hand*: Gmeline, p. 43.

181   *"I am going to tell you a secret"*: "Extrait du livret conçu pour l'exposition itinérante de 2005," Champagne Veuve Clicquot Ponsardin, quoted at www.reims-web.com/reims/champagne-reims-veuve-clicquot.html#.

183   *captured not far from the ancient province of the Champagne in the Battle of Sedan*: Located some fifty miles northwest of Reims, the battle took place on September 1, 1870.

183   *an important railway ran just below the outcrop*: Fiévet, *Madame Veuve Clicquot*, p. 16.

183   *nearly $10 million in damages*: 400,000 francs; Poindron, n.p.

183–184   *"I am an old man . . . and my life is not worth that sum"*: Ibid.

184   *"I thank my granddaughter . . . for the joy that she brought to the family"*: Gmeline, p. 63.

185   *through the phylloxera outbreak in the French wine country and the two world wars*: Henri Jolicoeur, *Description des ravageurs de la vigne: Insectes et champignons parasites* (Reims: Michaud, 1894); J. L. Rhone-Converset, *La vigne, ses maladies-ses ennemis-sa défense en Bourgogne et Champagne, etc.* (Paris: Châtillon-sur-Seine, 1889); also Don and Petie Kladstrup, *Champagne: How the World's Most Glamorous Wine Triumphed over War and Hard Times* (New York: William Morrow, 2005).

AFTERWORD

189   *"some of the largest commercial houses have women at their head"*: Linus Pierpont Brocket, *Woman: Her Rights, Wrongs, Privileges, and Responsibilities* (Cincinnati: Howe's Book Subscription Concern, 1869), p. 201; for a broader survey, see also Angel Kwolek-Folland, *Engendering Business: Men and Women in the Corporate Office, 1870–1930* (Baltimore: Johns Hopkins University Press, 1994).

Angela Georgina Burdett-Coutts (1814–1906) was the youngest daughter of the influential banker Thomas Coutts (1735–1822), who inherited the business from an aging female relation in 1837; she was

courted by Louis-Napoléon and was an intimate friend of France's
Louis-Philippe. Refusing all comers until 1881, she spent most of her
life as a businesswoman, philanthropist, and celebrity. She eventually
married, at the age of sixty-seven, her thirty-year-old secretary, William
Lehman Ashmead Bartlett (1851–1921). Edna Healey, *Lady Unknown:
The Life of Angela Burdett-Coutts* (New York: Coward, McGann & Geoghe-
gan, 1978).

190   *"after my mother the most remarkable woman in the country"*: Brocket,
p. 201.

190   *"many women in the eighteenth and nineteenth centuries participated in
commerce"*: Laura Cochrane, "From the Archives: Women's History in
Baker Library's Business Manuscripts Collection," *Business History Review*
74 (Fall 2000): 465–476.

190   *They ran plantations in the South and textile mills in the North*: On
middle- and upper-middle-class businesswomen in nineteenth-century
America, see, for example, Cara Anzilotti, "Autonomy and the Female
Planter in Colonial South Carolina," *Journal of Southern History* 63, no.
2 (1997): 239–268; David L. Coon, "Eliza Lucas Pinckney and the Re-
introduction of Indigo Culture in South Carolina," *Journal of Southern
History* 42, no. 1 (1976): 61–76; Eliza Pinckney, *The Letterbook of Eliza
Lucas Pinckney 1739–1762*, ed. Elise Pinckney (Chapel Hill: University of
South Carolina Press, 1997).

190   *seed merchant Carrie Lippincott or medicinal purveyor Lydia Pinkham*:
See Cochrane, pp. 465–469.

191   *"no single one has led to so much mischief"*: Charles Tovey, *Champagne
Revelations*, pp. 32–33. On this issue of monopoly in the modern context, Jancis Robinson observes that "the central feature of geographical
delimitation as it applies to wine is not just that it usually leads to an improvement in wine quality . . . it is [also] a legislative procedure whereby
a privileged monopolistic position is created for producers within a
demarcated area," quoted in Michael Maher, "In Vino Veritas?: Clarifying the Use of Geographic References on American Wine Labels,"
California Law Review 89, no. 6 (December 2001): 1881–1925, 1922.

Selected Bibliography

Amerine, Maynard A., trans. *Wines of Champagne and Sparkling Wines.* Paris: Encyclopédie Agricole, 1930.

Anonymous. *A Residence in France, During the Years 1792, 1793, 1794, and 1795; Described in a Series of letters from an English Lady.* Ed. John Gifford. London: T. N. Longman, 1797.

———. "The Comet." *Robert Merry's Museum* (November 1858): 137–139.

———. *A Glimpse of a Famous Wine Cellar, in Which Are Described the Vineyards of Marne and the Methods Employed in Making Champagne. Translated from the French.* New York: Francis Draz & Co., 1906.

———. "Entertaining the Son of the 'Bourgeois King.'" *Bulletin of the Business Historical Society* 3, no. 4 (June 1929): 15–17.

———. *Rheims and Battles for Its Possession.* Paris: Michelin, 1919.

———. *London at Table: or, How, When, and Where to Dine and Order a Dinner, and Where to Avoid Dining, with Practical Hints to Cooks.* London: Chapman & Hall, 1851.

———. *Description de la fête patriotique, célébrée à Rethel le 14 Juillet 1790, & jours suivants.* Reims: Jeunehomme, Imprimeurs du Rois, 1790.

Anzilotti, Cara. "Autonomy and the Female Planter in Colonial South Carolina." *Journal of Southern History* 63, no. 2 (1997): 239–268.

Assier, Alexandre. *Légendes, curiosités et traditions de la Champagne et de la Brie.* Paris: Techener Librairie, 1860.

Assier, Alexandre. *Napoléon Ier à l'École Royale Militaire de Brienne d'après des documents authentiques et inédits, 1779–1784.* Paris: n.p., 1874.

Aston, Nigel. *The End of an Élite: The French Bishops and the Coming of the Revolution, 1786–1790.* Clarendon: Oxford University Press, 1992.

Baines, Edward. *History of the cotton manufacture in Great Britain, with a notice of its early history on the East, and in all the quarters of the globe: A description of the great mechanical inventions, which have caused its unexampled extension in Britain: And a view of the present state of the manufacture, and the conditions of the classes engaged in its several departments.* London: H. and R. Fisher, P. Jackson, 1835.

Bakalinsky, A. T. "Sulfites, Wine and Health," in *Wine in Context: Nutrition, Physiology, Policy: Proceedings of the Symposium on Wine and Health.* Eds. Andrew L. Waterhouse and R. M. Rantz. Davis, Calif.: American Society for Enology and Viticulture, 1996.

Barker, Hannah. *Business of Women: Female Enterprise and Urban Development in Northern England 1760–1830.* Oxford: Oxford University Press, 2006.

Barker, Richard J. "The Conseil General des Manufactures under Napoléon (1810–1814)." *French Historical Studies* 6, no. 2 (Autumn 1969): 185–213.

Bercé, Yves-Marie. *Vignerons et vins, de Champagne et d'ailleurs, XVIIe-XXe siècle.* Reims: Université de Reims, Centre d'Études Champenoises, Departement d'Histoire, 1988.

Bésème-Pia, Lise. *Vignoble champenois: Lexique du paysan et du vigneron champenois.* Rethel: Binet Sarl, 1997.

Bidet, Nicolas. *Traité sur la culture des vignes, sur la façon du vin, et sur la manière de le gouverner: Ouvrage orné de figures, & en particulier de celle d'un pressoir d'une nouvelle invention.* Paris: Chez Savoye, 1752.

Bignicourt, Arthur Barbat de. *Les Massacres à Reims en 1792 après des documents authentiques.* Reims: n.p., 1872.

———. *Un salon à Reims en 1832.* Reims: n.p., 1879.

Black, Charles Bertram. *Guide to the North East of France, including*

Picardy, Champagne, Burgundy, Lorraine, and Alsace. London: Sampson Low & Co., 1873.

Blayo, Yves. "La mortalité en France de 1740 à 1829." *Population* (November 1975): 124–142.

Bonal, François. *Dom Pérignon: Vérité et légende.* Langres: D. Guéniot, 1995.

————. *Champagne Mumm: Un champagne dans l'histoire.* Paris: Arthaud, 1987.

————. *Le livre d'or du Champagne.* Laussane: Bonal Éditions du Grand Pont, 1984.

Bonnedame, Raphaël. *Notice sur la maison Moët et Chandon d'Épernay.* Épernay: Imprimerie de R. Bonnedame, 1894.

————. *Notice sur la maison Veuve Pommery, Fils & Cie.* Épernay: n.p., 1892.

Boralevi, Lea Campos. *Bentham and the Oppressed.* New York: Walter de Gruyter, 1984.

Bourgeois, Armand. *Le vin de Champagne sous Louis XIV et sous Louis XV.* Paris: n.p., 1897.

————. *Promenade d'un touriste dans l'arrondissement d'Épernay.* Châlonssur-Marne: Martin Frères éditeurs, 1886.

Briailles, Chandon, Raoul, de, and Henri Bertal. *Sources de l'histoire d'Épernay.* 2 vols. Paris: n.p., 1906.

Briailles, Chandon, Raoul, de. *Vins de Champagne et d'ailleurs: La bibliothèque de Raoul Chandon de Briailles.* Paris: Fédération française pour la coopération des bibliothèques, 2000.

Brennan, Thomas. *Burgundy to Champagne: The Wine Trade in Early Modern France.* Baltimore: Johns Hopkins University Press, 1997.

Brocket, Linus Pierpont. *Woman: Her Rights, Wrongs, Privileges, and Responsibilities.* Cincinnati: Howe's Book Subscription Concern, 1869.

Bruce, Evangeline. *Napoleon and Josephine: An Improbable Marriage.* New York: Scribner, 1995.

Buchan, William. *Domestic medicine, or, A treatise on the prevention and cure of diseases, by regimen and simple medicines: With an appendix, containing a dispensatory for the use of private practioners.* Philadelphia: Richard Folwell, 1797.

Buffenoir, Hippolyte. *Grandes dames contemporaines: La Duchesse d'Uzès.* Paris: Librairie du Mirabeau, 1893.

Busby, James. *Journal of a recent visit to the principal vineyards of Spain and France: Giving a minute account of the different methods pursued in the cultivation of the vine and the manufacture of wine.* New York: C. S. Francis, 1835.

Carmaran-Chimay, Jean, Princess, de. *Madame Veuve Clicquot Ponsardin: Her Life and Times.* Reims: Debar, 1956.

Carter, E. J. "Breaking the Bank: Gambling Casinos, Finance Capitalism, and German Unification." *Central European History* 39 (2006): 185–213.

Carter, Jenny, and Therese Duriez. *With Child: Birth Through the Ages.* Edinburgh: Mainstream Publishing, 1986.

Champenoises: Ecomusée de la région de Fourmies Trélon. Trélon: Atelier-Musée du Verre Trélon, 2000. Exhibit catalog.

Chandler, Alfred D., Jr. "The Emergence of Managerial Capitalism." *Business History Review* 58, no. 4 (Winter 1984): 473–503.

Chaptal, Jean-Antoine, Comte de. *L'Art de faire le vin.* Paris: Madame Huzard, 1819.

Chateaubriand, François-René de. *Memoirs from Beyond the Tomb* (*Mémoires d'outre-tombe,* 1849–1850). Trans. A. S. Kline, 31:8, www.tkline. pgcc.net/PITBR/Chateaubriand/Chathome.htm.

Choudhury, Mita. *Convents and Nuns in Eighteenth-Century French Politics and Culture.* Ithaca: Cornell University Press. 2004.

Clark, Christopher. *Iron Kingdom: The Rise and Downfall of Prussia, 1600–1947.* New York: Penguin, 2007.

Cochrane, Laura. "From the Archives: Women's History in Baker Library's Business Manuscripts Collection." *Business History Review* 74 (Autumn 2000): 465–476.

Code Napoléon; or, The French Civil Code. Literally Translated from the Original and Official Edition, Published at Paris, in 1804. Trans. George Spence. London: William Benning, 1827.

Conner, Susan P. "Public Virtue and Public Women: Prostitution in Revolutionary Paris, 1793–1794." *Eighteenth-Century Studies* 28, no. 2 (Winter 1994): 221–240.

Constant, Louis. *Mémoires de Constant, premier valet de chambre de l'empereur, sur la vie privée de Napoléon, sa famille, et sa cour.* Trans. P. Pinkerton. 4 vols. London: H. S. Nichols, 1896.

Coon, David L. "Eliza Lucas Pinckney and the Reintroduction of Indigo Culture in South Carolina." *Journal of Southern History* 42, no. 1 (1976): 61–76.

Craig, Béatrice. "Where Have All the Businesswomen Gone?: Images and Reality in the Life of Nineteenth-Century Middle-Class Women in Northern France," in *Women, Business and Finance in Nineteenth-Century Europe: Rethinking Separate Spheres.* Eds. Robert Beachy, Béatrice Craig, and Alastair Owens. Oxford: Berg Publishers, 2006.

Crestin-Billet, Frédérique. *La Veuve Clicquot: La grande dame de la Champagne.* Trans. Carole Fahy. Paris: Éditions Glénat, 1992.

Crouzet, François. *L'économie britannique et le blocus continental.* Paris: Economica, 1987.

Cuthell, Edith. *An Imperial Victim: Marie Louise, Archduchess of Austria, Empress of the French, Duchess of Parma.* London: Brentanto's, 1912.

D'Arnould, Charles-Albert. *La vigne, voyage autour des vins de France, étude physiologique, anecdotique, historique, humoristique et même scientifique.* Paris: Plon, 1878.

Daniels, Walter. *Saint-Évremond en Angleterre.* Versailles: L. Luce, 1907.

David, Jacques-Louis, and Studio. *The Death of Marat* (La mort de Marat), ca. 1794, oil on canvas. Reims: Musée des Beaux-Arts de la Ville de Reims, gift of Paul David, 1879.

Davis, C. R., et al. "Practical Implications of Malolactic Fermentation: A Review." *American Journal of Enology and Viticulture* 36, no. 4 (1985): 290–301.

DeGroat, Judith A. "The Public Nature of Women's Work: Definitions and Debates During the Revolution of 1848." *French Historical Studies* 20, no. 1 (Winter 1997): 31–47.

DeJean, Joan. *The Essence of Style: How the French Invented High Fashion, Fine Food, Chic Cafés, Style, Sophistication, and Glamour.* New York: Free Press, 2005.

Delpal, Jacques-Louis. *Merveilles de Champagne.* Paris: Éditions de la Martinière, 1993.

Delpierre, Madeleine. *Dress in France in the Eighteenth Century.* Trans.

Caroline Beamish. New Haven, CT: Yale University Press, 1997.

Desbois-Thibault, Claire. *L'extraordinaire aventure du Champagne Moët et Chandon, une affaire de famille.* Paris: Presses Universitaires de France, 2003.

Dexter, Elisabeth Anthony. *Colonial Women of Affairs: Women in Business and the Professions in America Before 1776.* Boston: Houghton Mifflin Co., 1924.

Diderot, Denis. *Encyclopédie; ou Dictionnaire raisonné des sciences, des arts et des métiers.* Neufchastel [*sic*]: Samuel Faulche, 1765.

Dion, Roger. *Histoire de la vigne et du vin en France.* Paris: n.p., 1959.

Dumbrell, Roger. *Understanding Antique Wine Bottles.* San Francisco: Antique Collector's Club, 1983.

Etienne, Michel. *Veuve Clicquot Ponsardin, aux origines d'un grand vin de Champagne.* Paris: Economica, 1994.

Evelyn, John. *Sylva, or, A discourse on forest-trees, and the propagation of timber in His Majesties dominions. By J. E. Esq. As it was deliver'd in the Royal Society the XVth of October, MDCLXII . . . To which is annexed Pomona; or, An appendix concerning fruit-trees in relation to cider.* London: Joseph Martyn & James Allestry, 1664.

Fagan, Brian. *The Little Ice Age: How Climate Made History.* New York: Basic Books, 2000.

Fauvelet, Louis-Antoine. *Memoirs of Napoleon Bonaparte.* London: Richard Bentley, 1836.

Fiévet, Victor. *Histoire de la ville d'Épernay.* Épernay: V. Fiévet, 1868.

———. *Jean-Rémy Moët et ses successeurs.* Paris: E. Dentu, 1864.

———. *Madame Veuve Clicquot (née Ponsardin), son histoire et celle de sa famille.* Paris and Épernay: Dentu, 1865.

Forman, Amanda. *Georgiana: Duchess of Devonshire.* New York: Random House, 1999.

Freeman, William G. *New Phytologist* 6, no. 1 (January 1907): 18–23.

Gabler, James. *Passions: The Wines and Travels of Thomas Jefferson.* Baltimore: Bacchus Press, 1995.

Galeron, Edmond. *Journal historique de Reims depuis la fondation de cette ville jusqu'à nos jours, avec les synchronismes de l'histoire romaine et de l'histoire de France.* Reims: n.p., 1853.

Gandihon, René. *Naissance du champagne, Dom Pierre Pérignon.* Paris: Hachette, 1968.

Gautier, Théophile. *Voyage en Russie.* 2 vols. Paris: n.p., 1867.

Geffré, Claude, and Jean-Pierre Jossua. *1789: The French Revolution and the Church.* Edinburgh: T. & T. Clark, 1989.

Gelbart, Nina Rattner. *The King's Midwife: A History and Mystery of Madame du Coudray.* Berkeley: University of California Press, 1998.

Gillespie-Peck, Helen. *Wine Woman@Bergerac.France.* Ely, UK: Melrose Books, 2005.

Glatre, Eric. *Chronique des vins de Champagne.* Paris: Castor et Pollux, 2001.

Glatre, Eric, and Georges Clause. *Le Champagne: Trois siècles d'histoire.* Paris: Éditions Stock, 1997.

Glatre, Eric, and Jaqueline Roubinet. *Charles Heidsieck: Un pionnier et un homme d'honneur.* Paris: Stock, 1995.

Gleeson, Janet. *Privilege and Scandal: The Remarkable Life of Harriet Spencer, Sister of Georgiana.* New York: Crown, 2007.

Gmeline, Patrick de, ed. *La Duchesse d'Uzès.* Paris: Librairie Académique Perrin, 1986.

Gmeline, Patrick de. *Ruinart, la plus ancienne maison de champagne, de 1729 à nos jours.* Paris: Stock, 1994.

Godinot, Jean. *Manière de cultiver et de faire le vin en Champagne* (1722). Ed. François Bonal. Langres: Dominique Guéniot, 1990.

Goode, Jamie. *The Science of Wine: From Vine to Glass.* Berkeley: University of California Press, 2005.

Goodrich, Frank. *Court of Napoléon; or, Society under the First Empire.* Philadelphia: J. B. Lippincott, 1880.

Gough, Jerry B. "Winecraft and Chemistry in Eighteenth-Century France: Chaptal and the Invention of Chaptalization." *Technology and Culture* 39, no. 1 (January 1998): 74–104.

Grosley, Pierre-Jean. *A Tour to London, or, New Observations on England and Its Inhabitants.* London: Lockyer Davis, 1772.

Guthrie, William. *Remarks upon Claret, Burgundy, and Champagne, Their Dietetic and Restorative Uses, Etc.* London: Simpkin, Marshall & Co., 1889.

Guy, Kolleen. *When Champagne Became French: Wine and the Making of*

National Identity. Baltimore: Johns Hopkins University Press, 2003.

———. "'Oiling the Wheels of Social Life': Myths and Marketing in Champagne During the Belle Epoque." *French Historical Studies* 22, no. 2 (Spring 1999): 211–239.

———. "Drowning Her Sorrows: Widowhood and Entrepreneurship in the Champagne Industry." *Business and Economic History* 26, no. 2 (Winter 1997): 505–512.

Hanson, Joseph Mills. *The Marne, Historic and Picturesque.* Chicago: A. C. McClurg, 1922.

Hau, Michel. *Croissance économique de la Champagne de 1810 à 1969.* Paris: Éditions Ophrys, 1976.

Healey, Edna. *Lady Unknown: Life of Angela Burdett-Coutts.* London: Sidgwick & Jackson, 1984.

Heidsieck, Marcel, and Patrick Heidsieck. *Vie de Charles Heidsieck.* Reims: Société Charles Heidsieck, 1962.

Hely-Hutchinson, Mary Sophia. *Fashion in Paris: The Various Phases of Feminine Taste and Aesthetics from the Revolution to the End of the 19th Century.* London: W. Heinemann, 1901.

Houssaye, Arsène. *Notre-Dame de Thermidor: Histoire de Madame Tallien.* Paris: H. Plon, 1866.

Houssaye, Henry. *Napoleon and the Campaign of 1814.* Uckfield, UK: Naval and Miltary Press, 2006.

Hughes, William. *The Compleat Vineyards, or, A most excellent way for the planting of wines not onely* [sic] *according to the German and French way, but also long experimented in England.* London: W. Crooke, 1665.

Jadart, Charles Henri. *Dom Thierry Ruinart . . . Notice suivie de documents inédits sur sa famille, sa vie, ses œuvres, ses relations avec D. Mabillon.* Paris: n.p., 1886.

James, David G. "Opportunities for Reducing Pesticide Use in Management of Leafhoppers, Cutworms, and Thrips." Conference proceedings of the Washington State Grape Society (2002), www.grape society.org.

James, Henry. *A Little Tour in France.* Leipzig: Bernard Tauchnitz, 1885.

Jefferson, Thomas. "Memorandum on a Tour from Paris to Amsterdam, Strasburg and Back to Paris" (3 March 1788). *Jefferson's Memorandum Books: Accounts, with Legal Records and Miscellany, 1767–1826.* 2 vols. Ed. James A. Bear Jr. and Lucia C. Stanton. Princeton, NJ: Princeton University Press, 1997.

Johnson, James H. "Versailles, Meet Les Halles: Masks, Carnival, and the French Revolution." *Representations* 73 (Winter 2001): 89–116.

Johnston, Hugh. *Wine.* New York: Simon & Schuster, 1979.

Jolicoeur, Henri. *Description des ravageurs de la vigne: Insectes et champignons parasites.* Reims: Michaud, 1894.

Joseph, Robert. *French Wine Revised and Updated.* London: Dorling Kindersley, 2005.

Jullien, André. *Manuel du sommelier, ou Instruction practique sur la manière de soigner les vins.* Paris: Encyclopédie de Roret, 1836.

———. *The Topography of All the Known Vineyards; Containing a Description of Their Kind and Quality of Their Products, and a Classification.* London: G. & W. B. Whittaker, 1824.

Kertzer, David I., and Marzio Barbagli. *Family Life in Early Modern Times, 1500–1789,* New Haven, CT: Yale University Press, 2001.

Kladstrup, Don and Petie. *Champagne: How the World's Most Glamorous Wine Triumphed over War and Hard Times.* New York: William Morrow, 2005.

Kriedte, Peter. *Peasants, Landlords, and Merchant Capitalists: Europe and the World Economy, 1500–1800.* Leamington Spa, UK: Berg, 1983.

Kwolek-Folland, Angel. *Engendering Business: Men and Women in the Corporate Office, 1870–1930.* Baltimore: Johns Hopkins University Press, 1994.

Lallemand, George. *Le Baron Ponsardin.* Reims: Chamber of Commerce/Société des Amis de Vieux Reims, 1967.

Lamartine, Alphonse Marie Louise de. *Histoire des Girondins.* Paris: Furne et Cie., 1847.

Laurent, Gustave. *Reims et la region rémoise a la veille de la Revolution.* Reims: Imprimerie Matot-Braine, 1930.

Le Play, Frederic. *La reforme sociale.* Tours: Mame, 1872. In *On Family, Work and Social Change.* Ed. Catherine Bodard Silver. Chicago: University of Chicago Press, 1982.

Lewis, Gwynne. "Proto-Industrialization in France." *Economic History Review* 47, no. 1 (February 1994): 150–164.

Liger-Belair, Gérard. *Uncorked: The Science of Champagne.* Princeton, NJ: Princeton University Press, 2004.

Ligne, Charles Joseph. *Mémoires et mélanges historiques et littéraires.* Paris: A. Dupont, 1827–1829.

Lloyd, Ward. *A Wine Lover's Glasses: The A. C. Hubbard Jr. Collection of Antique English Drinking Glasses and Bottles.* Yeovil, UK: Richard Dennis, 2000.

Loubere, Leo. *The Red and the White: The History of Wine in France and Italy in the Nineteenth Century.* Albany: State University of New York Press, 1978.

Louis-Perrier, Jean-Pierre Armand. *Mémoire sur le vin de Champagne* (1886). Reprint. Merfy: Librairie J.-Jacques Lecrocq, 1984.

MacLean, Natalie. "The Merry Widows of Mousse." *International Sommelier Guild* 3, no. 63AJ (December 2003): 1–2.

Maher, Michael. "On Vino Veritas?: Clarifying the Use of Geographic References on American Wine Labels." *California Law Review* 89, no. 6 (December 2001): 1881–1925.

Marchand, Leslie A. *Byron's Letters and Journals.* 10 vols. Cambridge: Harvard University Press, 1974.

Martineau, Harriet. *The Autobiography of Harriet Martineau.* Boston: James R. Osgood, 1877.

Matasar, Ann B. *Women of Wine: The Rise of Women in the Global Wine Industry.* Berkeley: University of California Press, 2006.

Maynard, Diane de. *La descendance de Madame Clicquot-Ponsardin, preface de la Vicomtesse de Luppé.* Mayenne: Joseph Floch, 1975.

Menon, Pierre-Louis, and Roger Lecotté. *Au village de France, les traditions, les travaux, les fêtes: La vie traditionelle des paysans.* Entrépilly: Christian de Bartillat, 1993.

Merey, Soufflon de. *Considérations sur le réetablissement des jurands et maîtresses; précédées d'observations sur . . . un project de status et règlements de MM. Les Marchands de Vin.* Paris: A. J. Marchant, 1805.

Merrett, Christopher. *Some Observations Concerning the Ordering of Wines.* London: William Whitwood, 1692.

Moore, Thomas. *Life of Lord Byron, with His Letters and Journals.* 6 vols. London: John Murray, 1854.

Moreau, Émile. *Le culte de Saint Vincent en Champagne.* Épernay: Éditions le Vigneron de la Champagne, 1936.

Moreau, Jacques. *De la connoissance* [sic] *des fièvres continues, pourprées et pestilentes.* Paris: Laurent D'Houry, 1689.

Murphy, Charles. *Observations on the character and culture of the European vine, during a residence of five years in the vine growing districts of France, Italy and Switzerland, to which is added, the manual of the Swiss vigneron.* New York: Oaksmith & Co., 1859.

Navier, Pierre Toussaint. *Question agitée dans les Écoles de la Faculté de Médecine de Reims. Le 14 Mai 1777. Par M. Navier fils, Docteur-Régent de la Faculté de Médecine en l'Université de Reims. Sur l'usage du vin de champagne mousseux contre les fièvres putrides & autres maladies de même nature.* Reims: Cazin, 1778.

Newman, Edgar Leon. "The Blouse and the Frock Coat: The Alliance of the Common People of Paris with the Liberal Leadership and the Middle Class During the Last Years of the Bourbon Restoration." *Journal of Modern History* 46, no. 1 (March 1974): 26–59.

Oeuvres complètes de Prosper Mérimée. Eds. Pierre Trahard and Edouard Champion. Paris: H. Champion, 1927.

Orton, Diana. *Made of Gold: Biography of Angela Burdett-Coutts.* London: Hamilton, 1979.

Pacottet, Paul, and L. Guittonneau. *Vins de Champagne et vins mousseux.* Paris: J.-B. Bailliere, 1930.

Paczensky, Gert von. *Le grand livre du Champagne.* Paris: Éditions Solar, 1988.

Pellus, Daniel. *Femmes célèbres de Champagne.* Amiens: Éditions Martelle, 1992.

Pevitt, Christine. *Madame de Pompadour: Mistress of France.* New York: Grove Press, 2002.

Peynaud, Émile. *Knowing and Making Wine.* Trans. Alan F. G. Spenser. [Chichester]: Wiley Interscience, 1984.

Phillips, Roderick. *A Short History of Wine.* New York: Harper-Collins, 2000.

Philpott, Don. *The Champagne Almanac.* Orpington, UK: Eric Dobby Publishing, 1993.

Picard, Liza. *Dr. Johnson's London.* New York: St. Martin's Press, 2000.

Pilbeam, Pamela. "The 'Three Glorious Days': The Revolution of 1830 in Provincial France." *Historical Journal* 26, no. 4 (December 1983): 831–844.

Pinckney, Eliza. *The Letterbook of Eliza Lucas Pinckney 1739–1762.* Ed. Elise Pinckney. Chapel Hill: University of South Carolina Press, 1997.

Pinkney, David H. "A New Look at the French Revolution of 1830." *Review of Politics* 23, no. 4 (October 1961): 490–506.

Poindron, Éric. "Promenade et *Conte rémois,* en guise d'introduction, ou, Tentative de nouvelle essai à la manière modeste des *Contes* de Louis de C[hevigné]," http://blog.france3.fr/cabinet-de-curiosites/tb.php?id=59083.

The Professional Chef: The Culinary Institute of America. New York: John Wiley & Son, 2002.

Rack, John. *The French wine and liquor manufacturer: A practical guide and receipt book for the liquor merchant . . . including complete instructions for manufacturing champagne wine.* New York: Dick & Fitzgerald, 1868.

Ray, Cyril. *Bollinger: The Story of a Champagne.* London: Peter Davies, 1971.

Redding, Cyrus. *A History and Description of Modern Wines.* London: Whittaker, Treacher, & Arnot, 1833.

———. *French Wines and Vineyards and the Way to Find Them.* London: Houlston & Wright, 1860.

Redlich, Fritz. "Jacques Laffitte and the Beginnings of Investment Banking in France." *Bulletin of the Business Historical Society* 22, nos. 4–6. (December 1948): 137–161.

Refait, Michel. *Moët & Chandon: De Claude Moët à Bernard Arnault.* Paris: Dominique Gueniot, 1998.

Rhodes, Anthony. *Prince of Grapes.* London: Weidenfeld & Nicholson, 1975.

Rhone-Converset, J. L. *La vigne, ses maladies-ses ennemis-sa défense en Bourgogne et Champagne, etc.* Paris: Châtillon-sur-Seine, 1889.

Ribiero, Aileen. *Fashion in the French Revolution.* New York, Holmes & Meier, 1988.

Roche, Emile. *Le commerce des vins de Champagne sous l'ancien régime.* Thèse pour le doctorat. Châlons-sur-Marne: Imprimerie de l'Union Républicaine, 1908.

Roman, Gustavo C. "Cerebral Congestion: A Vanished Disease." *Archives of Neurology* 44, no. 4 (April 1987), abstract.

————. "On the History of Lacunes, *État Criblé,* and the White Matter Lesions of Vascular Dementia." *Cerebrovascular Diseases* 13, no. 2 (2002): 1–6.

Rose, Elise Whitlock. *Cathedrals and Cloisters of the Isle de France: Including Bourges, Troyes, Reims, and Rouen.* New York: G. P. Putnam's Sons, 1910.

Rothenberg, Gunther. *The Napoleonic Wars.* New York: Collins, 2006.

Roubinet, Jacqueline, and Gilbert and Marie-Thérèse Nolleau. *Jean-Rémy Moët: A Master of Champagne and a Talented Politician.* Trans. Carolyn Hart. Paris: Stock, 1996.

Rudé, George. *Revolutionary Europe: 1783–1815.* Glasgow: Fontana Press/HarperCollins, 1985.

Saint-Marceaux, [Augustin Marie de Paul] de. *Notes et documents pour servir a l'histoire de la ville de Reims pendant les quinze années de 1830 à 1845.* Reims: Brissart-Binet, 1853.

Saint-Pierre, Louis de. *The Art of Planting and Cultivating the Vine; as also of Making, Fining, and Preserving Wines, &c.* London: n.p., 1722, *Research Publications, The Eighteenth Century,* Reel 6365, Item 1, Woodbridge, CT.

Salleron, Jules, and Louis-Joseph Matieu. *Études sur le vin mousseux.* Paris: Éditions J. Dujardin, 1895.

Schelleken, Jona. "Economic Change and Infant Mortality in England, 1580–1837." *Journal of Interdisciplinary History* 32, no. 1 (Summer 2001): 1–11.

Senior, Nancy. "Aspects of Infant Feeding in Eighteenth-Century France." *Eighteenth-Century Studies* 16, no. 4 (Summer 1983): 367–388.

Sharrer, G. Terry. "The Indigo Bonanza in South Carolina, 1740–1790." *Technology and Culture* 12, no. 3 (1971): 447–455.

Silverman, J. Herbert. "From Hautvillers to Waterloo: The First

Century of Champagne." *Wine and Spirits* (June 1992): 16–20.

Simon, André. *History of the Champagne Trade in England.* London: Wyman & Sons, 1905.

Smith, Bonnie G. *Ladies of the Leisure Class: The Bourgeoisies of Northern France in the Nineteenth Century.* Princeton, NJ: Princeton University Press, 1981.

Somerville, Edith, and Martin Ross. *In the Vine Country.* London: W. H. Allen, 1893.

Stevenson, Tom. *Champagne and Sparking Wine Guide.* San Francisco: Wine Appreciation Guild, 2002.

Stockley, C. S. "Histamine: The Culprit for Headaches?" *Australian and New Zealand Wine Industry Journal* 11 (1996): 42–44.

Sutaine, Max. *Essai sur l'histoire des vins de la Champagne.* Reims: L. Jacquet, 1845.

Taittinger, Claude, ed. *Saint-Évremond ou le bon usage des plaisirs.* Paris: Perrin, 1990.

Taylor, George V. "Notes on Commercial Travelers in Eighteenth-Century France." *Business History Review* 38, no. 3 (Autumn 1964): 346–353.

Techener, Jacques. *Catalogue d'une précieuse collection de livres anciens et rares . . . provenant de la bibliothèque de M. F. Clicquot, de Reims: La vente aura lieu de 22 avril 1843 et jours suivants.* Paris: Librairie Techener, 1843.

This, Hervé. *Molecular Gastronomy: Exploring the Science of Flavor.* Trans. M. B. Debevoise. New York: Columbia University Press, 2006.

Tomes, Robert. *The Champagne Country.* New York: Hurd & Houghton, 1867.

Tovey, Charles. *Champagne: Its History, Properties, and Manufactures.* London: James Camden Hotten, 1870.

———. *Wine Revelations.* London: Whittaker & Co., 1883.

Troyat, Henri. *Alexander of Russia: Napoleon's Conqueror.* New York: Grove Press, 2003.

Vitry, Paul. *L'Hôtel le Vergeur, notice historique.* Reims: Société des Amis du Vieux Reims/Henri Matot, 1932.

Vizetelly, Henry. *A History of Champagne, with Notes on the Other Sparkling Wines of France.* New York: Scribner & Welford, 1882.

————. *Facts About Champagne and Other Sparkling Wines, Collected During Numerous Visits to the Champagne and Other Viticultural Districts of France and the Principal Remaining Wine-Producing Countries of Europe.* London: Ward, Lock, & Co., 1879.

Vogüé, Alain de. *Une maison de vins de Champagne au temps du blocus continental, 1806–1812.* Thesis for the Diplôme d'Etudes Supérieures d'Histoire, June 1948.

Vogüé, Bertrand de. *Madame Clicquot à la conquête pacifique de la Russie.* Reims: Imprimerie du Nord-Est, 1947.

Wahrman, Dror. *The Making of the Modern Self: Identity and Culture in Eighteenth-Century England.* New Haven, CT: Yale University Press, 2004.

Walpole, Robert. *A Letter from a Member of Parliament to His Friends in the Country Concerning the Duties on Wine and Tobacco.* London: T. Cooper, 1733.

Weber, Caroline. *Queen of Fashion: What Marie Antoinette Wore to the Revolution.* New York: Henry Holt & Co., 2006.

Wheatcroft, Andrew. *The Hapsburgs.* New York: Penguin, 1997.

Whymark, H. J., and Alfred Lee. "Champagne Charlie Was His Name," sung by Billy Morris. Sheet music. Boston: Oliver Ditson, n.d. H-Music files, Sonoma County Library.

Williams, D. "A Consideration of the Sub-Fossil Remains of 'Vitis vinifera' L. as Evidence of Viticulture in Roman Britain." *Britannia* 8 (1977): 327–334.

Williams, Helen Maria. *Letters Written in France.* Ed. Neil Fraistat and Susan S. Lanser. Peterborough, ON: Broadview, 2001.

Wilson, Joan Hoff. "The Illusion of Change: Women and the American Revolution," in *The American Revolution.* Ed. Alfred F. Young. Dekalb, IL: Northern Illinois University Press, 1976.

Winik, Marion. "The Women of Champagne." *American Way* (March 1, 1997): 113.

Woodhall, Clyde E., and William H. Faver Jr. "Famous South Carolina Farmers." *Agricultural History* 33, no. 3 (1959): 138–141.

Woolf, Virginia. *A Room of One's Own.* New York: Harcourt Brace, 1981.

Wordsworth, Dorothy. *The Grasmere Journals*. Ed. Pamela Woof. Oxford: Oxford University Press, 1991.

Young, Arthur. *Travels in France and Italy During the Years 1787, 1788, and 1789*. London: J. M. Dent & Sons, 1927.

Young, David Bruce. "A Wood Famine?: The Question of Deforestation in Old Regime France." *Forestry* 49, no. 1 (1976): 45–46.

Zambonelli, Carlo, et al. "Effects of Lactic Acid Bacteria Autolysis on Sensorial Characteristics of Fermented Foods." *Food Technology/Biotechnology* 40, no. 4 (2002): 347–351.

Zoecklein, Bruce. "A Review of *Méthode Champenoise* Production." Virginia State University/Virginia Tech, Cooperative Extension Publication, Publication Number 463-017, December 2002, www.ext. vt.edu/pubs/viticulture/463-017/463-017.html.

Promotional materials from Champagne Château de Boursault, Champagne Taittinger, Champagne Cattier, Champagne Jeansson, Champagne Veuve Clicquot Ponsardin, Champagne Pommery, Champagne Moët et Chandon, Domaine Carneros, Château d'Yquem, Grgich Hills, Champagne Henriot, Champagne Laurrent-Perrier, Champagne Ruinart, and Champagne G. C. Kessler.

Veuve Clicquot Ponsardin Company Archives.

Index

About the Author

TILAR J. MAZZEO is a cultural historian, biographer, and passionate student of food and wine. She divides her time between the California wine country and Maine, where she is an assistant professor at Colby College. She can be reached at www.tilar-mazzeo.com.